Journalism
and the
Debate Over Privacy

LEA'S COMMUNICATION SERIES
Jennings Bryant / Dolf Zillmann, General Editors

For a complete list of titles in LEA's Communication Series, please contact Lawrence Erlbaum Associates, Publishers at www.erlbaum.com

Journalism
and the
Debate Over Privacy

Edited by

Craig L. LaMay
Northwestern University

 LEA

2003

LAWRENCE ERLBAUM ASSOCIATES, PUBLISHERS

Mahwah, New Jersey   London

Lawrence Erlbaum Associates, Inc., Publishers
10 Industrial Avenue
Mahwah, NJ 07430

Cover design by Kathryn Houghtaling Lacey

Library of Congress Cataloging-in-Publication Data

Journalism and the debate over privacy / edited by Craig L. LaMay.
    p. cm.
  Includes bibliographical references and index.
ISBN 0-8058-4626-3 (cloth : alk. paper)
1. Journalistic ethics—United States. 2. Privacy, Right of—United States.
    I. LaMay, Craig L.
PN4888.E8J67   2003
175—dc21   2002041678
                                                   CIP

Contents

Preface

George Bernard Shaw, speaking in New York in 1933, observed that "An American has no sense of privacy. He does not know what it means. There is no such thing in the country."[1] At times it may certainly seem so. On television talk shows, people unremarkable except for their desperation now routinely expose the rawest and most unpleasant details of their lives, and "reality" television elicits intimate and often humiliating disclosures from participants who are trying to win a prize, a date, a spouse, or a chance at celebrity. In 2000, ABC's *Good Morning America* featured a live broadcast of a woman giving birth; a few months earlier, NBC's Katie Couric, an advocate of preventative cancer screening, took *Today* viewers on a 2-day fiberoptic tour of her colon. In 1999, shortly after stepping down as executive editor of *The New York Times*, Max Frankel commented, with some incredulity, that he had lived to see the day when in "otherwise sober newspapers we read descriptions of the presidential penis and also the testimony of anonymous sources who were said to have watched that organ in action."[2]

At a time when the debate on privacy is largely captured by the Internet, this volume situates that discussion elsewhere, in the landscape of professional journalism. Other commentators have written about the conflict between rapid technological innovation and the much slower advance (some would say decline) of public morals, and any review of congressional activity over the past several years would turn up hundreds of bills dealing with some aspect of privacy and electronic data.[3] What were only recently innocuous terms—*cookies, filters, Spam*—are now freighted with privacy implications, and despite what Americans say about their desire for privacy they will indiscriminately engage in activities and transactions that they know, or should know, make widely available to private parties personal information that was once accessible almost exclusively to the government. Local, state, and federal governments themselves now control vast electronic databases with information about their citizens—from their driving records to the guns they own—of potentially significant value to both commercial users and journalists.

In this new context, the vantage point of professional journalism allows us to understand the conception of privacy as dependent on many factors, of which technology is just one. Just as important are social norms and practices. Today, for example, merchandisers collect information about consumer preferences with every purchase, information that they can use for their own internal purposes or sell to others. Many consumer groups find these practices invasive, but in another time the corner store supplied all of a person's needs, with the result that a person's needs were probably known by all. If anyone thought this an invasion of privacy it was also an accepted part of life, whether one lived in a farm community or on a block in Brooklyn.

The practice of daily journalism has always had a lot to say about the norms and practices that shape our notions about privacy. To take a well-known example, a press that once ignored President Kennedy's private life was willing, as Frankel observed, to explore the most sexually explicit details of President Clinton's. When the practice of journalism meets legal conceptions of privacy, the potential for normative change is even greater. Consider, for example, the implications of ABC's argument that the First Amendment should have barred *any* liability for the deceptive methods the network used in its 1992 *Prime Time Live* investigation of Food Lion grocery stores. Would ABC itself be willing to assume the risk that some of its employees are not there in good faith, but simply to eavesdrop and snoop around? If so, and if the rights of the press are no different than the rights of citizens generally, what does ABC's argument say for how we should behave in our daily lives, especially in an age when ever more people claim to be engaged in journalism? Should all of us assume that a conversation with the person in the next cubicle or at the next desk—whether a colleague, our boss, a student, or a lover—may be recorded and made public? Whatever one's responses to these questions, the answers are most interesting for what they say about what it is we are trying to achieve or react to by insisting on one or another form or understanding of privacy.

Privacy is inherently a social concept, important mostly because without it there is no conception of personhood. The conditions of slavery and serfdom, for example, are defined largely by the absence of any right of privacy for those who suffer their indignity.[4] People who have experienced totalitarian regimes conceive of privacy, publicity, and rights of information access quite differently than do those without similar memories of persecution and subjugation, which explains much of the difference between the European Union and the United States on this subject. Journalists, for their part, tend to view privacy issues in terms of social practice, which is both understandable and regrettable—absent a wider historical, cultural, and political inquiry, it is hard for journalists (or anyone else) to rise above their place in history and think about when they should support and when they should resist the dominant social practices that constitute their normative judgments about the world.

However, journalism is also uniquely valuable as a crucible for this kind of inquiry. Journalists, after all, are the social practitioners at the front lines in the debate over privacy's meaning, and because they seek news in places that are often grubby and mean they encounter dilemmas that most people do not. As Anthony Lewis writes in his contribution to this volume, journalists are the ones who must daily consider both law and ethics in making judgments about what they publish. Anyone who teaches journalism students knows that privacy issues, probably more than any other, present the widest gap between what ethics suggest and what the law allows. Journalism is the place where the tension between private and public is tested daily.

That tension is woven into the fabric of the Constitution, which includes both public aspects—such as making currency and regulating commerce—and private ones. The Bill of Rights is the best example of the latter; it is a statement of rights reserved to individuals apart from any public rights or obligations they may have. This tension plays out in lots of ways, but one is a system where, when we speak of "rights," an important subtext of that discussion concerns our ability to choose whether to keep matters private or to make them public. Constitutional law recognizes one line of cases that understands rights as grounded in private activity—the right to obtain an abortion, for example—and another that understands them as grounded in public activity.[5] First Amendment law specifically is notable for its public and private aspects: The freedom to speak is coupled with the freedom not to speak,[6] the freedom to associate is coupled with the right not to associate,[7] and the right of expression includes the right to speak anonymously[8] and in confidence.[9]

These aspects overlap, sometimes in confusing ways. In 1987, for example, the Supreme Court upheld the free speech rights of a clerk in a California sheriff's office who was fired when, after President Reagan was shot, she was overheard saying, "If they go for him again, I hope they get him."[10] Writing for the Court, Justice Marshall said the woman's remark was protected because of its public character. Relying on the principles articulated in *New York Times v. Sullivan*,[11] Marshall emphasized that "debate on public issues should be uninhibited, robust and wide-open and … may well include vehement, caustic and sometimes unpleasant attacks on government and public officials."[12]

Justice Powell concurred, but found the woman's speech protected because it was intended to be private: "She had no intention or expectation that [the remark] would be overheard or acted on by others.… [I]t will be an unusual case where the employer's legitimate interests will be so great as to justify punishing an employee for this type of private speech that routinely takes place at all levels in the workplace."[13]

If the justices recognized the contradiction in their views, there is no sign of it in their opinions. When *we* speak of privacy, then, it is important to understand what we might mean by the term, and for journalists the problem with all this is both conceptual and practical. Historically, American journalists have embraced both the private-regarding view of rights (particularly their own) that associates freedom with the absence of government interference, *and* the public-regarding view of rights that links freedom and citizenship with an active and competent government. Add to this the journalistic commitment to making all things visible and decision makers accountable, and the result is genuine confusion about what is legitimately private and what is properly public. Anyone familiar with journalistic codes of ethics, for example, knows that they struggle to reconcile libertarian with universalist impulses, often to the point of dissembling.

The chapters that follow examine journalism and privacy issues in both theoretical and practical terms. All the chapters were delivered originally as papers at an April

2000 conference organized jointly by Northwestern University's Medill School of Journalism, its School of Law, and its School of Speech (now School of Communication). Although most of the contributors to this volume are lawyers, two are journalists, and this book is intended for readers and students in both professions. All the pieces have been edited to make them more accessible to nonlawyers, and the endnotes—although preserving the style of legal citation—have been modified to make them easier to read and understand. Anthony Lewis's essay is adapted from his keynote speech at the Northwestern conference, and to help the reader, references have been added to the principal cases he discusses.

Part I of the book is an examination of privacy in theoretical terms, intended to get the reader thinking broadly about conceptual problems in discussions concerning journalism and privacy. The first chapter, "The Social Construction of Privacy," by Harvard's Frederick Schauer, explores the tendency in the modern debate to think of privacy as a moral absolute, a kind of fixed normative value under assault from changes in technology, journalism, and law, but which is itself uninfluenced by and immune to the changes in those fields. "Debates about privacy have had a singularly naturalistic tone," Schauer writes, "as if these rights were morally primary and socially antecedent." In fact, he argues, conceptions of privacy are products of widely varying social and cultural understandings, creating variations in understanding and expectation that are both geographic and temporal. Moreover, Schauer concludes, "[T]he very forces that have constructed the right to privacy are changing as quickly as anything we know," raising the question of what it is we wish to defend when we invoke the right of "privacy."

Following Schauer, Randall P. Bezanson of the University of Iowa looks at the public/private distinction in free expression theory and uses it to examine the principles that should apply to freedom of expression claims made by the press. Where traditionally the public/private distinction refers to the content of speech, the important thing in press claims, Bezanson argues, is the process, or manner, by which editorial judgment is exercised. Editorial judgment deserving of First Amendment protection can exist only in a system of private organizations engaged in meaningful competition, and for whom the important market guiding editorial judgment is readers and viewers—the public. Where the important market is something else—the financial markets or advertisers—it is not clear that the protections of the First Amendment should apply. Rather, those protections should be reserved for media organizations that are structurally independent and public regarding, free of coercive control by government or markets. In such a system, Bezanson argues, the way in which the law would regard invasions of privacy would be much different, focusing not on the content of speech or the conduct of news gatherers, as it does now, but instead on the exercise of editorial judgment in the service of public discussion and debate in a democratic society. To examine his theory, Bezanson reviews three well-known cases with privacy implications, including two of recent vintage—ABC's story about Food Lion, and CNN's 1993 ridealong with the U.S. Fish and Wildlife Service when it raided a Montana ranch—and considers how they might have turned out differently.

Part II of the book builds on this theoretical underpinning and looks at privacy problems as they are experienced by working journalists. Opening the section is former *New York Times* columnist Anthony Lewis, who is widely known for his uncompromising scholarly and journalistic writing on free expression issues. Here, however, Lewis tells his reader that "what I have written may not be what you expected," a critical analysis of several recent privacy controversies, including the Whitewater investigation of the Clintons, Paula Jones' sexual harassment suit against President Clinton, and two recent cases involving journalists who rode along with police and emergency crews into private homes. Lewis looks with a professional but compassionate eye at the humiliation that people can experience when, through no fault of their own, they suddenly become "newsworthy" and their lives are exposed to public examination. Acknowledging that the press must be "obstinate" and "cantankerous," Lewis asks whether "that requires us to treat the interest of privacy with contempt and disregard."

In response, Anita L. Allen of the University of Pennsylvania argues that journalists cannot respect privacy; indeed, that they have understandably "jettisoned" privacy values as inconsistent with their professional obligation to inform the public and the First Amendment's protections. Even normative discussions about ethics and news judgment have largely surrendered on this subject, Allen argues, noting that most of the current codes of professional ethics in journalism barely mention privacy, and some do not mention it at all. Journalists can be forgiven for some of this, she says, because public conceptions of privacy are so often idiosyncratic and even unreasonable. "Ascribed the unprecedented duty of ascertaining actual privacy preferences," Allen writes, "the community of journalists could quickly grow weary of the vexatious, expensive, and self-contradictory task of respecting individuals' privacy individually.... It is all too convenient for journalists, eager for lucrative stories, to claim that they do not know what respecting privacy entails; and yet, given cultural diversity, pluralism, and recent social change, they may be right."

Following Allen, Rodney Smolla of the University of Richmond examines what he calls the "striking imbalance" between the law's "hostile and curmudgeonly" treatment of revelation privacy claims and its "slavish submission" to intrusion claims. "To the extent one might hope or expect that the law would be a moral distillation of public sensibility on these issues, one would be disappointed," Smolla writes. "If it is true that the moral intuitions and sensibilities of many in our society about the propriety of intrusion and revelation are far more balanced and complex than the one-sided legal doctrines that currently exist, the questions become why this is the case and whether it ought to be." Smolla provides an engaging inquiry into the philosophical and First Amendment basis for the different treatment afforded these privacy invasions, and then looks closely at the Supreme Court's 2001 decision in *Bartnicki v. Vopper*, the Court's most important privacy case involving the press in more than a decade.[14] The press interests prevailed in that case, but the decision was far from a ringing endorsement for disclosure. Indeed, *Bartnicki* is perhaps most notable for the fact that the Court acknowledges a right of privacy with respect to revelation claims.

   The final two chapters in this volume concern privacy rights that are asserted as a kind of property right and used to conceal or control information. Jane E. Kirtley, the former director of the Reporters Committee for Freedom of the Press and now a professor at the University of Minnesota, writes about the collection and exchange of digitized personal information and the question of when and how the use of such information constitutes a violation of privacy. The Supreme Court has signaled that such information can be viewed as an economic commodity in which individuals have property rights, Kirtley says, which for the press means the possibility of liability for releasing it into the public domain. But of even greater significance, she argues, the risk of liability means that a government agency with limited resources will have to choose between "expending those resources to develop and enforce a complicated dissemination policy or simply closing its records altogether." If the latter, Kirtley writes, "one can assume that the agency will opt for secrecy," thus making news gathering more difficult.

   Closing the book is an essay by Northwestern University's Craig LaMay on the right of publicity, or misappropriation. One of Dean Prosser's original privacy torts, misappropriation is not really about privacy at all (at least not in the usual sense), but instead is about making one's person profitably and prominently public. As such, the right of publicity has more in common with intellectual property law than it does with the other privacy torts, providing a cause of action for the nonconsensual appropriation of a person's name and likeness for commercial purposes. The law has traditionally given news organizations a defense for the use of such material that is newsworthy, but in recent years some notable suits have raised the questions of what constitutes a "news" use and what uses of a person's "identity" are actionable. Some plaintiffs have used the right to seek damages they could not win under defamation or other privacy actions, whereas others have used it to seek to control forms of expression, such as parody, that would be protected under intellectual property law. As news organizations become smaller parts of large entertainment conglomerates, LaMay writes, the right of publicity may take on new significance for journalists who once did not have to worry about it.

   In the years to come, the First Amendment will have to navigate a series of increasingly difficult conflicts. The courts have already started down this road. One variety of case pits the expressive rights of one speaker against the expressive rights of another;[15] another conflict will match free expression rights against other, equally compelling rights. One of those countervailing rights, as the Supreme Court's dissenters made clear in *Bartnicki v. Vopper*,[16] is the right of privacy, however conceived. For journalists, journalism students, and law students, this volume is intended to provide a readable and thought-provoking introduction to current thinking on this subject, and to place it in the context of daily journalism, the place where theory meets practice head on. This volume has already benefited from the work of students who have read and commented on its chapters. For their help, thanks go to Northwestern Medill School of Journalism graduate students Malaika Costello-Dougherty and Stephanie Fosnight, and Northwestern Law students Claire Goldstein, Dorothy McLaughlin, and Eric Meyer.

—*Craig L. LaMay*
Northwestern University
August 2002

NOTES

[1]Quoted in Irving Louis Horowitz, *Networking America: The Cultural Context of the Privacy v. Publicity Debates*, ETC, 305–314, at 307 (Fall 1999).

[2]Max Frankel, *Media Madness: The Revolution So Far*, Catto Report on Journalism and Society, 1 (1999).

[3]See, for example, Fred Cate, *Privacy in the Information Age* (1997).

[4]Horowitz, 306.

[5]For discussion on the public–private distinction in constitutional law, see Louis M. Seidman, *Our Unsettled Constitution: A New Defense of Constitutionalism and Judicial Review* (2000).

[6]See *Wooley v. Maynard*, 430 U.S. 705 (1977), holding that New Hampshire's requirement that its citizens display the state motto—"Live Free or Die"—on their license plates violated their right to "refrain from speaking." See also *West Virginia Board of Education v. Barnette*, 319 U.S. 624 (1943), holding that a compulsory flag salute in public schools is a violation of the First Amendment.

[7]See *Boy Scouts of America v. Dale*, 530 U.S. 640 (2000), holding that the BSA does not have to accept gay scouts as members. See also *Hurley v. Irish-American Gay, Lesbian and Bisexual Group of Boston*, 515 U.S. 557 (1995), holding that a parade was not a public accommodation and that its organizers could exercise the "autonomy to choose the content" of the parade by excluding gay, lesbian, and bisexual participants.

[8]See *McIntyre v. Ohio Elections Commission*, 514 U.S. 334 (1995), holding that Ohio's prohibition against distributing anonymous campaign pamphlets was unconstitutional.

[9]See *Branzburg v. Hayes*, 408 U.S. 665 (1972), upholding a limited privilege for journalists to withhold the identity of confidential news sources.

[10]*Rankin v. McPherson*, 483 U.S. 378 (1987).

[11]*New York Times v. Sullivan*, 376 U.S. 254 (1964).

[12]Rankin v. McPherson, at 388.

[13]Ibid., at 394.

[14]*Bartnicki v. Vopper*, 532 U.S. 514 (2001).

[15]See *Arkansas Educational Television Association v. Forbes*, 523 U.S. 666 (1998) (involving the right of a state-run public television network to exercise editorial discretion in denying a political candidate the opportunity to participate in a televised debate) and *Turner Broadcasting System v. F.C.C.*, 512 U.S. 622 (1994) (involving the right of broadcast television stations to carriage on cable television networks).

[16]*Bartnicki v. Vopper*, at 544.

PART I

Theoretical Perspectives on Privacy and Free Expression

1

The Social Construction of Privacy

Frederick Schauer
John F. Kennedy School of Government, Harvard University

Debates about the social construction of reality are a persistent feature of contemporary academic debate.[1] At one highly implausible extreme are those who claim, or who are claimed to claim,[2] that the reality we experience is a social construction, and the "there" we believe to be there is a product not of a fixed external world, but of the way we contingently choose to organize the sense data that are the primary inputs of human experience.[3] Under this view, the things we perceive as real and fixed, from badminton to butterflies, are the contingent products of human perception and human categorization.

At the other extreme, equally implausible, is the radical rejection of the social construction account of reality. Those who strongly reject social constructionism claim, or again are claimed to claim, that the reason we perceive the external world as real is because it *is* real. From everything we see about mountains to everything we feel about our parents, the belief that what we perceive to be external maps onto the existence of a natural and external physical, conceptual, and moral world. Although we perceive this world, what we perceive exists is independent of human action, and stands apart from the contingencies of human perception and social categorization.[4]

Between these two highly implausible positions is a much more plausible one, and one that fits with the perspective informing this chapter. Under this position, much of the external world exists independent of human action, whether the action be that of individual perception or that of collective categorization. Zebras, bananas and gravity are not the products of social construction, but instead are just a few of the myriad examples of a mind-independent and society-independent reality.[5] Yet although much of the world we experience is thus not socially constructed (so this more plausible view maintains), much of it is. The existence of natural kinds and other forms of mind-independent reality is consistent with the existence of concepts and categories that are indeed socially and not naturally constructed. To put it differently, the proposition that some things are not socially constructed does not entail the conclusion that nothing is. And so we can readily and reasonably accept the nonsocial existence of much of the physical world, and much of science, while still believing, equally readily and equally reasonably, that chess, baseball, fashion, painting, and poetry, for example, and even the standards we use to evaluate performances in each, exist not as immovable and noncontingent objects of human perception but instead as the products of culturally contingent social conventions.

Even under this intermediate and much more plausible view, numerous issues remain. One of those issues is the classification, as socially constructed or not, of a large range of phenomena that are central to our everyday existence. Is law, for example, a feature of the prehuman world (as a caricatured version of natural law would have it),[6] or is it a social artifact (as legal positivists believe)?[7] Is morality itself part of the furniture of the world (as most moral objectivists believe),[8] or does it vary with individuals and societies (as those who are labeled subjectivists[9] or relativists,[10] respectively, insist)? Of course many of the debates about the existence of God are best understood as debates about whether God is a reality or a social construction.

IS PRIVACY SOCIALLY CONSTRUCTED?

As may now be apparent, given the title of this chapter, privacy appears to be a likely candidate for this middle ground, in which people who believe that some things are socially constructed and other things are not debate about which of these the item at issue is. Because privacy appears to be less fundamental than some things and more fundamental than others, we might have expected to discover that people have debated about where to array privacy on a scale of social construction (or not), and about the policy implications of placing it at one point rather than another along this scale.

Surprisingly, however, this debate about the ontological status of privacy is virtually nonexistent. Instead, the debates about privacy have had a singularly naturalistic tone, even more so as the Internet and other forms of cyberspace have given a special salience to debates regarding topics such as database privacy or the transmission of information about individuals that those individuals would prefer not to have transmitted.[11] In much of the modern debate, the right to privacy, the right to be let alone, and most importantly the right to control information about oneself, have been framed as if these rights were morally primary and socially antecedent. Consequently, as the claims typically go, those rights have been conceptually uninfluenced by social changes, even as the exercise of those rights is increasingly threatened by the social and technological changes associated with advances in information technology.

The structure of the contemporary claims exposes their naturalistic premises. Under the typical claim, there is a right to privacy—a right that is as conceptually primary and morally immovable as, for example, the right to equality. The right to privacy is, so it is said, part of the "inner person."[12] However, the argument goes that as technological changes make invasion of privacy easier, the right—itself conceptually immune from these changes—is increasingly under threat. Just as technological changes make racial profiling easier without affecting the moral wrongness of racism, so too do technological changes make privacy invasion easier without affecting the moral wrongness of those invasions, and therefore without affecting the moral necessity of increasing our safeguards so that the right to privacy remains as well protected as it was in the precyberspace age.

This view is not an unreasonable one. Assuming some version of moral objectivism (without which the view is incoherent), the question then arises as to which features of morality lie at the foundations of our moral universe. For some people these foundations are singular, as with Ronald Dworkin's view about the primacy of equal concern and respect,[13] the utilitarian's view about the primacy of the principle of utility,[14] and the views of many people about the primacy of the single value of justice.[15] For others these foundations are multiple, as with Bernard Gert's moral rules[16] and as with the views of those whom John Rawls refers to as "intuitionists."[17] But for both sets of views we do not typically see the right to control information about oneself listed among the moral primaries.

That the right to control information about oneself does not routinely (or ever, for that matter) appear as the single moral primary, or of the multiple moral primaries, is of course far from conclusive. Perhaps our moral monists have been mistaken in believing that the right to control information is not the single primary right from which all others are derived. And perhaps our moral pluralists (a less confusing appellation than *intuitionists*) have been equally mistaken in not listing control of personal information as among the small number of irreducible moral primaries. But the right to control personal information at least *seems* more specific than the typical moral primary, and thus it appears that the best argument for the nonsocially constructed nature of this right is not one that takes it be a moral primary, but instead one that takes it to be a secondary right that is related to primary rights (or other primary moral values) in a nonsocially constructed way.

There are two ways in which such a secondary right could be related to a primary right. One would be as an act of derivation or individuation. Although derivation and individuation are different from each other, the important point, and one that both derivation and individuation share, is that the relationship between the general and the particular is a logical, conceptual, or linguistic one. When Ronald Dworkin argues that a right to possess pornography is a component of the right to be treated with equal concern and respect,[18] he is not making an instrumental point about the empirical relationship between equal concern and respect and pornography possession, but is rather making a conceptual point about just what equal concern and respect *means*. And when John Rawls argues that justice requires and includes the right to political liberty consistent with an equal liberty for all,[19] his arguments are logical and conceptual, and in general not empirical.

Others would take the relationship between a primary right and a secondary one to be instrumental and empirical. To the utilitarian the right to free speech is recognized and protected because its recognition and protection would, as a contingent empirical matter, increase overall utility.[20] And even to someone who believes that something other than utility is the appropriate primary building block of morality, a right could still exist because of its empirical connection with the primary building block of morality, whatever it was. As long as recognition of some right would, instrumentally and thus empirically, increase the quantity or manifestation of the primary building block, then there would be an argument for recognizing the right. Even if a right is not primary, therefore, it could well be crucially important in this instrumental and empirical way.

Under either the conceptual or the empirical understanding, the right to privacy may exist as just such a secondary right, secondary not because it is unimportant, but because, like rights to freedom of speech, freedom of religion, and freedom from torture, it is typically understood, described, in a way that makes it more particular than the typical moral primaries of justice, equality, liberty, and utility. We understand what is being said when privacy is described as an aspect of human dignity,[21] but we also understand why it is understood that dignity is the moral primary of which privacy is only a component part.

With this distinction between moral primaries and secondary rights in hand, consider how one might justify a particular manifestation of the right to privacy. Take, for example, the German practice of concealing the names of civil litigants from the public record. If one brings a civil lawsuit in Germany, or if one is the defendant in a civil suit, one's identity is masked in the published opinions, so that all we know about the typical plaintiff or defendant is that he or she is the plaintiff or defendant in Case Number 1138-7, or such and such. This is in marked contrast with the practice in the United States, where the fact of bringing a lawsuit, or even the fact of being the defendant in a lawsuit (a less voluntary action), commits one to having one's name potentially disclosed in published opinions, and certainly available to all (except in rare exceptions involving trade secrets and a few other matters) in the publicly available court filings and other judicial records.

In Germany, the German practice is routinely defended on privacy grounds, even though such an argument is almost unheard of in the United States. In Germany, the right, albeit a secondary one, is thought of as an important component of, or importantly instrumental to, the right of personality, the right of personal sanctity, the right of personal integrity, or something of that variety. But when such arguments are raised in the United States in the same context, the reaction is little more than a raised eyebrow. Americans can get highly exercised about supposed invasions of their right to privacy, but they rarely appear to get exercised about the possibility that their names may appear in the *Federal Supplement*.

That an argument so well accepted in Germany is virtually unheard of in the United States is of course not conclusive of anything. It just might be that the Germans are wrong and we are right—or vice versa. Yet it is telling that Americans, who these days appear hardly reluctant to complain about violations of their privacy, rarely complain that they do not have the privacy protections available to Germans in the context of civil litigation. Again, this might simply be sheer ignorance, but it appears more likely that it is instead a matter of different expectations. Just as Americans do not think it an invasion of their privacy if people identify their faces as they walk down the street or observe the kind of car they drive, so too do they not seem to feel that their personal integrity has been violated if their names are attached to civil litigation. Just as people in some countries but not others think it prying if you ask about their salary, and just as people in some cultures but not in others readily invite guests into their homes, it should not be surprising to discover that the identity of the parties in civil litigation is something whose nonpublicity is considered highly important in some countries and part of living in society in many other countries. What this suggests, of course, is that privacy is not, like the moral repugnance of torture and slavery, culturally invariant.[22] Rather, it suggests that conceptions of privacy are themselves socially constructed, and that the domain people think it important to control is not morally fixed, but rather is a product of widely varying social and cultural understandings.[23]

CHANGING CONCEPTIONS OF THE "REASONABLE"

Thirty years ago, Justice Brennan observed, in the context of arguing that even private figures should be held to the actual malice rule in defamation actions if they were involved in matters of public concern, that "[v]oluntarily or not, we are all 'public men' to some degree."[24] And 4 years earlier, in a false-light privacy case, he had observed that "exposure of the self to others in varying degrees is a concomitant of life in a civilized country."[25] In both of these statements, Justice Brennan can best be understood as maintaining that the extent to which people are expected to expose their lives, their personalities, their attributes, and their behavior to public scrutiny is not for them to control, but is instead a function of the external understanding—the social construction of the world they and we inhabit.

Justice Brennan's views in *Rosenbloom v. Metromedia* may not have carried the day as a matter of the development of defamation law, but they do fit well with legal understandings of the common law tort of invasion of privacy.[26] In fact, this tort is not one but (at least) four, separated as such in the *Restatement (Second) of Torts*.[27] Putting aside the tort of appropriation of a name or likeness (as when a celebrity's picture, name, or slogan is used to sell a product without the celebrity's permission[28]) only because it is of less relevance to my themes here, we can focus on the three remaining branches of the common law tort. According to the *Restatement*, one of these torts is the "Intrusion Upon Seclusion," protecting people both against physical intrusion into the space they claim as their own, or against various forms of eavesdropping in that same protected space.[29] Electronic surveillance of my home is a tort of this variety,[30] and so too is when the intruder abjures electronic devices and simply breaks into my home and looks around.

The second, and indeed the most widely discussed, of the branches of the common law tort is the dissemination of private facts, a tort that is committed when— subject to numerous qualifications, exceptions, and defenses—widespread publicity is given to facts about a person that the person would prefer not be known.[31] Regardless of truth or falsity,[32] certain information about a person remains in the control of that person, and thus to disclose that information without the individual's consent is to violate a component of the individual's common law right to privacy.

Third, the common law right to privacy includes so-called "false light" invasion of privacy, in which publicity about a person not only publicizes facts about a person that the person would prefer not to have publicized, but also does so in a manner such that the person is portrayed in a way that diverges from the reality of the situation. Although this tort appears to be both conceptually and constitutionally problematic because of its apparent overlap with defamation law,[33] it remains the case that false light invasion of privacy is understood as a distinct tort both by the *Restatement*[34] and by the common law on which the *Restatement* is based.[35]

My concern here is not the taxonomy of the common law tort of invasion of privacy. Rather, it is with the fact that all three branches of the tort on which I have focused are ones in which the tort is explicitly premised on and thus bounded by changing social conceptions of "reasonable" behavior. Intrusion on seclusion is a tort only if the intrusion "would be highly offensive to a reasonable person"[36]; dissemination of private facts constitutes a tort again only when such dissemination "would be highly offensive to a reasonable person"[37]; and the same phrase is used in the context of defining false light invasion of privacy as well.[38] Unlike the naturalistic conceptions of privacy that dominate the modern debate, the legal recognition and definition of the very rights on which so much of the debate is premised sees these rights as necessarily dependent on a social and variable conception of the behavior that is alleged to constitute the tort. Just as the Germans find unreasonable a practice that almost all Americans take for granted without complaint, so too does the definition of the common law tort of invasion of privacy recognize that some behavior will be thought reasonable at some times and not others, and reasonable in some places and not others. Unlike most physical torts, in which the harm of the physical intrusion is taken to be largely unaffected by social values, invasion of privacy law is premised on the view that the harm that the recognition of the tort is designed to guard against is a socially constructed harm. When I attend a sporting event and then see my picture in the newspaper as part of a large crowd, I have no legal remedy—not because of some defense or constitutional side constraint, but because the law refuses to recognize that I have been harmed at all. The harm, says the common law, is not a function of my own preferences and my own feelings, but is instead a function of and socially constructed by the understandings of the larger world I inhabit. If in this world it is to be expected that my picture may at times appear in the newspaper without my consent, then the position of the law is simply that I have not been harmed in the first instance. Harm in this area, it is said, is precisely a function of going beyond what most of the people in the society have come to expect; so if those expectations change, then so too does the conception of harm that is based on them.

Much the same can be said about the notions of privacy that inform the Fourth Amendment's protection against unreasonable searches and seizures. For not only does the Fourth Amendment itself pivot on the term *unreasonable*, it also does so in order to protect the expectation of privacy "that society is prepared to recognize as 'reasonable.'"[39] As a matter of Fourth Amendment doctrine, the question of whether one's privacy is invaded by listening in on a telephone conversation from a telephone booth,[40] searching an automobile,[41] or conducting aerial surveillance of an open field[42] is not to be determined by moral or scientific absolutes, or even by logical application of formal legal doctrine. Instead, it is determined by looking at society as it is and by looking at what society now thinks of as an area that is understood as a sanctuary. As with the law relating to the tort of invasion of privacy, the law of the Fourth Amendment recognizes and hinges on the idea that what society understands as a sanctuary and a haven from government intrusion is itself inevitably dependent on changing social values and social expectations.

In 1929, U.S. Secretary of War Henry L. Stimson disbanded an American facility for breaking the codes being used by foreign governments, sniffing that "Gentlemen do not read other gentlemen's mail."[43] In embodying not only a nostalgic view of the nature of war but also an equally nostalgic view of the nature of gentlemen, Stimson provided a vivid reminder of the fact that the intrusions considered morally unacceptable in one era may be considered morally necessary in another. And as a consequence, expectations of privacy change as well. Whatever a 21st century spy may think about other 21st century spies reading his or her mail, it is hard to imagine that the spy would complain of a violation of privacy. Society had constructed a set of expectations that supported Stimson's view in 1929, but between 1929 and now society has reconstructed those expectations, and has thus reconstructed the understandings on which the very idea of privacy rests.

THE TECHNOLOGICAL CONSTRUCTION OF PRIVACY

To note that conceptions of privacy are socially constructed is only the beginning. What comes next must be an inquiry into the phenomena on which the social construction is based. Although there are as many sources of social construction as there are of society itself, three sources of the social construction of privacy are of particular concern to me here: the technological, the journalistic, and the legal. Indeed, it is likely that these three social phenomena are especially relevant in shaping our conception of privacy, even if they are less so in shaping our conceptions of other socially constructed phenomena, and that is why I concentrate on them here. In this section I deal with the technological; in the sections that follow I address the journalistic and the legal.

There can be little doubt that we are in the middle of a dramatic social transformation as a consequence of rapid and dramatic advances in information technology. Whether it be widespread use of the Internet, or the burgeoning use of electronic mail and electronic publishing, or a host of other dimensions of the modern informational world that were scarcely imaginable even a generation ago, there can be little quarrel with the proposition that changes in information technology have revolutionized the way in which most people conduct their lives, and the way in which most people interact with each other.

This observation is banal, but I make it to underscore the irony that is the central theme of this chapter. Although numerous people, especially self-styled privacy advocates, are quick to identify the innumerable ways in which changes in information technology have altered our lives, they have failed to recognize the way in which those same changes in information technology have the potential to, and may already have, altered our conception of privacy as well. In the eyes of the typical privacy advocate, everything changes except the conception of privacy on which the advocacy is based. So if, for example, a new form of infrared technology makes it possible to see photolike details of human behavior through the walls of a typical house or apartment, the view I am questioning would treat this as a plain invasion of the privacy rights we have, rather than even asking whether the new technology has changed that conception of privacy. If the existence of windows, or telephoto lenses, for example, has changed the very notion of what it is to be private (at least compared to 500 years ago), then perhaps the hypothetical new infrared technology would do the same thing. Now if the invasion of privacy, like the wrongness of rape and torture, were a fixed moral absolute, it would make perfect sense to treat the concept of privacy as immune from technological modification. But once we see that conceptions of privacy—and thus necessarily conceptions of invasion of privacy—are socially constructed, the irony of perceiving everything as changing except this social construction is particularly apparent. To put the same point differently, once it is understood that the reasonableness of an expectation of privacy depends on existing social practices, it is hard to see why the Internet, e-mail, and innumerable other technological changes can be understood as being cordoned off from those social practices.

Thus, to the extent that electronic mail is less secure than some other forms of correspondence, one might have less of an expectation of privacy in this medium than in some other. To the extent that we understand that one of the chief ways of making money from a dot.com is by "mining" information from users and selling that information to others, then we have less reason to be surprised or offended when the information about us is part of the information that is mined. To the extent that we now perceive that the Internet in general is a less "secure" environment, one whose social rules appear less constrained, we understand privacy differently in that environment than we do in others.[44] To the extent that we're aware that people we call on the telephone may know the number we are calling from even before they pick up the phone, we no longer have privacy concerns that we had just a few years ago.[45] The changes in information technology that are routinely thought of as threatening our right to privacy must also be thought of as constituting our conception of privacy. If the same technology that to some is threatening our privacy is the technology that leads us to think of ourselves, recalling Justice Brennan, as more public than we thought of ourselves in the past, then this is but another manifestation of the phenomenon of the social construction of privacy. If privacy is socially constructed, and if technology is part of society, then it follows that privacy, and our conception of what constitutes an invasion of it, is technologically constructed as well.

THE JOURNALISTIC CONSTRUCTION OF PRIVACY

Although it is easy these days to focus on the electronic and cyberspace dimensions of our changing informational lives, it is worthwhile to recall that Justice Brennan was making his point not in the context of changing information technology, but instead in the context of changes in our conception of public physical space[46] and changes in the actual practices of journalism. If, so he supposed, the media was becoming more aggressive in what it reported and what it did not, legal rules aside, then this social fact was relevant in determining the extent to which so-called private individuals should be able to bring lawsuits based on what was said about them when they were involved in public events.

It is a mistake to think that all or even much of this is attributable to law. Just as vast differences between American and Australian media law overpredict differences between American and Australian media,[47] so too is it a mistake to attribute too much of journalistic behavior to legal incentives.[48] Although I briefly discuss the law in the following section, here I am concerned instead with the legally unmediated effect of press practices in general. Consider, for example, American political journalists' widespread historical practice of not publishing information about the sex- and alcohol-related behavior of public officials and public figures. Even though the publication of such information was plainly legally protected, and even though many citizens would have used such information in making their voting and other decisions, the rules of the game kept such matters from public view. Starting with Gary Hart, and probably not finishing with President Clinton, the rules have changed, and public officials no longer have the expectation of privacy with respect to sex-related or alcohol-related behavior that they enjoyed prior to the late 1980s. Unlike the expectations of President Kennedy, President George W. Bush would in 2003 have no expectations of privacy, reasonable or otherwise, with respect to sexual behavior with a woman who was not his wife, regardless of where that behavior occurred.

This is not the place to discuss whether the change I have just described is for better or worse.[49] The point is only that we have witnessed a substantial change in what a class might reasonably have expected, and that change is largely a consequence of legally uninfluenced alterations in journalistic behavior. Nor is there any reason to believe that the phenomenon is restricted to public officials and public figures. Insofar as similar changes in journalistic mores and practices make it more likely that ordinary people will see their pictures in the newspaper, more likely that they will be approached by a journalist in the immediate aftermath of a tragic accident, and more likely that those who are the victims (or perpetrators) of crimes will be described in some detail in the press, then it is more likely that people's understanding of what privacy is will be influenced as well. This is not just a matter of people becoming psychologically or sociologically inured to things that previously would have appalled them, although this factor is at work as well. Rather, changing journalistic practices, by altering people's empirical expectations of the space that is theirs alone to control, have changed, in what is ultimately a conceptual and not empirical way, people's understanding of just what privacy *is*.[50]

THE LEGAL CONSTRUCTION OF PRIVACY

Although technological changes and journalistic practices influence our understanding of what privacy is, it is also the case that law does not just stand by as an innocent observer. Especially in a law-soaked society like the United States, our social and cultural practices, our institutions, and our conceptual understanding are highly influenced by the law.[51] Law creates possibilities—conceptual, institutional, and empirical—and extinguishes them. Law can mold and remold our understanding of the world. To take the First Amendment as an example, many people in the United States understand incitement to racial hatred as a free speech issue and not as a crime—as an issue of communication and not as an issue of equality—largely because of the way in which the highly salient First Amendment has shaped our practices of cultural categorization.[52] Similarly, Americans increasingly categorize hostile- environment sexual harassment as a free speech issue, although they did not only a few years ago,[53] largely because of the salience of the First Amendment and its doctrines.

In much the same way, we can see the distinct possibility that the law of privacy informs our conception of what privacy is. With some topics, of course, this is highly unlikely. Our conception of what a horse is remains largely untouched by equine law, and so too with the law pertaining to rivers, food, and chemicals. In all of these cases the law operates on a prelegal world, and although the law may affect that world it is unlikely to affect our conceptual understanding of what that world is all about. Not so, however, with privacy. Although the concept of privacy does have a moral, social, and philosophical prelegal existence (and in this respect differs from the First Amendment, which does not have a prelegal existence),[54] a great deal of our understanding about the concept of privacy appears to be influenced by judicial decisions invoking the right to privacy,[55] and by legal categories (including the common law tort of invasion of privacy) that inform our language and our practices of categorization. The person in the street might think of elephants and rivers without thinking of the law, but that same person is unlikely to think of privacy without thinking of the *right* to privacy and *invasion* of privacy. The intrusion of these legal terms and legal ideas makes it far less likely that a widespread understanding of the concept of privacy can exist without being created and recreated by the law itself. Even if privacy has a prelegal existence, therefore, the ordinary understanding of it is infused with law in ways that our ordinary understanding of natural kinds is not, and to that extent the ordinary understanding of privacy, like the ordinary understanding of the First Amendment, is at least partially at the mercy of legal changes.

If this is so, then our conception of privacy is likely to be as influenced by legal change as it is by changes in technology and changes in journalistic practices. As courts and legislatures identify as privacy violations some things that would not previously have been so categorized, this will likely inform public understanding of the idea of privacy itself. In a world in which the law is especially important, those who have the power to make the law—legislatures, judges, administrative agencies, and occasionally authoritative commentators on the work of legislatures, judges, and administrative agencies[56]—are likely to be the ones who have a disproportionate power over our conceptual apparatus in those areas in which the concepts have at best a thin prelegal existence. As a largely socially constructed concept, privacy is particularly at the mercy of society's constructors; in the United States, at least, law is one of the most important of our constructors.

CONCLUSION

The claims of social construction are important, but cannot be pressed too far. That privacy is socially constructed does not mean that it is not subject to normative critique and evaluation, nor that privacy is immune from legal and political influence. But once we understand that privacy—arguably unlike justice, utility, and other moral primaries, and certainly unlike rabbits, tulips, and other natural kinds—is largely a function of a socially constructed and contingent way of organizing the world, we can understand as well that this social construction is as variable as the forces that create it. As we now live in a world in which changes in law, changes in journalistic practice, and, most of all, changes in technology are accelerating, we consequently live in a world in which the very forces that have constructed the right to privacy are changing as quickly as anything we know. One approach to all of this, an unfortunately common one, is to shore up the barricades and guard against the intrusions to our privacy. But, as I hope to have shown here, the barricades themselves are made of the same material as the forces that are alleged to threaten them. As a result, there is something strangely circular and anachronistic about contemporary fears concerning our privacy. Those fears may be real, but insofar as those fears are expressed in terms of social understandings that are themselves changing, they may turn out to be as short-lived as the technologies that are thought to threaten them.

NOTES

[1]See, for only the tip of the iceberg, Peter L. Berger & Thomas Luckman, *The Social Construction of Reality: A Treatise in the Sociology of Knowledge* (1966); John Searle, *The Construction of Social Reality* (1995); David Weissman, *Truth's Debt to Value* (1993); Sheila Jasanoff, *The Eye of Everyman: Witnessing DNA in the Simpson Trial*, Social Studies of Science, 713–40 (1998); Marilyn MacCrimmons, *The Social Construction of Reality and the Rules of Evidence*, University of British Columbia Law Review 36–63 (1991); John R. Searle, *Rationality and Realism: What Is at Stake?* 122 Proceedings of the American Academy of Arts and Sciences 55–73 (1993); Symposium, *Philosophy and Literary Theory*, 69 The Monist 3ff (1986).

[2]The entire topic of social construction is one that is especially fraught with caricature, and thus I find it necessary to signal early on that the gap between what some scholars maintain and what they are claimed to maintain is wider here than in many other areas of academic inquiry.

[3]The statement in the text is a loose summary of various social constructivist, deconstructionist, and postmodernist claims. For a much deeper exploration, see Christo-

pher Norris, *What's Wrong With Postmodernism: Critical Theory and the Ends of Philosophy* (1990). See also James McGowan, *Postmodernism and Its Critics* (1991).

[4]Labels often obscure more than they illuminate, but the view in the text is often described as "positivism" or "realism," and has both its vulgar and its sophisticated versions. See Moritz Schlick, "Positivism and Realism," in Richard Boyd, Philip Gasper & J. D. Trout, *The Philosophy of Science* 37–56 (1991).

[5]Philosophers often call these things "natural kinds." See D. M. Armstrong, *A Theory of Universals: Universals and Scientific Realism* 65–67 (1978).

[6]For arguments coming close to the caricature, see Cicero, *De Legibus* (C. W. Keyes, trans.) book I Sec. 6, book III Sec. 19 (1928). See also William Blackstone, *Commentaries on the Laws of England*, 44 (vol. 1, 165).

[7]See, for example, H. L. A. Hart, *The Concept of Law* (Oxford: Clarendon Press, 1961); Hans Kelsen, *Pure Theory of Law* (Max Knight trans.; 2d. ed., 1967); Jules Coleman, *Negative and Positive Positive Positivism*, 11 Journal of Legal Studies 139–62 (1982); Frederick Schauer & Virginia J. Wise, *Legal Positivism as Legal Information*, 82 Cornell Law Review 1080–1110 (1997). For a contemporary collection of perspectives, see Robert P. George, ed., *The Autonomy of Law: Essays on Legal Positivism* (1996).

[8]See, for example, G. J. Warnock, *Contemporary Moral Philosophy* (1967).

[9]See, for example, C. L. Stevenson, *Ethics and Language* (1944).

[10]See, for example, "Moral Relativism Defended," in Michael Krausz & Jack W. Meiland, eds., *Relativism, Cognitive and Moral* (1982).

[11]See Frederick Schauer, *Internet Privacy and the Public-Private Distinction*, 38 *Jurimetrics* 555–64 (1998), in which I first hinted at some of the ideas I develop at greater length in this chapter.

[12]Thomas I. Emerson, *The Right of Privacy and Freedom of the Press*, 14 Harvard Civil Rights–Civil Liberties Law Review 329–53, at 339 (1979).

[13]See Ronald Dworkin, *Freedom's Law: The Moral Reading of the American Constitution* (1996).

[14]See John Stuart Mill & Jeremy Bentham, *Utilitarianism and Other Essays* (Alan Ryan, ed.; 1987).

[15]See John Rawls, *A Theory of Justice* (1971).

[16]Bernard Gert, *Morality: Its Nature and Justification* (1998).

[17]Rawls, 34–40.

[18]Ronald Dworkin, "Do We Have a Right to Pornography," in *A Matter of Principle* 335–72 (1985).

[19]Rawls, *passim*.

[20]If one takes John Stuart Mill to be a utilitarian, itself a debatable proposition, this is the best understanding of his *On Liberty* (David Spitz, ed.; 1975).

[21]Edward J. Bloustein, *Privacy as an Aspect of Human Dignity: An Answer to Dean Prosser*, New York University Law Review 962–81 (1964).

[22]The moral relativist, of course, would take varying degrees of social or cultural acceptance or rejection of these practices as evidence of the social construction of morality. The moral objectivist, however, whose views are presupposed in any statement critical of a practice of social or cultural acceptance, would take the fact of social acceptance of an immoral practice as irrelevant to its moral status.

[23]See Rendall P. Bezanson, *Privacy, Personality, and Social Norms*, 41 Case Western Reserve Law Review 681–87, 684 (1991).

[24]*Rosenbloom v. Metromedia, Inc.,* 403 U.S. 29, at p. 47 (1971) (plurality opinion of Brennan, J.).

[25]*Time, Inc. v. Hill,* 385 U.S. 374, 388 (1967) (Brennan, J., for the Court).

[26]See, generally, Robert C. Post, "The Social Foundations of Privacy: Community and Self in the Common Law Tort," in *Constitutional Domains: Democracy, Community, Management* 51–88 (1995).

[27]*Restatement (Second) of Torts, "* 652 B, C, D, E.

[28]See *Carson v. Here's Johnny Portable Toilets Inc.,* 698 F.2d 831 (6th Cir. 1983).

[29]See Richard C. Turkington & Anita L. Allen, *Privacy Law: Cases and Materials* 399–449 (1999).

[30]See *Hamberger v. Eastman,* 206 A.2d 239 (N.H. 1964).

[31]See, generally, Frederick Schauer, *Reflections on the Value of Truth,* 41 Case Western Reserve Law Review 699–724 (1991); Diane L. Zimmerman, *Requiem for a Heavyweight: A Farewell to Warren and Brandeis's Privacy Tort,* 68 Cornell Law Review 291–354 (1983).

[32]Samuel D. Warren & Louis D. Brandeis, *The Right to Privacy,* Harvard Law Review, 193–224 (1890).

[33]*Time, Inc. v. Hill* (1967).

[34]*Restatement (Second) of Torts* Sec. 652E.

[35]See *Leverton v. Curtis Publishing Co.,* 192 F.2d 974 (3d Cir. 1951).

[36]*Restatement (Second) of Torts* Sec. 652B(1).

[37]*Restatement (Second) of Torts* Sec. 652D(1)(a).

[38]*Restatement (Second) of Torts* Sec. 652E (1).

[39]*Katz v. United States,* 389 U.S. 347, 361 (1967) (Harlan, J., concurring).

[40]*Katz v. United States,* at 349.

[41]*California v. Carney,* 471 U.S. 386 (1985).

[42]*Florida v. Riley,* 488 U.S. 445 (1989); *California v. Ciraolo,* 476 U.S. 207 (1986).

[43]See John MacDonald, *Keep Journalists Out of the Spook Business,* Hartford Courant 8 (March 30, 1996).

[44]See Katrin Schatz Byford, *Privacy in Cyberspace: Constructing a Model of Privacy for the Electronic Communications Environment,* 24 Rutgers Computer and Technology Law Journal 1–34 (1998).

[45]See Arthur R. Miller, *The Right to Privacy—A Look Through the Kaleidoscope,* 46 SMU Law Review 37–46, at 40 (1992), describing Caller ID as "a paradigm of privacy issues we are experiencing today."

[46]Although he did not say so, it is not unreasonable to suppose that Justice Brennan was thinking not only of defamation, and not only of privacy, but also of (then) recent changes in First Amendment doctrine marked by cases such as *Cohen v. California,* 403 U.S. 15 (1971). If the "shell" with which one surrounded oneself was becoming more permeable with the possibility of affront, offense, and verbal assault of the kind protected in cases like *Cohen* and then-pending cases like *Gooding v. Wilson,* 405 U.S. 518 (1972), then it was not unreasonable for someone in Justice Brennan's position to suppose that the increasing permeable shell provided less of a protection for personal privacy in public space.

[47]Although Australian defamation law, by contrast to the American, has historically been both well used and among the most press restrictive in the English-speaking world, the actual content of the Australian press, in terms of the "wide-open" and "robust" criticism of government and officials (*New York Times Co. v. Sullivan,* 376 U.S. 254 (1964)), is strikingly similar

to that of the American press. See, generally, New South Wales Law Reform Commission, *Defamation*, (Discussion paper 32) (August 1993).

[48] At least some journalists and editors, for example, claim that their publication decisions are largely uninfluenced by considerations of defamation law. See David A. Anderson, *The Economics of Libel Litigation*, 53 Texas Law Review 422–71, at 422 (1975); David A. Hollander, "The Economics of Libel Litigation," in Everette Dennis & Eli Noam, eds., *The Cost of Libel: Economic and Policy Implications* 257–84, at 257, 258 n.3 (1989); Barry F. Smith, *The Rising Tide of Libel Litigation: Implications of the Gertz Negligence Rules*, 44 Montana Law Review 71–92, at 87 (1983).

[49] For the record, I believe it more for the better than the conventional wisdom supposes, partly because I think that journalistic covering up of information that some voters would have thought relevant to *their* voting decisions is more for the worse than the conventional wisdom believes. See Frederick Schauer, *Can Public Figures Have Private Lives?* 17 Social Philosophy and Policy 293–309 (2000).

[50] There is an interesting issue here, and with other First Amendment-related reporting as well, of journalists' ethical responsibilities when reporting on privacy issues. Given that individual privacy and freedom of the press are often thought to be in conflict, see Peter B. Edelman, *Free Press v. Privacy: Haunted By the Ghost of Justice Black*, 68 Texas Law Review 1195–1211 (1990); Terence J. Clark, *When Privacy Rights Encounter First Amendment Freedoms*, 41 Case Western Reserve Law Review 921–28 (1991), much of reporting on privacy issues will involve, whether explicitly or implicitly, reporting on free press issues as well, issues in which the reporters, the editors, the publishers, and the newspaper (or magazine, or radio station, or television station, or whatever) have strong views, and are themselves interested parties. If a reporter for *The New York Times* is ordinarily expected to recuse himself/herself when the issue on which he/she is reporting is one in which he/she has especially strong moral or political views, and to identify any potential conflict of interest, then what are the implications for this when reporters are reporting on issues centrally about, or touching on, issues of freedom of the press—issues on which reasonable people often disagree, and on which there are often two sides (as especially with privacy versus free speech conflicts), but in which journalists are more uniformly on one side rather than the other?

[51] See generally Robert W. Gordon, *Critical Legal Histories*, 36 Stanford Law Review 57–126 (1984).

[52] See Frederick Schauer, *Exceptions*, 58 University of Chicago Law Review 871–99 (1991).

[53] See Frederick Schauer, "The Speech-ing of Sexual Harassment," in Catharine MacKinnon & Reva Siegel, eds., *New Directions in Sexual Harassment Law* (2003).

[54] Note that I say "First Amendment" and not "freedom of speech" or "freedom of expression" or "freedom of the press." The point here is only that legal concepts do not and cannot have a prelegal existence, even if laws can and often do protect prelegal rights.

[55] Especially decisions such as *Roe v. Wade*, 410 U.S. 113 (1973), and *Griswold v. Connecticut*, 381 U.S. 479 (1965). See Thomas Gerety, *Doing Without Privacy*, 42 Ohio State Law Journal 143–44 (1981).

[56] There is also the interesting phenomenon by which influential public understanding of what the law is may diverge from the formal or technical understanding of what the law is, a phenomenon with interesting implications for the point I make in the text. See Robert C. Ellickson, *Order Without Law: How Neighbors Settle Disputes* (1991).

2

The Structural Attributes of Press Freedom: Private Ownership, Public Orientation, and Editorial Independence

Randall P. Bezanson
University of Iowa College of Law

The distinction between the public and the private—between speech about public matters and speech concerning private matters, between censorship by public agencies and by private parties, between private speakers and government speech—permeates free speech doctrine. It accounts for the law of state action,[1] for the public forum doctrine,[2] for the gradients of constitutional protection accorded speech whose content is more or less public or political in character,[3] and for one of the mainstays of First Amendment theory, which is that speech is free as a means of facilitating self-government.[4]

Much has been written about the distinction between the public and private in free speech law, not all of it favorable.[5] The distinction has grown up and matured in the crucible of free speech; in the tension between individual liberty of belief and the collective interests in the effective functioning of democratic government;[6] in the need to assign value to the artifact of expression even when it bears slim relationship to individual liberty;[7] and in the concomitant need to rationalize protection of speech acts that are grounded in liberty but bear scant relationship to self-government, culture, and general social and economic facts of life.[8]

Although the distinction, ironically, has partly been forged in cases involving the press, such as *New York Times Co. v. Sullivan*,[9] there has been little if any systematic attention in the judicial opinions or the academic literature to the distinction's possible relevance to the constitutional law of freedom of the press, or indeed to the possible, and possibly different, meanings of the concepts of public and private in the press setting. This is no doubt largely due to the fact that there is no distinct law of freedom of the press. Until recently at least, the free press guarantee has been seen as identical to the free speech guarantee.[10] Speech by journalists has as a theoretical matter been protected under the general guarantee of free expression, with no recognition of relevant differences between the journalist's expression of his or her private views and the way in which the journalist chooses to speak in his or her capacity as a journalist. There is, even today, no large and coherent body of case law and theoretical writing on the distinct subject of freedom of the press. If free speech law didn't really emerge until the 1920s and 1930s, the law of freedom of the press began to emerge only in the 1970s and 1980s, and it remains largely unarticulated to this day.

As one who has written about many specific issues involving the press—ranging from privilege claims, news gathering, defamation and privacy, taxation, editorial judgment, institutional speech, and the organization and economics of news enterprises (especially newspapers)—I have long held the conviction that a distinct and coherent set of principles should apply to free expression claims by the press.[11] Getting beneath the exigencies of particular claims and issues to more broadly theoretical or generalized principles that animate press freedom, however, has proved difficult, and the Supreme Court understandably has been reluctant to rush unnecessarily into uncharted waters. For the Court, free speech doctrine has proved serviceable enough for most issues.[12]

A useful analytical tool is needed to probe beneath the surface. One such tool is editorial judgment—a belief-forming judgment protected for journalists that, I have recently claimed, differs in some marked and revealing ways from the belief formation and expressive judgments of individuals.[13] Another such tool, I think, is the public/private distinction. Does the distinction have any useful place in the protections accorded a free press? If so, do the concepts of public and private take on different meaning in the press context than in the free speech context, drawing us in different directions and yielding different results?

In undertaking this inquiry, I begin with the intuition that the public/private distinction, as it has come to be employed in speech cases, has little relevance to journalism and its constitutional freedom. The press cannot be free if it is tethered to a special obligation to report on matters judged to be of public importance and relevance to politics or to the current conceptions of public interest or value. The press' freedom is the freedom to judge for itself. Moreover, the press' freedom connotes independence. But it is an independence grounded not in free will, but in structure and process. And its freedom is freedom not just from government, but also from other, often privately originated, pressures and inducements that would undermine its structural independence.

But in a different sense a distinction between the public and the private is at the heart of journalism and freedom of the press. This different sense of the "public" is not grounded in content of expression, but instead in its manner, in the orientation of publication judgment toward a general public audience, in the public rather than private purpose served by a publication, and in the ownership and organizational structure of the firm.[14] The press is a public speaker; it is much more than that, of course, but at base its expression must be public. News and journalism occupy a uniquely public space, performing a uniquely public function of transforming the particular into the general, converting the private into the public. The press' standard of selection of material to publish must be oriented to public need. At the same time, control of the selection process must be private, and thus ownership must be private.

Thinking about individual speech and press speech—by which, of course, I mean news and journalism—in terms of their public and private qualities and functions thus leads to a set of new and systematic distinctions between "public" and "private," distinctions that may help us better understand the constitutional guarantees of the "freedom of speech … and of the press."

My conclusions about the essential differences between the public and private qualities of individual and press speech are as follows:

1. Individual speech is, by its very nature, personal and therefore private. Press speech is public.
2. The content of individual speech is personal, dictated by the individual speaker. It is an exercise of free will deeply personal to the speaker and serving only the speaker's interests. The content of press speech, in contrast, is public in design, dictated by the speaker's judgment of audience, public interest, and relevance. The culture and conventions of journalism and news induce a measure of depersonalization of a story from an individual reporter, and an accounting of the audience in the selection and construction of content and composition.[15]
3. Individual speech serves personal and private ends—of self-expression, individual free will, personal belief, and the conduct of atomized social relationships. Press speech serves public ends—of collective fact and information and knowledge, of culture and social organization, and of assimilation.[16]
4. Individual speech has value to the individual and at the level of local groups; press speech has value to the public or polity. In traditional societies, local and rural, information is contextualized by the interests and understandings of the community. This is the business of individual speech. With industrialization and the emergence of a mass working class in urban areas, and now with the revolutionary changes in communication, many former social organizations, which served as contexts for meaning, have broken down. Mass media are a reflection of this change. News in mass media is information decontextualized from community. Meaning, then, becomes in this mass media setting a function of ideology, not of shared values and experiences at a more personal and less ideological level.[17] This is the nature of press speech.
5. Individual speech produces public value through the systematic effects of individual, atomized, and personally focused instances of expression. Press speech produces individual value through the receipt and use of a public message by unique individuals for their own purposes.[18] Public value is thus a secondary (and unpredictable) consequence of individual speech. Individual speech serves personal ends; only secondarily, when

aggregated at a societal level, does it serve public ends. In contrast, public value is a primary consequence of press speech; a personal value is achieved derivatively, if at all, through the individual's conversion of press speech to his or her own uses.

6. An individual speaker uses information about others in order to translate the public to the private—to give significance and meaning in the speaker's private terms and for the speaker's private purposes. Press speakers use information about others to convert the private to the public—to give private or personal information public significance.

7. Restrictions on individual speech must rest in part on the content of the message. Restrictions on press speech must rest largely on process-based criteria.

Individual speech originates in a person's free will (if a group, in the aggregated free will of each member). Press speech originates in a group or organizational setting (institutional) and serves the expressive purposes of the institution, not any specific individual. Individual speech involves all subject matters—fact, fiction, art, gossip, opinion, history. Press speech involves fact and opinion (nonfiction) regarding matters of current general relevance to the public.

Thus, individual speech, being a reflection of personal freedom and creativity, is not easily susceptible to process-based constraint; its limitations must rest largely on content. Press speech, being a reflection of public knowledge and elucidation, rests explicitly on process-based qualities, and thus cannot be effectively limited by content-based criteria.

These conclusions have interesting implications for existing doctrine under the speech and press guarantees, and useful practical consequences for many press claims, including news-gathering claims.

I begin my analysis with the free speech doctrine of privacy, identifying the various ways in which the public and private manifest themselves at the definitional, doctrinal, and balancing levels in First Amendment analysis. I explore the meaning and theoretical footings of the public/private distinction, and then inquire into its useful or logical application to free press claims. Next, I turn to the possibly new and distinct ways in which the ideas of "public" and "private" may play a useful and theoretically critical role in claims of journalistic freedom. I conclude, in the end, that putting journalism to use as a specially privileged instrument of speech on public issues would be a serious mistake and would deprive journalism of its very identity and independence. I also conclude that speech by journalists—speech by the press—is by definition public regardless of its content, although this is paradoxically true only if the press is private; and that the public quality of press speech serves both as the fundamental premise for its protection and as a precondition to that protection. Substantive or content-based definitions of the "public" have no place in the press' freedom.

It is in the public quality of press speech—its necessary orientation to broad audiences and to matters of interest and usefulness to a broad public, to public need as well as to public preference—that the distinction between claims of freedom of the press and claims of free speech lie. But paradoxically, the instruments the law uses to ensure and protect the public quality of press speech must rest on process-based and structural considerations, not on the content or value of the press' expression.

DISTINGUISHING THE FREE SPEECH MODEL: "PUBLIC" AS SUBSTANCE

In this section, I review the ways in which the public/private distinction manifests itself in free speech doctrine and theory of privacy. The public/private distinction in free speech doctrine is a manifestation of the tension between the private and public faces of individual expression, the individual and collective goals of free speech. The tension is negotiated through the dominantly content-based standards on which the rules governing the permissible restrictions on speech rest. The animating content standard, of course, is the preference for speech on public rather than private subjects.

Privacy cases can be read as implying greater justification for invading privacy when the topic is of public importance—judged not by the fact of publication but by legal criteria based on public relevance and value of the disclosed information. Indeed, this is precisely what many common law privacy cases hold,[19] but they do so largely by virtue of the common law rules of privacy and the common law privilege of newsworthiness, not because the Constitution demands it.[20]

Moreover, even the common law cases can be read to imply a quite distinct and content-neutral proposition. They can be seen to rest on a neutral question of relevance of fact to theme—and with the press, at least, a *chosen* theme, not a theme judged useful by anyone other than the publisher. The question, in other words, is not whether the invasive disclosure or the subject to which it relates (if different from the disclosure itself) is of public importance, but instead whether and how the disclosure is relevant—a neutral inquiry—to the subject the publisher chose to write about, whatever its public or private stripe.[21]

But seeing the common law tort rules in terms other than public/private ones is not, in the end, the main point. My principal interest is in the constitutional standards, not the common law doctrine. From a constitutional perspective it is fair to say that virtually nothing can be said about privacy, much less its public/private basis. At least this is so in the decisions of the Supreme Court, because the Court has managed effectively (and perhaps wisely) to reserve for future decision the very central constitutional issue of whether a truthful communication by the press that otherwise qualifies for free press protection can ever be subjected to liability.[22] In the absence of an answer to that question, no conclusion can be drawn from the privacy cases—at least those that turn on publication rather than conduct related to publication, the latter being news-gathering and distribution questions of a different stripe.

In the end, the essential immunity of the press from invasion-of-privacy liability speaks loudly of the irrelevance of a substantive public/private distinction to freedom of the press.[23] Indeed, the difficulty of subjecting the press to harm for privacy invasion that arises from the content of a press publication may represent but a manifestation of a press freedom premised not on content or on ideas of the "public" or "value," but on standards of structure and process alone. Such an approach would effectively formalize the death of the privacy tort as applied to news on the simple ground that the tort eviscerates any semblance of editorial freedom by a press publisher. It would replace protections for privacy instead with rules that are content neutral and generally applicable, such as a statutory or tort-based right of control over information about oneself, a right akin to that protected under the heading of breach of confidence.[24] This seems, in fact, to be where the privacy debate is going, especially with the advent of invasive technologies for information collection and use on the Internet; it is also a direction that the Supreme Court seems to be signaling in some of its recent decisions.[25]

With the press, independence is the heart of press freedom, and independence comprehends a larger set of concerns, larger than just the state or what is formally public. Independence for the press is a more full-bodied idea, requiring a different conception of the "public" and "private" that in turn reflects a distinct set of purposes served by the press' constitutional freedom, purposes such as ensuring an independent source of information to the public, providing a structural means of limiting the accretion of power, and serving as a force of egalitarianism and assimilation for the culture and social order. Substantively grounded public/private distinctions, much less sharp distinctions between the state and private interests, do not fit well into this distinct framework of purposes and functions.

THE PROCESS BASIS OF THE FREE PRESS MODEL: OWNERSHIP, AUDIENCE, INDEPENDENCE

The public/private distinction does have a place in the press setting, but it does not fall along lines of substance, content, or value; rather, it rests on structure and process. In this section, I explore the three principal elements of structural public/private distinctions and the constitutional ends of press freedom that explain them. The three structural elements of a free press are: private ownership, public audience, and editorial independence. Following a general and brief discussion of the three elements, I explore their specific application and meaning through three cases involving, respectively, news gathering, press independence, and the right of privacy.

Private Ownership: A Private Rather Than Public Forum.   Perhaps the most fundamental public/private distinction in free press law and theory concerns ownership: A free press must be a private press, free of government ownership and even involvement in its editorial affairs. As Frederick Siebert put it in his famous description of libertarianism, "[T]he underlying purpose of the media [is] to help discover truth, to assist in the process of solving political and social problems by presenting all manner of evidence and opinion as the basis for decisions. The essential characteristic of this process [is the press'] freedom from government controls or domination."[26] Freedom of the press accordingly belongs to private organizations and publishers; the government may not, at least as such, exercise the rights protected by the free press guarantee.[27]

The "Private" Press: Ownership and Audience.

This central premise of press ownership rests on one of two possible public/private distinctions. The first distinction is between government and nongovernment actors: Presses owned by all forms of private arrangements—whether business firms, individuals, groups, or ideological, political, or social organizations—are protected by the free press guarantee of the First Amendment *because* they are private. Only presses owned or controlled by the government fail to qualify for constitutional protection. An alternative view would limit "private" owners to those organizations and firms that operate in the broad capitalist market, free of ideological or special interest obligation and thus are, in Siebert's phrase, "completely free from control or domination."[28] The distinction is an important one, because it has to do with expectations of objectivity and dedication to seeking information useful to the public, wherever that might lead.

But if objectivity and public service are the standards by which to judge the public/private distinction in ownership, why would one interpret the First Amendment as preferring capitalist business organizations? Private corporations are clearly as embedded in ideology and committed to their own interests as are more explicitly partisan or social organizations that own presses, such as labor unions, universities, or political parties. The classic defense of private ownership of the press has been based on the capitalist model, consisting of profit-driven and nonideological firms competing in the market (the market, of course, being defined narrowly as the capitalist market). The justification for singling out business firms as the paradigmatic private form of ownership is that the firms "respond rationally to market demands and provide the goods and services the public wants."[29] As Siebert wrote, "Anyone with sufficient capital could start a communication enterprise ... [and] the success of the enterprise would be determined by the public which it sought to serve."[30] The private press model, in other words, is premised on a privately owned business firm whose product is directly responsive to the market, by which is meant, for the press, a market consisting of a *public* readership or audience.

Responsiveness to the public audience in a capitalist market is critical to this view of private ownership, because if a firm need not respond to the public readership it could easily become an instrument of the private ideology or political interests of its owners and thus no longer independent, incapable of aspiring to objectivity or neutrality and indifferent to the interests of its audience. Historically, this has occurred when a newspaper, for example, exercises monopoly power, freeing the publisher of the restraints of competition and enabling the paper to follow editorial courses even in the face of reader resistance.[31] In such cases the competitive model has broken down and the assumptions supporting a free, private press have been undermined, if not destroyed.[32] For this reason, if no other, the Supreme

Court years ago rejected the argument that freedom of the press means freedom from application of the antitrust laws.[33]

The underlying issue of what qualities the press must possess, and their relationship to forms of ownership, is of course a subtle and complicated one. Is a press freed from the will of a public audience not a "press" for purposes of the First Amendment? Is the central question one of freedom from all allegiances and controls on editorial content and choice, thus suggesting that the union newsletter and ideologically committed magazine, for example, fail fully to qualify as "press"? Is an audience's control different from other forms of control? An audience for a union newsletter may exercise control in as ideological a fashion as the union leadership. Alternatively, must audience control be "public" in the sense that it is broad and not ideologically monolithic (except perhaps by happenstance of buying preference)? Why is audience control more benign than ownership control? Are the difficult issues raised by the issue of ownership form and audience control the very reasons that the public/private distinction in the ownership context ultimately comes down to a prohibition on government ownership or control, with the privately owned but ideologically committed press qualifying for constitutional protection on the assumption that freedom of the press consists not simply of atomized publications but rather of *a system of competition* in news and opinion by various publications?

Monopoly power that forecloses competition among types of publications undermines the premise of the *system* of a free press. Viewing freedom of the press in systematic terms—as a system consisting of private and competing voices—is perfectly sensible, so long as the voices qualifying for the competition share attributes that distinguish them from all other speakers, such as fiction writers, humorists, and painters, even as they distinguish themselves from each other—daily, weekly, aligned, independent, agnostic, political, or economic in focus, and so forth. After all, a free press consisting of identical, cookie-cutter publications would hardly serve the interest in dissemination of information from all perspectives and all quarters, much less opinions of all sorts.

Such a diverse and wide-open press is not what we enjoy today, however. The fact is that the dominant press has always been, and remains, the purely private, profit-driven, capitalistic business firm.[34] The alternative press is small, atomized, and marginal, hardly a large enough competitive force to offset the ideological interests and business behaviors of the private business firm if, and when, those interests and behaviors compromise the press' obligation to be free from "control or domination." Thus we must examine the business firm, in particular, to judge whether its actions are consistent with its claims to protection under the First Amendment.

Two things must be noted in any critical examination of the business firm. The first is that the business firm is not, by definition, free of allegiance to an ideology that could systematically undermine its capacity for objectivity and public responsiveness. As John Nerone expressed it in his critique of the libertarian and liberal press theories:

There is a dilemma here, and it comes from the (characteristically liberal) failure to recognize forms of power other than that of the state. How can the press ... be "completely free from control or domination" when it is part of the business system and driven by the same kinds of economic concerns and motives that drive other businesses? The press cannot logically be free from capital because it is capital in form and use.... [A] press driven by capital cannot be expected to provide a thorough critique of the economic system or to offer alternatives.... Naturally, from its very beginning, the capital-driven press did not have as its aim to be a watchdog over the system of which it is a part. Watchdogs do not bite their owners.[35]

A private, capitalist press is a press committed to the ideology of capitalism and, ironically, to the importance of distinguishing the private from the public. These are, of course, deeply political convictions to which the business firm is committed for the very preservation of its ability to publish, and therefore these are assumptions that animate in one way or another virtually all, if not all, editorial choices the firms make. Capitalism is a product of law and political choice. A view of freedom of the press that is premised on capitalism is thus a product of the government that creates, through law, the very rules and privileges under which the capitalist press organization operates. Can a government-created right or privilege be public and private at the same time?

The answer to this dilemma in free press theory is the audience. The capitalist press may be a creature of government—created by law in fairly detailed terms—and it may thus, without more, be truly a government actor owing allegiance to the public law and political philosophy of the existing order. At least this is so with such fundamental premises as private capital, private economic markets, individual freedom of choice, and the preservation of the private realm—and hence the imperative of a limited realm of governmental action. But if, notwithstanding this, the private, capitalist press' editorial choices and publication activities can be shown to be controlled not by government, nor even by allegiance to an ideology of self-preservation, but instead by individual consumers in the public marketplace, the business firm's claim to freedom can be redeemed. The firm's inclination to act in ways that preserve its political and economic identity is offset by the forces of the very market to which it owes its primary (because it is financial and thus necessary) allegiance—forces of an ideologically diverse and heterogeneous market of consumers of news and journalism.

Corporate Organization and Press Independence.   This conclusion, in turn, requires that we explore a second question: whether the private press' claim to control by the public—the subscribers or viewers who possess the capacity of individual choice and discernment—is well founded. What are the market forces that explain and shape the behavior of private press organizations? What influence does the news consumer actually wield? What is the definition of the "market" in which news organizations compete? Isn't press freedom the freedom to *do more* than simply publish what the audience wants?

A study that I recently conducted with my colleagues Gil Cranberg and John Soloski explored these and related issues in the context of the publicly traded newspaper company. Our study arrived at a disturbing conclusion: In the publicly traded newspaper firms, the dominant market forces that influence the firm and its editorial choices come not from the reader or consumer, nor from the advertiser (at least in any primary sense), but instead from the investment markets.[36] The investment markets strictly and rigorously orient—indeed, incentivize—the news organizations, from top to bottom, to maximize investment yield and financial performance. For the publicly traded newspaper company, the business of news is often not news, but just business. News product is incidental, even unimportant. Audience is significant only in instrumental ways, not in terms of satisfaction with published content but rather in terms of nonnews consumer buying preferences and socioeconomic characteristics.

What impact does the consumer have in shaping the editorial character of the firm? Our conclusion, applicable to the "pure" publicly held newspaper company, was that the reader/consumer has surprisingly little influence in shaping or checking the firm's behavior. Consumer preferences and reactions to a publication and its quality were essentially unimportant, except when subscription levels fell and consequently so too did the audience for advertisers. The principal consumer for the newspaper is the advertiser. Advertisers supply 80% or more of the revenues to the firm; they are interested in reaching audiences efficiently, and often in targeted ways; and their "market" is liquid in the sense that if the newspaper doesn't deliver a desirable and acquisitive audience as effectively as another medium, they will simply go elsewhere.

Newspapers, in short, are the victims of the advertisers' perfectly understandable interest in providing information to *their* customers, who are also the newspapers' customers. But advertisers' dominance is systematic, not specific, and results not from pressures exerted by advertisers themselves but instead from forces emanating from the investment markets; forces that ironically lead the firm itself to structure its news operations in ways that will maximize appeal to advertisers.

The metamorphosis effected by the investment markets is perhaps most apparent in the changing organizational structure of the news firm, and particularly the publicly traded newspaper firm. When audience and public preferences dominated the news firm's attention, companies adopted a form of internal organization that separated the news function from the business function of the firm. This separation preserved, symbolically and imperfectly, the independence of news judgments from advertisers and business considerations. It also provided a needed buffer between those who make news decisions and the audience that may dislike some of them. The audience should control the firm's editorial choices through subscription decisions, but at a wholesale level only, not at the retail level of specific content of the individual stories that are published.

The shift from the audience as principal constituency to the advertiser as principal market has led to a breaking down of the organizational wall between news and business. Advertisers are now seen as partners; advertising personnel in the newspaper firm are seen as editorial colleagues who have something to contribute to decisions about the form and content of editorial and news matter. The audience is treated differently as well. Subscribers are no longer discouraged from having direct influence on the editorial decisions. Indeed, news organizations now conduct substantial market research with subscribers to ascertain their raw preferences and to find ways in which to make the newspaper and its advertising more appealing and comfortable to the readers.

Finally, the gravitational force of the investment market's expectations serve to shape the organization of the firm, its priorities, and the definition of the market to which the paper is most responsive. The investment market's influence might well be capable of exerting itself from the top down by edict or fiat. However, in the publicly traded newspaper companies this difficult form of control has been effectively avoided by the introduction of pervasive bottom-up incentives throughout the firm, including in the newsroom. The incentives are designed to merge investment market demands with personal self-interest. In their most corrupting form, the incentives consist of compensation based heavily, and often predominantly, on strictly formulaic and financial criteria, coupled with generous stock options tied, by definition, to investment market performance. Options, in particular, have proved to be a subtle, popular, and extremely effective way to shift priorities and alliances in the news operation and in the newsroom. To put the point less delicately, stock options in public companies are corrupting news traditions and undermining audience influence, a corruption stemming, remarkably, from within the newsroom itself.

Does the private market function to encourage the press' independence? The answer is far from clear, based on our findings and on studies undertaken by others. The press—as a private, capitalist, business firm—is a bit different from most other firms. A news organization is not subject to only one principal consumer market— the car buyer, for example, whose choices clearly influence General Motors. Instead, the newspaper business (and other media businesses, too) participate and compete in two distinct, and sometimes clashing, markets: the market for consumers of the manufactured product (news) and the market for advertisers who pay the bills if they decide to support the product.[37] As it happens, the advertisers provide most of the cash, most of the profits. They also have the greatest range of choices about where to spend their money. In the newspaper business, subscribers have relatively few choices if they want the movie listings, obituaries, want ads, local sports, business news, and so forth—unless they are Internet users and are familiar with ways in which to obtain this information at low cost electronically. Because the advertisers provide the most money and have the most choices, they shape and constrain the press' publication activities. They are reinforced in their influence by the investment market demands that the firms have strategically distributed throughout the firm, from top to bottom, in the form of incentives.

The 17 largest privately owned, publicly traded newspaper firms account for over 50% of the daily and Sunday newspaper circulation in the United States. In the publicly traded newspaper firm, the private, free, and competitive market works very well. But it's the wrong market. Free press theory rests on the assumption that the control of the press in a capitalist system comes from the market of news consumers—individual persons expressing and acting on their preferences and thus forcing the press to act independently of government and other ideological commitments even though it is a creature of both. Advertisers cannot fill the same role: They are not interested in content as such. To the extent that content matters, their preference is for blandness and consistency with the status quo, not for fierce independence; and their audience members, which they effectively transfer to the news organization, are their customers, not a broad public audience reflecting all sides and dimensions of society.

A Public Press?   With the recent Supreme Court decision in *Arkansas Educational Television Commission v. Forbes*,[38] the possibility of a public press and its constitutional status has been brought to the forefront. The *Forbes* case involved a decision by the staff of a government-owned and operated public television station to exclude a congressional candidate from a political debate, a decision which, if made by a private news organization, would clearly fall within the organization's constitutionally protected editorial freedom.[39] The decision concerned a news program, rested expressly on a content-based editorial decision about the candidates and views to be represented, and was the product of a specific and discretionary programming decision (not the product of a generally applicable rule evenly applied without regard to content).[40] The candidate, Forbes, claimed that the decision was government action based on the content of his views and the quality of his candidacy, and therefore was strictly prohibited by the First Amendment.[41]

The Court rejected Forbes' claim on grounds that are, at best, peculiar. The Court did not conclude that the content discrimination was justified under the conventional First Amendment standards. Indeed, the Court did not view the decision to exclude Forbes as a regulatory action subject to the First Amendment. Instead, the Court held that the decision represented government expression resulting from an exercise of editorial judgment by state employees/editors and, as such, it was either protected under the First Amendment or, in the alternative, it represented a form of expressive, nonregulatory government action that is not subject to the normal scrutiny demanded by the First Amendment.[42] Under either view, the government's expression and the underlying editorial decisions were given special constitutional status under the First Amendment guarantees.

The *Forbes* case, and its companion, *National Endowment for the Arts v. Finley*,[43] raise important questions. Can freedom of the press be exercised by government or public presses as well as private ones? Can *Forbes* be seen as placing Arkansas Educational Television on the "private" side of the divide, notwithstanding its government ownership?[44] The first question can be addressed briefly and decisively. A government-owned press can hardly be seen as likely to engage in the monitoring and checking functions performed by the press. This is evident with respect to the checking of government power and the conduct of government officials, which perhaps is the most important (although not the only) structural assumption of the free press guarantee. As to checking the exercise of private power, government already has sufficient tools at its disposal to do that[45]—more tools than the press possesses, especially in the news-gathering setting. It hardly needs the power of a free press too. But the critical fact is the absence of independence that a government press would possess, whether from government self-interest or from government temptation to control how public business is conducted.

This does not exhaust the list of difficulties. A government press would possess, presumably, all of the powers of government to investigate, discover, coerce, prosecute, and to make law, because these are powers that accompany all constitutional acts of government. The government press would thus be able to arm itself with the investigative authority of government—subpoenas, wiretaps, regulatory reporting requirements—and hence possess awesome news-gathering capacities that would swamp those held by the private press. It would be able to dominate news and public affairs in ways almost as effective as direct prohibitions on competition from private firms. The government press could hardly be said, then, to comport with the model of competition that underlies the private press. Additionally, being supported by government appropriations, not advertising or subscription revenues, it would not be subject to consumer or audience control in the marketplace. Its claim to legitimacy would be that it is responsive to democratic control by the whole public, a claim that would, even if believable in a remote representative form of government, literally ring with irony. Were this reasoning adequate as a means of controlling government, why guarantee freedom of the press, thus visiting power on a wholly private and nondomesticable set of people and organizations? The idea of a government-owned "free" press simply cannot be squared with the First Amendment.

But what about a narrower idea: a publicly owned press structured in a way that preserves the attributes of the private press—independence, market responsiveness, editorial decisions made professionally and with a view to the editors' own (not the government's) view of truth and of what is important for a public to hear or see? Indeed, might such a press be seen as really private, and the private press as partly public? The "private" press' position and power are, at base, the product of positive law, and thus the way in which they conduct their business—poor quality, violence, degradation, and so forth—might be seen as a form of state action. Many argue that the power of the media to exclude fringe views is just that: nominally private editorial authority sanctioned or at least authorized by the state's conferral of power on the private media, power that doesn't exist except as a product of our system of law. If this is so, couldn't the government's step of creating a press of its own, and claiming First Amendment protection for it, be seen as really a "private" act, one designed to counterbalance the exercise of government-conferred (and government-reinforcing) power by the private press? Isn't this precisely the argument often made about access by citizens to the press, or about limitations on editorial freedom in the name of fairness and balance and representation of minority points of view? These are steps, like the creation of a government free press, that are taken in the interests of the individual citizens, and thus are properly seen as private in aspiration even if not in inspiration or execution.

These are arguments that editors and publishers fear and hate, and for good reason. If the divide between the public and the private in ownership of the press, or in ownership of a claim of freedom of the press, is breached even a little, can the tide be stopped? Can we stop short of turning the public into the private and vice versa, and thus turning the Constitution inside out? To put the point a bit differently, can any stopping point be set that rests on ideologically neutral grounds? The answer is likely "no." One need only look at the *Forbes* and *Finley* cases to see why. The government's editorial choice in *Forbes* had the effect of eliminating Forbes' reactionary, some would say hateful, views from the principal political debate in a congressional election. Those views had already received ample attention in the private press, and they had failed to measure up because Forbes' support in the polls was small.[46] The government's action, then, was taken to restore a balance that better reflected the public's preferences. But what if the decision had been to exclude a gay candidate on the ground that his or her views were hateful and in any event garnered little support in the polls? Can the interests of gay voters be distinguished from those of deeply conservative voters on ideologically neutral grounds? Clearly not.

The *Finley* case presents an even starker illustration of the impossibility of an ideologically neutral stopping point.[47] The denial of NEA support to an applicant of performance art deemed "indecent and inconsistent with traditional American values" might be seen as a private act of restoring balance and general standards of taste to a program that rewarded artists whose work appealed to only a few or reflected the basest in artistic standards.[48] The government's decision to limit grant support to art that satisfies a standard of public decency might be seen as a truly "private" act by a government acting in the capacity of private patron,[49] ensuring that the tastes of the general public would be represented too in the world of fine arts. The need to do so was particularly important, the argument might run, because the general public's tastes had been submerged by a system of private and public grants and patronage that existed only by virtue of government action. That system reserved the enforcement of aesthetic standards for those with sufficient wealth to find patronage profitable (from a tax and estate planning standpoint).

It is hard, perhaps impossible, to distinguish the benign exercise of government power in *Forbes* from the malignant narrow mindedness of *Finley*. It is thus impossible to limit the authority government might claim once it is permitted to breach, even in a small and well-intentioned way, the divide between private and public ownership of the press. Once the divide is breached, even in small measure such as in *Forbes*, the larger problems of government monopoly and domination, the application of government power toward expressive ends, and the absence of independence loom large. Too large, even, for some of the Justices in *Forbes*, who might have been generally agreeable to a claim of editorial freedom comparable to that enjoyed by the private press. The Justices worried that the exercise of editorial freedom, in *Forbes* itself, disturbingly involved access to participation in the very government powers being wielded by the station (a true conflict of interest for government to select those who are "elected" to it) and smacked of monopoly power by the government press, as the debate was to be the only debate among the candidates in the entire election period.[50] These difficulties, unsurprisingly, are but manifestations of the concrete risks that a government-owned "free press" would present. They therefore provide perhaps the best evidence of the value, and indeed the necessity, of a public/private distinction in the specific setting of ownership of the press.

The public/private ownership question presents an interesting and important application of the public/private distinction in freedom of the press. It is clear that the public/private distinction is fundamental to the very idea of freedom of the press. It is also clear that for the distinction to function as it must to preserve press independence—and thus to preserve the press' constitutional function—press organizations must be protected from government allegiance and influence, and this must be accomplished by the firm's dependence on the private marketplace of individual reader or viewer preference. At a systematic level, this model largely reflects the actual development and growth of the private press in the United States. In significant respects, however, it no longer reflects the organization and behavior of substantial segments of the private, capitalist press today, where the focus on investment-based profits and the dominance of advertiser preferences have become so acute that the audience's voice, so necessary to editorial independence in a private news company, is either lost or, even more distressingly, consciously ignored.

The most obvious conclusion to draw from this is that although the public/private distinction is and should be fundamental, even definitional, to press freedom, it cannot be taken for granted or viewed as a natural result of the invisible hand of the market. Indeed, in some parts of the "press," positive measures, such as antitrust laws, may be needed to ensure that the market assumptions of private ownership are realized. In other quarters of the press, specific firms and forms of ownership should be subjected to serious scrutiny to determine whether those organizations still possess the attributes of public orientation, responsiveness to audience, and editorial independence that are definitional to a free press and, therefore, to the protections of the First Amendment. The ultimate and broad conclusion, in short, is that although government-owned and controlled presses should never enjoy First Amendment protection, neither should *all* private organizations claiming or even appearing to conduct the business of journalism. A precondition of a private press serving the ends of the First Amendment is a press that competes for the news preferences of a public audience, in a market where the competition is among publishers seeking readers, not among advertisers or investors.

PUBLIC ORIENTATION AND EDITORIAL INDEPENDENCE: THREE INSTRUCTIVE CASES

I have argued that in the setting of journalism the public/private divide manifests itself differently than it does in the setting of individual freedom of expression. In the press setting, the distinction rests on process and structure, on independence and public mission served by editorial freedom; in the speech setting, the distinction rests more dominantly on content and subject matter of speech, in the interest of fostering expression on matters of self-government and democracy. The process or structural characteristics of journalism are definitional. That is, in some forms at least, they are the standards by which claims of freedom of the press are judged.

The three definitional characteristics of press publication that I have identified are public orientation in publication judgments, private ownership in a form consistent with the exercise of editorial judgment, and independence from forces that would compromise editorial freedom.[51] Although these three characteristics are interdependent, I focus in this section chiefly on public orientation and editorial independence, often building on what I have said previously in the discussion of private ownership.

A publication restricted in its scope, orientation, or purpose—available, for example, to a narrow audience for limited private purposes—cannot claim to serve the public function of press publication.[52] For example, Dun & Bradstreet's private sale of useful commercial information to subscribers is not a publication by the press.[53] This is not because of its content, but rather because of structural features of the publication decision.

Likewise, a publication whose content is determined by wholly personal or private criteria, with no view to a public audience, or a publication whose content is in no material way the product of anyone's editorial choice, fails at a definitional level to qualify as a press publication.[54] Thus, the information- packed commercial advertisement dedicated strictly to selling widgets,[55] or the Web provider's sale of gateway access to otherwise unsorted and unedited raw material,[56] is not a press publication.

Of course, a publication whose content is the product of choices or standards given over to another—even to government—or whose choices are even sold off or bargained away by a publisher, cannot be described as independent.[57] Such publications—for they are that—lack the structural qualities of availability to a public audience; orientation to a public audience's needs and interests; and independent, particularized choices about information and opinion to be disseminated. They lack, in short, independently arrived-at, publicly oriented choices about material to be published that are characteristic, even definitional, of the press.

In this section, I discuss three concrete controversies, two of them recent, that present important and difficult questions about freedom of the press and journalism. They allow me to explore at a concrete and detailed level the meaning and interrelationships among the three definitional elements of private ownership, public orientation, and editorial independence. The controversies force us to think about some difficult and uncomfortable questions: Are news-gathering claims (i.e., claims of exemption from law by the press) inherently inconsistent with press freedom?[58] Might privacy claims, redefined as an individual's general right of control over use of information, have greater legal force in a structurally defined free press guarantee?[59] When might self-interested behavior by the press defeat the press' claimed freedom to engage in it?[60] Are certain forms of private ownership and organization of the press simply inconsistent with press freedom, and indeed with definitional assumptions underlying journalism itself?[61] Must the law impose structural requirements on who qualifies as a press speaker in order to prevent the press from selling its very own soul?

The controversies I discuss are, respectively, the *Food Lion* case;[62] the *Berger v. Hanlon* case;[63] and an older but most instructive invasion of privacy case, *Howard v. Des Moines Register & Tribune Co.*[64] In the course of the discussion of these cases, I also touch on two quite recent, and equally instructive, incidents: the Staples Center controversy;[65] and the sad tale of soul-selling by TV networks and newspapers to the White House Office of National Drug Control Policy.[66]

The *Food Lion* Case: The Ends of Editorial Judgment

The Food Lion story is a familiar one. The ABC television network received allegations of unsafe and unhealthy food handling practices[67] from a number of former and current employees of the large regional Food Lion grocery store chain. After looking into the allegations, ABC decided to do a segment for *Prime Time Live*. Many of the current and former Food Lion employees were interviewed. Not all of them were supporters of the United Food and Commercial Workers Union, which was engaged in a battle with the nonunionized Food Lion chain.[68] Their allegations, if true, were serious. ABC decided to attempt to film the practices, and assigned two *Prime Time Live* producers, Lynne Litt (then Dale) and Susan Barnett, to apply for positions in Food Lion stores with the purpose of filming the food handling practices through hidden cameras secreted in their wigs.[69] Each applied, giving false employment backgrounds, false references, and other false information. They were hired and worked for a period of time in different Food Lion stores.

Together the undercover producers shot 45 hours of tape, which was edited down to about 10 minutes of footage that was used in the *Prime Time Live* broadcast that aired on November 5, 1992.[70] The *Prime Time Live* report was powerful and, for Food Lion, devastating. It showed redating of meat for which the sale date had passed, unsanitary practices, and the trimming of apparently rotten meat or produce and then repackaging the items for sale. The piece was graphic. It was hard hitting. It was right there before us on film, which meant, to virtually every viewer, that it was *real*.

But was ABC's segment really real? Marshall McLuhan warned us long ago that what appears real may only be the message of the medium.[71] Walter Lippmann implored journalists to strive to represent reality, by which he meant not events themselves but events in perspective and in a context that would lend them meaning.[72] ABC's Food Lion segment appeared on the surface to do just that: The film of Food Lion's practices gave the practices meaning—indeed, all the meaning that was necessary.

However, was there more here than ABC and *Prime Time Live* revealed? Did the *Prime Time Live* piece effectively carry the implication that there was *not* more? The "more" that I am interested in involves the news decisions made by ABC: the decision to pursue the story for *Prime Time Live*; the decision to go undercover with cameras; and the decision to air the segment on November 5, 1992. It is these critical choices—not the deception, staging, or sloppy editing—that reveal the most about the news-gathering process and the nature of ABC's claim of immunity from generally applicable law.

Why did the Food Lion story become a *Prime Time Live* story? In the view of many journalists, ABC could have done the story without hidden cameras.[73] Indeed, with the information gathered from the disgruntled employees (including affidavits), for news purposes ABC almost certainly had enough to broadcast the story immediately.[74]

The decision to go undercover in order to obtain filmed footage of the practices for *Prime Time Live* was thus not, at base, a news decision. It was instead a *broadcast* news decision, and more particularly it was a *television newsmagazine broadcast* news decision. Filmed footage was not needed to establish the newsworthiness of the story. It was, instead, a necessary step to producing a television news story, a piece of investigative journalism in which the hard-hitting facts and allegations could be established because they were shown and thus were real. This is the message of the broadcast news medium: a message not of truth but of power and force and image.

The decision to air the segment on November 5, 1992, during the fall sweeps week, is perhaps the most interesting one.[75] The undercover work had been done over a 2-week period in late April and early May.[76] Little else by way of investigation, such as further interviews, tracking down health department records or speaking to health department employees, and the like, was conducted—a surprising fact, in retrospect. But *Prime Time Live* was not doing particularly well at the time. Its ratings were low.[77] A hard-hitting, undercover expose of a very large grocery chain in the Southeast might help the struggling newsmagazine in the ratings game. And what better week to run such a universally appealing, titillating piece, promoted by 15-second spots announcing an "investigation into rotten food at a well-known [but unidentified] supermarket chain,"[78] than a fall sweeps week?

Freedom of the press rests, at its core, on editorial judgment. With respect to news at least, editorial judgment consists of choices about whether and what to publish based on what an audience needs to know, not simply what it might wish to know—based, in other words, on the editor's own independent decision about a subject's importance and usefulness as news, and not on the will of a publisher or advertiser or the whim of an audience.[79]

Were ABC's decisions to delay publication of the Food Lion story in order to obtain a filmed (and thus more powerful and apparently real) account of Food Lion's practices, and its further delay of publication until sweeps week, the kind of judgments we should protect under the mantle of editorial freedom? Or were those judgments so affected by (a) considerations of audience want, not audience need, (b) "values" of forcefulness, narrowing of focus and perspective, and power of the visual medium of television, and (c) purely market-based and commercial considerations, that they should not qualify for protection as editorial judgment?

As to the first decision—filming undercover to maximize the impact of the medium—it can't be said that medium is irrelevant to news. News, after all, must be presented in a way that people will read or watch.[80] This presentation may involve some delay: delay in the writing and editing process to make the story clear and accurate and appealingly written; and delay in the news-gathering process to obtain and process film footage for use on television.

Yet the question whether a decision constitutes an exercise of editorial judgment by the press is not, strictly speaking, an objective one. It concerns not just what was done, but what factors motivated the decision to do something.[81] Nothing in the circumstances surrounding ABC's decision to engage in illegal news-gathering tactics negates the possibility that the decision was, in critical measure, a product of ABC's desperation to jumpstart a failing competitor of *60 Minutes* and *20/20*. The decision to delay the broadcast of the Food Lion story for up to 5 months in order to run it as a well-advertised segment during sweeps week, when ratings and thus advertising revenues are determined, is more difficult to rationalize as protected editorial judgment, unless, of course, the First Amendment is interpreted as protecting nonnews decisions to maximize revenues and ratings in a competitive market. If decisions about conduct leading to publication, including decisions about the strategic timing of publication, are to be protected by the First Amendment, they ought to be protected in the name of editorial judgments about the public's need for information, not the publisher's profits.[82] It is hard, I think, to understand ABC's decision to delay broadcast for months in order to hit sweeps week as resting in any fashion on public need; as grounded on an independent decision based on what the public needs to know, rather than on what it might wish to know; or as based on the reasoned judgment of an editor rather than on the commercial will of a publisher.

The press is now being transformed from a world of monopoly to one of unrestrained competition; from a concentrated market with few choices to a decentralized market of almost unlimited choices; from an economic model of heavy fixed costs and high barriers to entry to one of low fixed costs and few barriers to entry; from a model of the press in which editors needed protection from the will of powerful publishers to one in which editors need protection from the new imperative of audience preference, advertiser influence, and investment market incentives.[83] Increasingly news, like entertainment, is devoted to the enterprise of "delivering eyeballs to advertisers,"[84] and in a localized and decentralized market with wide choices advertisers are increasingly the most effective surrogates for the audience in its newly defined market segments.[85]

In this economic environment, ABC's decision to delay the Food Lion story in order to maximize the power of the television medium in its telling and as a means of resuscitating ABC's poor ratings is a perfectly rational and understandable one. However, that is an entirely different matter from whether it was an exercise of editorial judgment about news that should be protected by the First Amendment.

In expressing skepticism about ABC's decision, I am not suggesting that the law permit the parsing of every publication decision to determine what considerations it rests on, and thus to second guess the judgments made by editors. Instead, I am suggesting that when the press decides to engage in news-gathering conduct that violates generally applicable law, it should bear the consequences. If it seeks exemption from the law it has violated, the press, not the party enforcing the law, should bear the burden of proving that the decision to employ illegal means was a product of protected editorial judgment, not a decision based only on medium and commerce rather than message and public need; that the means employed in obtaining the published news were necessary to serve the public need, not just necessary to achieve the commercial or other interests of the publisher; and that the public need is in fact so great that it subordinates the public interest—and the press' constitutional interest—in equal enforcement of law.

The *Food Lion* case involves decisions about conduct (news gathering) preceding publication; indeed, conduct that may or may not lead to any published news. The decision to employ illegal news-gathering techniques is thus based on a prediction about their results, and it is fraught with temptation because of the potential commercial value that undercover and invasive news-gathering techniques can produce.[86] It is reasonable, therefore, to place the burden of proof of proper motive and necessity of means on the press, for the claim is one of immunity from general law governing conduct, not publication; the conduct may not, originally, have been related to a publication decision; and the claim of exemption or immunity for the press jeopardizes the independence on which protected editorial judgment ultimately rests under the First Amendment.

The *Berger* Case: Press Independence and the Duty of Civil Disobedience

Paul Berger was 71 years old when it happened. His wife, Erma, was 81. They lived on a 75,000-acre ranch in Montana—Big Sky country.

Mr. Berger appears to be something of a character, independent and even perhaps a bit crusty, acclimated to the outdoors and to nature, but also mindful of his livelihood and his livestock and thus not unwilling to use a strategically employed chemical or two, even a shotgun, to control the damage done by prey, including birds such as eagles and hawks. In this we might assume that Berger was typical, hardly the exception. He was a rancher in the Western mold.

Mr. Berger's alleged strategic use of poison and his use of a shotgun to kill eagles, it turns out, came to the attention of the U.S. Fish and Wildlife Service and its agents in January 1993.[87] Two of the Bergers' former employees reported to Fish and Wildlife Service agents in Montana that they had seen Mr. Berger poison and shoot eagles a few years earlier. An investigation immediately ensued. It was short and, it appears, yielded little more than the informants' tales, but it was not confidential. Montana is a country of big spaces and small places, so it is not surprising that word of the investigation got out fairly soon after it began. In this area, everyone tends to know everyone else's business, and the doings of the federal government, whether the IRS or the more benign yet powerful Fish and Wildlife Service, were no doubt the subject of public curiosity.

Among those who found out about the investigation was Cable News Network (CNN) employee Jack Hamann, and Turner Broadcasting System employees Robert Rainey and Donald Hooper. Jack Hamann worked in CNN's Environmental Unit. The Berger investigation naturally was of interest to Hamann—so much so, in fact, that it inspired him to think of developing a story about environmental predation by fiercely independent, land-loving, government-despising ranchers in the West. The drama of a federal raid, complete with calvary coming full speed to the rescue of the eagle, would add to the impact of the story.[88] As the imagining grew, so too did the CNN and TBS staff involvement, with lawyers from the CNN Legal Department and others from the Environmental Unit now added to the investigating team.

It was thus a delegation of CNN and TBS people who, in early 1993, approached the Fish and Wildlife Service agents in Montana with a proposal. It was a straight and simple television deal: If the government would let CNN accompany the agents on a raid of the Bergers' ranch, hidden cameras running, CNN would use the footage to help the government "publicize its efforts to combat environmental crime."[89] In return, CNN and TBS would get real-life action footage that could be used on its environmental programs—maybe the environmental equivalent of *COPS, Rescue 911*, or *Justice Files*.[90] The price was small: CNN would keep editorial control but would agree to embargo its telecast until charges were brought, the trial was underway, and the jury was empaneled. And, as if to confirm the stakes for each party and to confirm the arrangement's deal-like quality, a written contract was signed by Kris McLean, an Assistant U.S. Attorney in Montana, and by Jack Hamann for CNN. The contract, dated March 11, 1993, provided:

> This confirms our agreement that the United States Attorney's Office for the District of Montana agrees to allow CNN to accompany USFWS [United States Fish and Wildlife Service] Agents as they attempt to execute a criminal search warrant near Jordan, Montana, some time during the week of March 22, 1993. Except as provided below, CNN shall have complete editorial control over any footage it shoots; it shall not be obliged to use the footage; and does not waive any rights or privileges it may have with respect to the footage. In return, CNN agrees to embargo the telecast of any videotape of the attempt to execute the search warrant until either: (1) a jury has been empanelled and instructed by a judge not to view television reports about the case; or (2) the defendant waives his right to a jury trial and agrees to have his case tried before a judge; or (3) a judge accepts a plea bargain; or (4) the government decides not to bring charges relating to the attempt to execute the search warrant.[91]

The contract was executed on March 11, 1993.[92] A search warrant for the Bergers' ranch, but excluding the residence, was issued on March 18. The judge who issued the warrant was not told of the contract.[93] With the warrant issued, activity picked up speed. Presearch planning and briefings were scheduled. CNN was in attendance, it appears, and was thus made aware of the material included in the warrant and other information that was supposed to be sealed until after the warrant was executed. What then transpired is described in the opinion of the Ninth Circuit as follows:

> On the morning of the search, the government team, accompanied by a media crew, gathered on a county road leading to the ranch, to discuss the execution of the warrant.

The cameras videotaped that gathering. The broadcast team then proceeded with the federal agents and [Assistant U.S. Attorney] McLean in a caravan of approximately ten vehicles to a point near the Bergers' ranch. Media cameras mounted on the outside of government vehicles, or placed in their interior, documented every move made by the federal [agents]. At all times during and immediately prior to the search, [Fish and Wildlife] Special Agent Joel Scrafford was wired with a hidden CNN microphone which was continuously transmitting live audio to the CNN technical crew.

Mr. Berger approached and met the caravan in a pickup truck on the road leading up to the ranch. Agent Scrafford proceeded to inform Mr. Berger of the search warrant, and asked him whether he could ride to the house in Mr. Berger's truck so that he could explain to Mrs. Berger what they were going to do. Mr. Berger allowed Agent Scrafford to ride with him in the pickup truck. Upon arriving at the Bergers' residence, the two men entered the house together. Audio recorded at the site indicates that Mr. Berger consented to Agent Scrafford's entry into the home at this time. The parties disagree on whether the agents who entered the residence with Agent Scrafford searched the residence for incriminating evidence, and whether Agent Scrafford's subsequent entries into the home were consented to. However, it is undisputed that Agent Scrafford recorded all his conversations with the Bergers inside the house.

The Bergers were not informed that Agent Scrafford was wearing a microphone or that the cameras that were visible during the search belonged to the media. The media recorded more than eight hours of tape and it broadcast both the video footage and the sound recordings made in the house.[94]

Mr. Berger was charged with the taking of one or more golden eagle, multiple ferruginous hawks and one ring-billed gull, and with the use of a registered pesticide, Furdan, "in a manner inconsistent with its labeling."[95] The latter charge was a misdemeanor. Mr. Berger was acquitted of all charges except the misdemeanor of using the pesticide inconsistently with its labeling.

Then the Bergers sued. They sued the government for violation of their constitutional right to be free from unreasonable searches and seizures under the Fourth Amendment.[96] They sued CNN and TBS for violation of the Federal Wiretap Act,[97] and for state law claims including trespass and intentional infliction of emotional distress.[98] Most notably, the Bergers sued TBS and CNN for violating their constitutional rights on the ground that "the 'inextricable' involvement of the media with both the planning and execution of th[e] search, the government's active involvement with the media's news-gathering activities, and the mutually-derived benefits, is more than enough to make the media government actors."[99] All of the Bergers' claims were denied by the district court, which granted summary judgment to the government and to TBS and CNN. On appeal to the Ninth Circuit, however, the district court's grant of summary judgment was reversed and most of the Bergers' claims, including all those mentioned previously, were allowed to proceed to trial.[100]

The press' editorial freedom depends on the press' independence from those persons and institutions, most notably (but not only) government institutions and officials, about which it must make judgments in the interest of the public's need to know.[101] Government is neither a friend nor foe to the press. It is, instead, a frequent object of the press' editorial judgments and therefore an institution on which the press cannot afford to be reliant. Reliance on government, or dependence on government, would threaten to skew and shape judgments that might otherwise be made in the interest of public need: whether to investigate and publish, what to publish, how to publish, and when to publish. Independence of the press thus connotes non-dependence, not hostility. It requires that the press' interests vis-à-vis government not be at stake in any publication decision, that the press not be singled out in its political interests but instead, to the extent possible, that the press' interests be the same as those shared generally by larger political constituencies of which it is but a small part.[102]

As the *Berger* case reveals, it is all too tempting for a competitive press to sacrifice its long-term interests in independence in order to achieve short-term advantages. In order to get a good story, CNN was willing enter into a joint venture with the government agents. CNN would assist the government in achieving its political ends in exchange for a license to engage in cooperative activity that, if done alone, would amount to criminal trespass and invasion of privacy, if not more. What, we must ask, did CNN give up in exchange?

First, CNN gave up control over what was filmed, for its agreement was that CNN would be permitted to accompany and film only the agents conducting the search. Did CNN accompany and film all of the agents, or only some? Who decided which? Second, CNN gave up control over the "when" of its publication decisions, agreeing in a written contract to withhold publication until a specified point in time that was set to serve the government's prosecutorial interests.

Third, CNN compromised, and therefore effectively gave up, its ability to criticize the very government decisions in which it had become a complicit party. It is unlikely, we might assume, that CNN would criticize the government's decision to conduct the search, given CNN's joint involvement in its planning and execution. It is unlikely that CNN would criticize the government for allowing CNN to participate in the search, even though the occasional press commentary since the raid became public suggests that CNN's participation itself was a significant news story and subject of public controversy. And it is unlikely that CNN would use the fruits of its participation to reveal wrongdoing committed by the government agents in the course of the search. Examples of wrongdoing might include the fact, known to CNN,[103] that the judge who issued the warrant was not apprised of CNN's involvement in the search,[104] and the fact, also known to CNN,[105] that CNN's recording equipment was employed to effect an unconsented and unconstitutional search of the Bergers' *home*, which was not covered by the warrant.[106] Both examples of wrongdoing benefitted CNN, and disclosing them would have jeopardized the prospect of future advantageous arrangements between CNN and the government.

CNN, in short, gave up a great deal. It gave up much more, in fact, than it cares to admit. However, these are not the only things that CNN gave up. At a more fundamental level, it was CNN's later claim to immunity from liability in the Bergers' lawsuit that jeopardized not only CNN's independence but that of the press in general. CNN's claim of First Amendment privilege, or immunity, for otherwise illegal news-gathering activities legitimated what CNN had done. By this I mean that a finding of constitutional immunity for news-gathering would have freed any news organization not only to violate general law, but also to conspire with government or even with private parties to facilitate the press' law-violating techniques. Unbeknownst to CNN (and even to CNN's lawyers), we must assume, such a claim would have placed the press in a vastly increased position of dependence on government for leads, information, and the facilities of privacy invasion,[107] trespass,[108] or harassment, fraud, and deception.[109]

Independence and immunity, independence and dependence, do not coexist well. One or the other must ultimately win out, and it is too often the more tempting pair—immunity and dependence—that prevail.

A rule of exemption or immunity or privilege, even if absolute and certainly if presumed but conditional, reduces rather than enhances the independence of the press when making decisions about whether, what, how, and when to publish information that the public needs to know. A press that is specially exempt from law is by that exemption given a special allegiance to that law, and to the legal and political system that maintains the press' special legal status.[110] A benefit specially conferred is one that can be specially withdrawn. Finally, a press possessed of a special stake in the existing legal or commercial order is not in a position to fiercely and independently criticize that legal order. It is more likely to curry the order's favor, to cooperate with it, to join it,[111] and to benefit further from it.[112]

Howard v. Des Moines Register & Tribune Company: Privacy Protection and the New News- Gathering Question

> *"Objectivity resides not in the quality of the product*
> *but in the mode of its performance."*   —Bernard Roshko[114]

By the time the *Des Moines Register* story was published, Robin Howard was 24 years old. She was married. She had a new name, a new home, in a new city. In 1970, 6 years earlier, she was Robin Woody, a young girl of 18 who had been committed to the Jasper County Home in Iowa. According to the *Register* story, she "was not retarded or mentally disabled, but an 'impulsive, hair-triggered, young girl.'"[115] In 1970, at the age of 18, she was involuntarily sterilized. Her parents and the home's doctor decided sterilization was for the best. Robin "didn't want it at all.… She was told," according to one source, that it was "the only way she could be dismissed from the home."[116] The doctor described her as "a very explosive, impulsive young girl … [who] would be a very questionable risk as far as having and rearing a baby."[117]

All of this, and more, was published in 1976 in the *Des Moines Register*, a newspaper of which (at the time) all Iowa was proud. The *Register*'s story was not about Robin Woody, as such, but about alleged illegal activities that had taken place in the Jasper County Home (where Robin had been sterilized), activities that included poor care, patient deaths, scalding baths, and improper sterilizations of women. Robin was the story's rhetorical instrument, ceremoniously swept up into a larger public controversy uncovered through the investigative reporting of a very good newspaper. Robin's role in the controversy was not to prove its allegations, but to bring them to life and to drive them home. This she did very well.

That she was a less than enthusiastic participant in the *Register*'s news is perfectly understandable, as was her decision to sue for invasion of privacy. But she met with no more satisfaction in court than she had in the pages of the *Register*. Summary judgment was awarded to the *Register* before trial, and the decision was affirmed on appeal.[118] This was a proper conclusion to a tragic episode.

"[N]ews and truth," Walter Lippmann said, "are not the same thing.... The function of news is to signalize an event.... "[119] This is the dilemma presented when the privacy tort is applied to news or to the press. Our conventional ideas of privacy focus on the point of publication and on the substance of what is published; this, certainly, is of what the tort-based idea of privacy consists. For the privacy tort, and certainly for Robin Woody, the tortious act was "publication," and the underlying wrong was the publicity thus given to information (content) that was personal, embarrassing, and deprived Robin Woody Howard of control over her personal and social identity.[120] For the law, the question was whether Robin's story was *newsworthy*.

But for news and journalism, at least the news and journalism practiced by the *Des Moines Register*, the decision to publish the private material had little to do with Robin Woody, herself, or with her story, as such. To thus rest liability on the thoughtlessness and unnewsworthiness of the *Register*'s editorial decision is to focus on the wrong (and indeed an irrelevant) question. This is because the decision to disclose Robin's tragic experience was compositional, not substantive; it was a choice of process, of how to communicate an issue or event to a public audience, not a choice of substance.

The significance of Robin's story was its allegorical force, its capacity to transform the private into the public. This is what news can, and must, do.[121] Robin's tragic story captured the imagination and focused the attention of a public audience on a current event or issue about which the audience should be informed and with which it should, in the editor's view, be concerned. The editorial decision by the *Register* was to "signalize" the issue of illegal treatment in county homes with Robin's story. It was, without doubt, an editorial decision in the best of journalistic tradition. However, we can reach this judgment only in terms of process, not in terms of content; in terms of means, not in terms of ends. To do otherwise is to substitute the law—the judge and jury—for the editor.

"Objectivity," Bernard Roshco has said, "resides not in the quality of the product but in the mode of the performance."[122] The *Register*'s decision in Robin Woody's case, in other words, can be judged not by its quality—its rightness or wrongness, the harm it produced, the importance of its subject or even its object—but by the mode of its performance. To put it another way, was the decision the product of an editorial choice about current information and opinion needed by a public audience—a choice arrived at in an institutional setting marked by independence from corrupting influences (or even corrupting conflict of interests), public or private in origin? If not, freedom of the press should not be the shelter in which it seeks protection. If so, the publication should be absolutely secure from regulation or liability. It is newsworthy in the sense—and only in the sense—that the editorial process has earned that title. Perhaps this is the best explanation for the utter failure of invasion of privacy actions against the press.[123] News, after all, is as much a product of process as it is of substance. In judging news or journalism, process contributes three important qualities: It explains how it is that selection of material for publication can represent more than caprice or the mere accommodation of audience preferences (a claim often made in privacy cases); it reflects a measure of needed consistency in publication judgments across the profession and within given organizations;[124] and, especially with privacy claims, it avoids intruding into an editor's substantive choices, which are an inescapable part of both publication and the more aesthetic compositional choices. Substantive criteria are and should be elusive and aspirational, and therefore judicially unmanageable.

What happens, then, to privacy under a guarantee of freedom of the press based only on process? There are two answers to this question, both interesting.

The traditional form of privacy—protected by restrictions visited on the point of publication and resting on the substantive content of a publication—is extinguished with respect to the press. Freedom of the press forecloses legal superintendence of the content of the decision to publish; it permits inquiry only into matters of process. Acknowledging this would simply formalize a deed already done.

This does not mean, however, that the interest of privacy is extinguished in relation to the press. The privacy question is instead transformed into a question of control over information, of ownership of information, and of access to information. Privacy, in short, becomes a question of news gathering, not of substantive limitation on publication. Control over information about oneself, and the resultant ability to shape one's own identity in a large and impersonal social order, seem on reflection to be truer ways to think about privacy at the start of a new millennium—preferable and more fitting, certainly, than Warren and Brandeis' condemnation of fallen standards of decency, and their celebration of personal freedom from public humiliation and embarrassment.[125] The time has long passed for clinging to, much less recapturing, delicate and refined standards of taste and decency, much less a now-lost collective sense of shame.

The threat to privacy today comes not from the occasional salacious news publication, but instead from the collecting, organizing, and selling of identifiable information for use not just by news organizations but more often by commercial organizations, employers, and government. The publishers of the information are not, really, the news publishers, but instead the states that collect it in connection with taxation, recording, licensing, and the like, and the companies that gather information about our purchases, our demographics, our habits, our health, and so on.

Even if a manageable standard of newsworthiness and substantive privacy could be crafted, it would be foolish in today's technological world to think that a restriction visited on the act of publication would be effective in protecting privacy. Publication is simply too diverse, omnipresent, technological to think of patching the dike when information leaks through. The focus of privacy, instead, must be on the point of collection and assembly of information, and its control must be accomplished by empowering the subject of the information to maintain and exercise control over its disclosure and dissemination at the point of collection. Precisely how this might be accomplished is well beyond the scope of this chapter, although I did suggest some years ago that a legally enforceable obligation of confidentiality by recipients of private information might serve as a useful analytic tool in shaping specific rights of control.[126]

My point here is that privacy protection has *already* been transformed into a question of ensuring the individual control over information, and therefore that the constitutional issues pertaining to privacy have already been assimilated into the distinct and largely process-based principles governing news gathering and access claims by the press. The *Food Lion* and *Berger* cases, in short, extend well beyond the press' liability for trespass or deceit or violation of constitutional rights. They reflect also the regime of rules that will govern the protection of privacy and the press' claim to news-gathering protection when seeking private material: rules focused on process and structure and related not to the substance of publication but to independence of editorial judgments made with a view to a public audience and its needs in a free and democratic society.

Means *and* Ends

I have said that the press' liberty should not depend on the publicness, or the value, of its stories, but instead should rest on structural and content-neutral premises, thus freeing the press to publish what it deems publishable. Only under such a view of press freedom can meaning and content be given to the Supreme Court's seemingly vacuous dictum, "Editing is what editors are for."[127] I have suggested that the chief end of the First Amendment guarantee of freedom of the press is independence, not freedom to publish; that the way in which publication decisions are made is more important than the act of publication, itself, or its content; that although the First Amendment restricts the government's ability to interfere with editorial freedom and with resultant publication, news-gathering activity bears only an incidental relationship to editorial freedom; and most important that in the areas of press conduct—news gathering, distribution, and the like—the greatest risks to press independence lurk just beneath the surface.

The press' independence is not freedom from law, but freedom from special legal status. The press must be institutionally agnostic in its editorial choices. The press' freedom is freedom from having to expend its energies, or bend its critical faculties, in order to maintain its special position and its station above the public interest. To serve this role the press must share equally the benefits and burdens of public and private life. It cannot be privileged to enter into special arrangements with government, arrangements that must inevitably make the press dependent on government or jointly culpable with government, and therefore unwilling to risk its well-being by staking out editorial positions that threaten embarrassment or reprisal and loss of advantage. It cannot allow itself to be seduced by special benefits or corrupting incentives, be they increased corporate revenue or the promise of personal wealth so alluringly held out by stock options.

The press crossed this line in the *Food Lion* case, but the consequences of doing so were not easily detected there. Only after digging could one discover that ABC sacrificed all semblance of devotion to the public's need to know in order to achieve its own corporate interests. The consequences became apparent in the *Berger* case, however, where the press crossed the line by entering into a formal arrangement with the government, making itself a party to, and thus an unlikely critic of, the government's action. To privilege CNN's short-sightedness by excusing it from liability would be to legitimate conduct that undermines the very independence that the press has achieved only after hundreds of years of struggle. The better rule, and the one more consistent with the independence and central constitutional functions of the press, would be to presume, with news-gathering activities, that the press should be subject to general legal rules, and thus aligned with the broader public constituency that it serves.

A rule that takes as its starting point—its presumptive result, if you will—that the press should be subject to generally applicable law respects the press' constitutional interest in independence from government and respects the moral force of the press' self-conscious decision to violate law in pursuit of ends it considers more important.[128] Such a rule does not, however, demand an unyielding application of any form of generally applicable law, criminal or civil, in any circumstances. Instead, it sets up a presumption but can admit exceptions. It justifies placing the burden of persuasion and proof for an exception to the general legal rule on the press in a manner similar to the operation of the common law necessity defense.[129]

The necessity defense is a one of common law origin that operates to excuse or justify criminal violations on a case-by-case basis.[130] To succeed in making out the defense the defendant must show that the illegal act was taken "to avoid imminent harm; ... that no reasonable legal alternatives existed; ... that the harm of [the] act was not disproportional to the harm avoided; and ... that there was a direct causal relationship between [the] act and the harm avoided."[131] The defense, of course, need not be imported directly from the criminal law to the civil disobedience and news-gathering setting, but it is instructive in articulating criteria that might govern the burden of proof that the press would have to bear to free itself from liability by making out a case-specific "necessity" justification.

The difficulty ABC would confront in proving necessity in the *Food Lion* case is highlighted by the criteria the defense requires. Although ABC presumably would have little difficulty establishing an imminent harm (and indeed a subordinating one) by virtue of the public health risks of which ABC was already aware at the time of the undercover decision and up until the story was run in November, it appears unlikely (at least on the facts here hypothesized about ABC's decisions) that "no reasonable alternatives existed." ABC knew enough to take steps—by publication or reporting to authorities—to avert any imminent health risks to the public, but decided to *increase* those risks by delaying publication while undercover film was shot, and to delay publication *further* in order to broadcast the segment in the November sweeps week. Even more difficult would be ABC's burden of proof that "there was a direct causal relationship between [the] act and the harm avoided." The only possible causal relationship would be malignant, not benign, because ABC's editorial decisions to film undercover—the conduct that violated the generally applicable law—and to delay broadcast until November caused the harm to be increased, not decreased as the necessity defense requires.

The *Berger* case presents different problems under the necessity rubric. In *Berger* the problem for CNN would not be available alternatives or causation, but instead establishing that there was an identifiable public harm to which the law-violating cooperative behavior related at all. The public harm might, for example, be imminent risk of death to future birds, but there was really no basis in fact for CNN to rationalize its news-gathering decisions in terms of that risk, rather than in terms of greater impact, larger audiences, and thus higher profits. With little or no justification grounded in risk of harm, it is by definition impossible for CNN to establish that the illegal act "was not disproportional to the harm avoided." Indeed, there is no real basis on which to conclude that any harm was, or was likely to be, avoided by CNN's actions.[132] Instead, there were simply costs: costs to CNN's editorial independence, costs to CNN's journalistic integrity, and costs to the trust CNN's audience places in CNN's work.

Civilization consists largely of a compromise struck between means and ends: I can achieve my own ends only by certain means. Hunger doesn't justify my stealing from another. Saving "life" doesn't justify my blocking entry into an abortion clinic. Ends, in other words, don't justify any means. Means are important.

ABC justifies its use of fraud, deception, trespass, and entrapment in the Food Lion story because its ends were important. But who decides in a civilized society what ends justify means that violate the rules of the society?

A wise person (I think it was Edmund Burke[133]) said that violence must be the monopoly of the state: The "means" of violence, at least, must be reserved only to collective action, not individual choice. What about trespass, fraud, entrapment? How much of their use ought to be left to the discretion of the individual or the corporation?

The answer is not absolute, of course, but neither is it as simple as ABC made it appear. If babies are being injured (as was the case in one example ABC used to publicly justify its hidden camera practices), ABC's responsibility is not to stop it—if it were, secret taping and delayed broadcast were not very effective ways of doing that. ABC's responsibility, instead, is to report it publicly, without delay caused by producing a more "compelling" peak through hidden cameras, so that people and government are put on notice, and then to report on what government does about it.

ABC may think of itself as part of a Fourth Estate (a deeply unfortunate metaphor), but it is not a fourth branch of government and it possesses neither the power nor the responsibility of government. There seems to be a deep confusion about this on ABC's part.

The law's normal response when an individual violates the society's rules for a moral or just end is to give the act a decent name—civil disobedience—and then to hold the law violator to account, on the theory that if the "end" is very important, it must be important enough to achieve at the price the law exacts. In the *Food Lion* case, a jury decided that ABC violated the law, perhaps for a just cause, but the price of doing so is the jury's damage award.

Jesse Jackson recently went to jail overnight, a price he was willing to pay for taking the law into his own hands in service of his own ends.[134] Whether we agree with him or not, we should respect him for that. We would discount the importance of Jackson's act by ignoring it or excusing it.

Why should ABC or CNN or the *Los Angeles Times* or the *Washington Post* be treated differently? Let's hope the Food Lion story was worth the legal consequences, not to mention the lawyers' bills, which were surely high.

Indeed, let's hope, at least, that it was true.

FREEDOM OF THE PRESS AND THE "PUBLIC": MEANS AND ENDS, PROCESS AND SUBSTANCE

What can we conclude from the public/private distinction about the meaning of "press" and the difference between press speech and other forms of expression? A number of possible conclusions emerge. The first is that in exercising its editorial freedom, the press must be independent, at least in structural terms. The independence must be from coercion or dependence that would compromise its organizational capacity to reach reasoned conclusions in the interest of the audience, or public, that the press serves. This necessarily implies independence from government coercion, control, or inducement—as well as freedom from conferral of benefit or imposition of burden, as Phillip Kurland expressed in another setting,[135] for without such independence the press' claim to serving a public of its own definition collapses into a government claim that *its* public is the true public and *its* judgment of public preference is determinative. This result would make a meaningless shambles of the free press guarantee. Thus, this line of reasoning is constitutionally foreclosed.

The second conclusion is that, in order for the press to be truly independent, it must be structurally able to make its judgments free of control, coercion, or dependence on other corrosive influences—including the power of capital markets, the dominant culture it must represent in its pages, and the governmental and business interests it must check. This degree of independence implies the existence of some form of structural or organizational barrier between news judgments and the commercial and capital market forces bearing on the firm engaged in journalism. The separation has traditionally been reflected in a loose "wall" between the news and business side of news organizations, a wall now being increasingly breeched.

Today the needed separation may also imply freedom of the news organization and its editorial and news staff from direct inducements intended to secure greater allegiance to the organization's corporate, rather than journalistic, welfare. Stock options and bonuses, for example, are becoming an increasingly common and substantial part of editorial staff compensation in publicly traded news companies, and they are explicitly based on management's desire to provide positive incentives for employees to consider revenues, margins, and stockholder value as part of their decision-making processes. Options and similarly structured incentive compensation schemes in the newsroom should stop. These and other devices through which the priorities of the newsroom can be reshaped, and therefore with which the independence of news judgments can be compromised, undermine the organization's claim to independence.

A third conclusion concerns the dominance of editorial freedom as the central guarantee of press freedom. If press freedom consists largely of—and depends in all its applications on—freedom in making independent editorial judgments for a public audience, then the speech/conduct distinction takes on a very narrow and limited role. The press' business is not simply to decide whether or not to publish a story; it is instead to judge stories that might be worthy of publication, to pursue the truth about those stories, and to compose them and reach conclusions on those stories that ultimately warrant publication. Press speech, in short, is not a largely internalized, reflective instance of judgment and belief, but an elaborate and often ritualized process of iterative judgment and forming of belief.

Protecting editorial judgment requires protection of the entire news publication process, not just its penultimate stages. Thus, choices about inquiries; decisions about obtaining information (news gathering); and judgments about exclusion and inclusion, judgments about public need and usefulness, and particularly compositional judgments about how information is conveyed—these must all be fully protected, seen as part and parcel of editorial judgment. This is so as long as the decisions made at any stage (e.g., a decision to guarantee confidentiality to a source, to go undercover, or to trespass) are in fact decisions grounded on obtaining for publication the information that is independently judged useful or needed by a public audience. Just as the calculated lie is disqualified as a public-oriented independent judgment, so too should decisions of purely commercial or self-interested nature be disqualified from protection under the free press guarantee, even when they are draped in the appearance of editorial process.

Including news-gathering decisions and actions within the embrace of the free press guarantee (and thus disposing of the artificial—for editorial judgment purposes, at least—distinction between speech and conduct) does not imply that countervailing First Amendment concerns don't serve to limit the right to gather material for press publication. The limitation, however, should not be based on a wooden application of the expression/action distinction, nor on a wooden application of a principle that the press is subject to generally applicable law. Instead, it should be based on the paramount importance of maintaining the independence of editorial judgments and resulting publications for the audience they serve.

Thus, exemption from general law may, in many (although surely not all) instances, undermine independence. In the tax setting, for example, a special exemption for the press could undermine its independence by giving the press a particular stake in the outcome of the political process and an incentive, much like the editor's stock option, to steer clear of a person or issue if continued exemption might be affected. This, of course, is the relatively clear lesson of the Supreme Court's sales tax cases.[136] Likewise, when the press is so intent on a story that it joins or conspires with individuals or organizations whose own actions might themselves be newsworthy—whether advertisers, competitors, or even government agencies—the price of the story may be lost independence.[137] As a result, news- gathering activities that jeopardize press independence must be avoided. If generally applicable law provides the deterrent and punishment for engaging in those types of activities, then generally applicable law should equally be available for use against the press *in the name of its independence, and thus ultimately in the name of the free press guarantee.*

The final conclusion concerns ownership of the press. First Amendment freedom of the press should be available only to private publishers and organizations. Public ownership has no place under the First Amendment. This is not to say that government may not start and operate a newspaper, for example, and even compete, as PBS does, with private organizations in news and public affairs programming. Much benefit can result from such government action. But the government's newspaper, or the broadcast channel it owns and/or funds in whole or in part, should not be able to raise a First Amendment claim, or even enjoy special immunity under the First Amendment if that immunity limits the freedom of a private press.

On the other hand, all private persons and organizations involved in publishing current information of a nonfictional character should not, by that fact alone, be deemed press publishers for First Amendment purposes. Only private organizations and publishers whose publication processes and decisions are structured in ways that preserve the capacity for independent and public-oriented decisions should qualify for the First Amendment's protection. Commercial advertisements, even if truth seeking, would not qualify because they are governed by the private purposes of a firm or organization, not by the public's need independently judged. Likewise, publishers of purported fact that have no organizational pretense or concern about truth, and that indeed value fiction in the garb of truth most highly, should not be able to claim free press protection. Their claim to freedom should rest on the less certain marketplace of ideas and public value-based free speech analysis, where their arguments about harm, satire and humor, fiction, and the usefulness of falsity make sense (even if they may not prevail). A free press must be a private press, but it must also be more than just private.

I conclude, in the end, that the distinction between press publications and nonpress publications rests not (only) on certain attributes of its speech—nonfiction, current, relevant—but more basically on the purposes that animate the judgments that result in the speech's selection and publication. Press judgments are animated by a public audience, information and opinion that is deemed useful to a public audience, and judgments about what information and opinion is needed by the audience in the conduct of their personal, social, economic, and political affairs. The purpose, or orientation, of press publication is therefore public and indeed a reflection, in a sense, of the distinction between matters of public importance and those only of personal or private interest. However, the public/private distinction in this particular form is not imposed as a duty from outside, but instead is the result achieved, at a systematic level, by a structurally independent group of press speakers whose specific decisions are made independently, against an aspiration for truth seeking, and with a firm view to the audience's need. Except in the setting of ownership, the public/private distinction under the free press guarantee is assumed, but not enforced.

NOTES

[1]*Abrams v. United States*, 250 U.S. 616, 664 (1919) (Holmes, J., dissenting); Thomas Irwin Emerson, *The System of Freedom of Expression* (1970).

[2]*International Society for Krishna Consciousness, Inc. v. Lee*, 505 U.S. 672 (1992).

[3]See, for example, *Miller v. California*, 413 U.S. 15 (1973) (obscenity); *New York v. Ferber*, 453 U.S. 747 (1982) (indecent speech harmful to children); *Gertz v. Robert Welch, Inc.*, 418 U.S. 323 (1974) (public and private defamation); *Central Hudson Gas & Elec. Corp. v. Pub. Serv. Comm'n*, 447 U.S. 557 (1980) (commercial speech); *FCC v. Pacifica Found.*, 438 U.S. 726 (1978) (indecent broadcast speech); *Denver Area Telecommunication Consortium v. FCC*, 518 U.S. 727 (1996) (indecency on cable).

[4]*Abrams*, 250 U.S. at pp. 664 (Holmes, J., dissenting); *Mills v. Alabama*, 384 U.S. 214 (1966); *New York Times Co. v. Sullivan*, 376 U.S. 254 (1964); Emerson, supra note 1; Alexander Meiklejohn, *The First Amendment Is an Absolute*, 245 Sup. Ct. Rev. (1961) [hereafter Meiklejohn, *The First Amendment*]; Cass Sunstein, *Democracy and the Problems of Free Speech* (1993).

[5]See, for example, Lillian BeVier, *The First Amendment and Political Speech: An Inquiry Into the Substance and Limits of Principle*, 30 Stan L. Rev. 299 (1978).

[6]Compare, for example, C. Edwin Baker, *Human Liberty & Freedom of Speech* (1989), with Sunstein, supra note 4.

[7]See Randall Bezanson, *Institutional Speech*, 80 Iowa L. Rev. 735 (1995) [hereafter Bezanson, *Institutional Speech*]; Randall Bezanson, *Artifactual Speech*, 3 U. Penn. J. Const. Law 819 (2001).

[8]See note 6 *supra*.

[9]376 U.S. 254 (1964).

[10]A theoretical and historical debate about a distinct constitutional guarantee of freedom of the press occurred in the 1970s and 1980s. See e.g., David Lange, *The Speech and Press Clauses*, 23 UCLA L. Rev. 77 (1975); Potter Stewart, *Or of the Press*, 26 Hastings L. Rev. 631 (1975); David Anderson, *The Origins of the Press Clause*, 30 UCLA L. Rev. 455 (1983); Randall Bezanson, *The New Free Press Guarantee*, 63 Va. L. Rev. 731 (1977) [hereafter Bezanson, *The New Free Press Guarantee*]. More recent articles continue to address the question. See, for example, David Anderson, *Freedom of the Press*, 80 Texas L. Rev. 429 (2002); Jon Paul Dilts, *The Press Clause and Press Behavior: Revisiting the Implications of Citizenship*, 7 Commun. Law & Policy 25 (2001); C. Edwin Baker, *The Media That Citizens Need*, 147 U. Pa. L. Rev. 317 (1998); Randall Bezanson, *The Developing Law of Editorial Judgment*, 78 Neb. L. Rev. 601(2000) [hereafter Bezanson, *Editorial Judgment*]. The Supreme Court has been unsympathetic to special or different protections for the press than for free speech. See *First Nat'l Bank v. Belotti*, 435 U.S. 765, at 798 (1978) (Burger, C.J., concurring).

[11]Bezanson, *The New Free Press Guarantee, supra* note 10, 731.

[12]For example, the court has uniformly applied doctrine in both speech and press cases in the fields of: defamation—*Gertz v. Robert Welch, Inc.*, 418 U.S. 323 (1974); privacy—*Florida Star v. B.J.F.*, 491 U.S. 524 (1989); prior restraint—*New York Times Co. v. United States*, 403 U.S. 713 (1971); and privilege and access claims—*Bransburg v. Hayes*, 408 U.S. 665 (1972) and *Houchins v. KQED, Inc.*, 438 U.S. 1 (1978).

[13]Bezanson, *Editorial Judgment, supra* note 10, 604–609.

[14]For fuller development of these elements, see Bezanson, *Institutional Speech, supra* note 7, at 735; Randall Bezanson, *The Atomization of the Newspaper: Technology, Economics and the Coming Transformation of Editorial Judgments About News*, 3 Comm. L. & Poly 175 (1998) [hereafter Bezanson, *The Atomization of the Newspaper*]; Gilbert Cranberg, Randall Bezanson & John Soloski, *Taking Stock: Journalism and the Publicly Traded Newspaper Company* (2001) [hereafter Cranberg, Bezanson, & Soloski, *Taking Stock*]; Bezanson, *Editorial Judgment, supra* note 10.

[15]Michael Schudson, *The Power of News*, 9–16 (1995). As Michael Schudson has put it: "[T]he news constructs a symbolic world that has a kind of priority, a certification of legitimate importance. And that symbolic world, putatively and practically, in its easy availability, in its cheap, quotidian, throw-away material form, becomes the property of all of us." *Ibid.*, 33.

[16]News

is a kind of moral amplification and moral organization. News ... produced by journalists is different from messages [of a] government official or corporate executive.... The difference is not only that the journalist has the opportunity, indeed the professional obligation, to frame the message. It is also that the newspaper story or television broadcast transforms an event or statement into the cultural form called news. A news story is an announcement of special interest and importance. It is a declaration by a familiar private (or sometimes public) and usually professional (but occasionally political) entity in a public place that an event is noteworthy. It suggests that what is published has a call on public attention.

Ibid., 20–21.

[17]See Alvin Gouldner, *The Dialectic of Ideology and Technology*, 97–98 (1976).

[18]Gouldner's discussion is revealing:

It was central to the pioneering analysis of the public ... that news *constructed* a public [in the newly industrialized and urban and centralized society of the late 19th century] by stimulating face-to-face conversations.

***

Publics imply a development of rational discourse because they imply the existence of a cleared and safe space in the community available for *face-to-face* discourse, concerning a commonly shared body of news-disbursed information, that is motivated by a quest for the interpretation of that shared news. Such open discourse is "rational" precisely in the sense that it is *critical*.... This, in turn, is possible if and only if people may speak "openly" without fear of sanctions, other than those imposed [on] deficient logic ... by co-speakers in their *private* capacity.... *Publics thus require [individuals] to be treated as "private" persons.*

Ibid. (last emphasis supplied).

[19]See, for example, *Green v. Chicago Tribune Co.*, 675 N.E.2d 249 (Ill. App. 1996); *Briscoe v. Reader's Digest Ass'n*, 93 Cal. Rptr. 866 (Cal.1971); *Hall v. Post*, 355 S.E.2d 819 (N.C. Ct. App. 1987).

[20]See *ibid.*; Bezanson, *Editorial Judgment, supra* note 10, 624–37.

[21]The conflict between the "descriptive or normative" meaning of newsworthiness was the focus of the court's analysis in *Shulman v. Group W Publications, Inc.*, 74 Cal. Rptr. 2d 843, 855 (Cal. 1998). As the court put it: "Is the term 'newsworthy' a descriptive predicate, intended to refer to the fact that there is widespread public interest? Or is it a value predicate, intended to indicate that the publication is a meritorious contribution and that the public interest is praiseworthy?" A third alternative would defer to the press' decision to publish, but measure the use of invasive facts in terms of their relevance, in the context of news, to the story's theme. See *Howard v. Des Moines Register & Tribune Co.*, 283 N.W.2d 289 (Iowa 1979); Randall Bezanson, *Public Disclosures as News: Privacy Invasions and Injunctive Relief Against the Press*, 64 Iowa L. Rev. 1061 (1978) [hereafter Bezanson, *Public Disclosures as News*].

[22]*Florida Star v. B.J.F.*, 491 U.S. 524, 531 (1989): "[We do not] accept [the] invitation to hold broadly that truthful publication may never be punished consistent with the First Amendment. Our cases have carefully eschewed reaching this ultimate question."

[23]For a discussion of the dearth of successful privacy cases against the press, and the reasons news judgments cannot and ought not to be submitted to a privacy test, see Randall Bezanson, *The Right to Privacy Revisited: Privacy, News, and Social Change, 1890–1990*, 80 Cal. L. Rev. 1133 (1992).

[24]A right of confidentiality based on individuals' control over information about themselves is discussed in Randall Bezanson, *The Right to Privacy Revisited: Privacy, News, and Social Change 1890–1990*, 80 Cal. L. Rev. 1133 (1992).

[25]See *Los Angeles Police Dep't v. United Reporting Publishing Corp.*, 120 S.Ct. 483 (1999).

[26]Fred Siebert, T. Peterson, & W. Schram, *Four Theories of the Press*, 51 (1956) [hereafter *Four Theories of the Press*].

[27]The court lately has begun to address the constitutional status of expressive claims by government in both the free speech and free press settings: *Arkansas Educ. Television Comm'n v. Forbes*, 118 S. Ct. 1633 (1998); *National Endowment for the Arts v. Finley*, 118 S. Ct. 2168 (1998). Although government speakers and publishers have not been recognized as acting under the First Amendment, a degree of immunity from First Amendment scrutiny has been accorded government action in its expressive capacities. See Randall Bezanson, *The Government Speech Forum: Forbes and Finley and Government Speech Selection Judgments*, 83 Iowa L. Rev. 953 (1998) [hereafter Bezanson, *The Government Speech Forum*].

[28]Fred Siebert, "The Libertarian Theory," *Four Theories of the Press, supra* note 26, p. 51.

[29]John Nerone, *Last Rights: Revisiting the Four Theories of the Press*, 27 (1995), [hereafter *Last Rights*].

[30]Fred Siebert, "The Libertarian Theory," *Four Theories of the Press, supra* note 26, 52.

[31]This was the explicit rationale for the Supreme Court's decision in *Red Lion Broadcasting Co. v. FCC*, 395 U.S. 367 (1969).

[32]Such a condition was the premise supporting the *Hutchins Commission Report*. Commission on Freedom of the Press, *A Free and Responsible Press* (1947).

[33]*Associated Press v. United States*, 326 U.S. 1 (1945).

[34]This was a major premise of the recommendations of the *Hutchins Commission Report, supra* note 32. The recently published study of the publicly traded newspaper companies reveals a similar dominance by large firms and, particularly today, those whose ownership is widely held and whose stock is publicly traded in the securities markets. Cranberg, Bezanson, & Soloski, *Taking Stock, supra* note 14.

[35]John Nerone, "Revisiting Four Theories of the Press," *Last Rights*, *supra* note 29, 26.

[36]Cranberg, Bezanson, & Soloski, *Taking Stock*, *supra* note 14.

[37]See C. Edwin Baker, *Giving the Audience What It Wants*, 58 Ohio St. L.J. 311 (1997).

[38]523 U.S. 666 (1998).

[39]*Ibid.*, 670.

[40]*Ibid.*, 674, 683.

[41]*Ibid.*, 676.

[42]*Ibid.*, 682–83. For further analysis of the opinion and its implications for free speech, and particularly the public forum doctrine, see Bezanson, *The Government Speech Forum*, *supra* note 27, 953.

[43]524 U.S. 569 (1998).

[44]There is, of course, some precedent for this in the setting of public broadcasting at the federal government level, but the structure of National Public Broadcasting preserves independence from the federal government and the federal support represents only a portion of the financing of NPR or PBS programming. See *FCC v. League of Women Voters*, 468 U.S. 364 (1984).

[45]Examples would include investigatory powers, subpoena powers, powers to search, and powers of law enforcement and prosecution, to name but a few.

[46]*Arkansas Educ. Television Comm'n v. Forbes*, 523 U.S. 666, at 670 (1998).

[47]*Finley*, 524 U.S. 569 (1998).

[48]The challenged amendment to the NEA statute supports just such a construction. *Ibid.*, 572.

[49]*Patron* is the term the majority used to describe the government's actions. *Ibid.*, 589.

[50]*Forbes*, 523 U.S. at 684–87 (Stevens, J., concurring).

[51]See *New York Times Co. v. Sullivan*, 376 U.S. 255 (1964) (stating that to prevent a chilling effect on debate of public issues, the editors must be allowed to publish critiques of public officials, even when half-truths or misinformation is included, unless actual malice is proven); *Miami Herald Publ'g Co. v. Tornillo*, 418 U.S. 241 (1974) (editors of publications dealing with matters of public debate must be granted independence to determine what material will be published); Bezanson, *Editorial Judgment*, *supra* note 10.

[52]See *Ibid.*; *Florida Bar v. Went For It, Inc.*, 515 U.S. 618 (1995); *Dun & Bradstreet, Inc. v. Greenmoss Builders, Inc.*, 472 U.S. 749, at 762 (1985).

[53]*Dun & Bradstreet, Inc. v. Greenmoss Builders, Inc.*, 472 U.S. 749, 762 (1985); Bezanson, *Editorial Judgment*, *supra* note 10.

[54]See Bezanson, *Editorial Judgment*, *supra* note 10, 647–76.

[55]*Virginia State Bd. of Pharmacy v. Virginia Citizens Consumer Council*, 425 U.S. 748, 760 (1976) (advertisements that do no more than "simply propose a commercial transaction" constitute commercial speech; not political speech), *Board of Trustees v. Fox*, 492 U.S. 469 (1983) (information about sales presentations for housewares products qualifies as commercial speech).

[56]See *Pittsburgh Press Co. v. Pittsburgh Comm'n on Human Relations*, 413 U.S. 376 (1973); *Cubby, Inc., v. CompuServe, Inc.*, 776 F. Supp. 135 (S.D.N.Y. 1991).

[57]For a discussion of such cases and the way courts treat them under the First Amendment or in response to claims of editorial freedom, see Bezanson, *Editorial Judgment*, *supra* note 10, 830–53.

[58]*Food Lion, Inc. v. Capital Cities/ABC, Inc.*, 964 F. Supp 956 (M.D.N.C. 1997), aff'd in part, 194 F.3d 505 (4th Cir. 1999); *Berger v. Hanlon*, 129 F.3d 505 (9th Cir. 1997), aff'd in part and remanded sub nom., 119 S.Ct. 1706 (1999).

[59]See Randall Bezanson, *The Right to Privacy Revisited: Privacy, News, and Social Change, 1890–1990*, 80 Calif. L. Rev. 1133 (1992).

[60]*Food Lion, Inc. v. Capital Cities/ABC, Inc.*, 964 F.Supp 956 (M.D.N.C. 1997), aff'd in part, 194 F.3d 505 (4th Cir. 1999).

[61]See Cranberg, Bezanson, & Soloski, *Taking Stock, supra* note 14.

[62]*Food Lion, Inc. v. Capital Cities/ABC, Inc.,* 964 F. Supp 956 (M.D.N.C. 1997), aff'd in part, 194 F.3d 505 (4th Cir. 1999). The following discussion of the *Food Lion* and *Berger* cases draws on an article the author published in the *Emory Law Journal*. Randall Bezanson, *Means and Ends and Food Lion: The Tension Between Exemption and Independence in Newsgathering by the Press*, 47 Emory L.J. 895 (1998).

[63]*Berger v. Hanlon*, 129 F.3d 505 (9th Cir. 1997), aff'd in part and remanded sub nom., 119 S.Ct. 1706 (1999).

[64]3 Media L. Rep. (BNA) 2304 (Iowa Dist. Ct. 1978), aff'd, 283 N.W.2d 289 (Iowa 1979), cert. denied, 445 U.S. 904 (1980). I have previously written about the *Howard* case; Randall Bezanson, *Public Disclosures as News: Injunctive Relief and Newsworthiness in Privacy Actions Involving the Press*, 64 Iowa L. Rev. 1061 (1979).

[65]See William Prochnau, "Paradise Lost?" *Am. Journalism Review* (January 10, 2000); David Shaw, "Crossing the Line," Special Supplement, *L.A. Times* (December 20, 1999).

[66]Daniel Forbes, *Prime-Time Propoganda*, available at www.Salon.com (last visited January 13, 2000); Howard Kurtz, "Drug Office Ad Deal Included Newspapers," *Washington Post* C1 (January 20, 2000).

[67]The practices were alleged to center on the meat and deli departments. *Food Lion, Inc. v. Capital Cities/ABC, Inc.,* 964 F. Supp. 956, at 958 (M.D.N.C. 1997).

[68]Russ Baker, *Damning Undercover Tactics as "Fraud"* Columbia Journalism Review 28, 31 (March/April 1997).

[69]*Food Lion, Inc. v. Capital Cities/ABC, Inc.,* 951 F. Supp. 1224, at 1226–27 (M.D.N.C. 1996).

[70]*Ibid.*; William Powers, "Making Sausage," *The New Republic* 15–16 (January 20, 1997).

[71]Marshall McLuhan, *Understanding the Media* (1964).

[72]Walter Lippmann, *Public Opinion* 54–55, 222 (1965).

[73]Baker, *supra* note 68, 32.

[74]*Ibid.*

[75]See Richard Starr, "What ABC Thinks of You," *The Weekly Standard,* 13 (February 10, 1997).

[76]See *Food Lion, Inc. v. Capital Cities/ABA, Inc.,* 951 F. Supp. 1224 (M.D.N.C. 1996); Thomas McArdle, "ABC's Food Lyin'," *Nat'l Rev.* 42 (February 10, 1997); Rance Crain, "Food Lion Injured But Journalism Takes Bigger Hit," *Advertising Age* (May 12, 1997).

[77]See Starr, *supra* note 75, 13; Russ Baker, *Truth, Lies and Videotape*, Columbia Journalism Review 25 (July/August 1993).

[78]Starr, *supra* note 75, 13.

[79]See Bezanson, *The Atomization of the Newspaper, supra* note 14; *CBS, Inc. v. FCC*, 453 U.S. 367, at 395 (1981); *Miami Herald Publ'g Co. v. Tornillo*, 418 U.S. 241 (1974). See J. Herbert Altschull, *From Milton to McLuhan: The Ideas Behind American Journalism* (1990); Lippman, *supra* note 72; Michael Schudson, *Discovering the News: A Social History of American Newspapers* (1978).

[80]See Lippman, *supra* note 72, 221–24, 355, 363: "News which does not offer [the] opportunity to introduce oneself into the struggle which it depicts cannot appeal to a wide audience"; Bernard Roshko, *Newsmaking* 15–17 (1975); G. Tuchman, *Making News* 182–197 (1978); Bezanson, *Public Disclosures as News, supra* note 64, 1061. As Oliver Wendell Holmes, Sr. put it: "[T]echnology itself does not inform anyone. Someone or something

must produce the almost hourly paragraphs in a form that provides an accurate representation of what is happening, in a form that the audience can comprehend.... And this information must be what its audience *needs* to know." Altschull, *supra* note 79, 14 (quoting Oliver Wendell Holmes, Sr., "Bread and the Newspaper," *Atlantic* (September 1861).

[81] See *New York Times Co. v. Sullivan*, 376 U.S. 254 (1964); *Herbert v. Lando*, 441 U.S. 153 (1979).

[82] For example, claims of First Amendment protection for "editorial judgments" have been denied when the purposes served by the publication of information were purely commercial and related to a limited audience, even though the information, if published by the press—or by a publisher with a view to public need—would be highly important. See, for example, *Dun & Bradstreet, Inc. v. Greenmoss Builders, Inc.*, 472 U.S. 749 (1985); *Lowe v. SEC*, 472 U.S. 181 (1985); *SEC v. Wall St. Publ'g Inst. Inc.*, 851 F.2d 365 (D.C. Cir. 1988), cert. denied 489 U.S. 1066 (1989); *Wainwright Sec. Inc. v. Wall St. Transcript Corp.*, 558 F.2d 91 (2nd Cir. 1977), cert. denied, 434 U.S. 1014 (1978).

[83] See Cranberg, Bezanson, & Soloski, *Taking Stock, supra* note 14.

[84] Gilbert Cranberg, *Trimming the Fringe: How Newspapers Shun Low Income Readers*, Columbia Journalism Review 52 (March/ April 1997) (quoting Miles Groves, Newspaper Association of America Chief Economist); See Ken Auletta, *Peering Over the Edge*, 5 Media Stud. J., 83, 91; (Fall 1991); Bezanson, *The Atomization of the Newspaper, supra* note 14.

[85] See Katherine Fulton, *A Tour of Our Uncertain Future*, Columbia Journalism Review (March/April 1996).

[86] See, for example, cases cited notes 107–109 *infra*.

[87] *Berger v. Hanlon*, 129 F.3d 505, at p. 508 (9th Cir. 1997).

[88] The real story, as it turned out, was dramatically titled "Ring of Death." According to Max Frankel, the story "implied that Berger had killed hundreds of protected eagles and ascribed his acquittal to jury bias. The program was shown at least 10 times on CNN, TBS, CNN International and TNT Latin America." Max Frankel, "A Case of Sheep v. Coyotes," *New York Times Magazine* 30 (December 21, 1997). CNN might be seen as having a stake in continuing, even after the acquittals, to make the Bergers the evil characters and the fish and game agents, with whom CNN cooperated, the heroes.

[89] *Berger*, 129 F.3d, at 508.

[90] See note 88 *supra*.

[91] *Berger*, 129 F.3d, at 508.

[92] *Ibid.*

[93] *Ibid.*, 508–09.

[94] *Ibid.*, 509.

[95] *Ibid.*

[96] *Berger*, 129 F.3d, at 510.

[97] 18 U.S.C. Sec. 2511 et. seq. (1994).

[98] See *Berger*, 129 F.3d, 516. Other state law claims, such as conversion, were not allowed to go forward. See *Ibid.*

[99] *Ibid.*, 515.

[100] *Ibid.*, 505.

[101] See Bezanson, *The New Free Press Guarantee, supra* note 10, 731; Blasi, *The Checking Value in First Amendment Theory*, Am. Bar Found. Res. J. 521 (1977).

[102] See Bezanson, *Taxes on Knowledge in America: Exactions on the Press from Colonial Times to the Present* 256–286 (1994); *Leathers v. Medlock*, 499 U.S. 439 (1991); *Minneapolis Star & Tribune Co. v. Minnesota Comm'r of Revenue*, 460 U.S. 575 (1983).

[103]CNN was given a copy of the warrant in advance of the search, although such warrants are not to be publicly disclosed until after a search has taken place.

[104]See *Berger*, 129 F.3d, at 508–09.

[105]CNN personnel witnessed Mr. Berger's limited consent to an agent's presence in the Bergers' house during the search.

[106]*Berger*, 129 F.3d, at 508.

[107]See, e.g., *Shulman v. Group W Prod.*, 51 Cal. App. 4th 850 (1996) (videotaping and later broadcast of rescue operation in car accident and in emergency helicopter pursuant to agreement between television production company and local hospital); *Baugh v. CBS*, 828 F. Supp. 745 (1993) (CBS news crew accompanying crisis counselor to home in which domestic dispute was taking place); *Ayeni v. Mottola*, 35 F.3d 680 (2nd Cir. 1994) (press admitted to home by officers during a search); *Dietemann v. Time, Inc.*, 449 F.2d 245 (9th Cir. 1971) (reporters cooperating with law enforcement in recording and transmitting conversations with fraudulent doctor).

[108]See e.g., *Copeland v. Hubbard Broad., Inc.*, 526 N.W.2d 402 (1995) (nonconsented [deception] entrance with secret camera by reporter); *United States v. Sanusi*, 813 F. Supp. 149 (2nd Cir. 1992) (unconsented-to participation of CBS news crew in execution of warrant for search of house); *Anderson v. WROC-TV*, 109 Misc.2d 904 (1981) (Humane Society investigator with warrant invited television stations to accompany him on raid and search of house without owner's consent); *Le Mistral v. CBS*, 61 A.D.2d 491 (1978) (CBS camera crews enter restaurant unannounced with cameras rolling in order to catch occupants by surprise).

[109]See, e.g., *Desnick Eye Services, Ltd. v. ABC*, 851 F. Supp. 303 (1994) (misrepresentation of purposes and techniques by press); *Sanders v. ABC*, 52 Cal. App. 4th 543 (1997) (deception in obtaining employment and secret taping); *Wolfson v. Lewis*, 924 F. Supp. 1413 (1996) (television journalists engaging in unlawful harassment of company executive in order to obtain, according to the court, "entertaining background for their TV expose"); *New Jersey v. Cantor*, 221 N.J. Super. 219 (1987) (newspaper reporter misrepresented self as county official to gain access to interview with homicide victim's mother); *Belluomo v. KAKE TV*, 3 Kan. App. 2d 461 (1979) (fraudulently obtained videotape of steakhouse).

[110]See Bezanson, *The New Free Press Guarantee*, *supra* note 10, 731; Bezanson, *Taxes on Knowledge in America*, *supra* note 102, 252–286.

[111]This, of course, is precisely what happened in the *Berger* case. See Frankel, *supra* note 88, 30; *Cohen v. Cowles Media Co.*, 501 U.S. 663 (1991); authorities cited notes 107–109 *supra*.

[112]The concept of special benefit and the close relationships such benefits may foster is analogous to the entanglement principle that the Supreme Court has often voiced under the Establishment Clause of the First Amendment. See *Lemon v. Kurtzman*, 403 U.S. 602, at 612–13 (1971); *Jones v. Wolf*, 443 U.S. 595 (1979). Although the constitutionally guaranteed relationship between government and religion and religious institutions, which might be described as "arms-length," agnostic, or "neutral," is distinct from that between government and the press, many of the basic concepts—such as independence, nondependence, and freedom to exercise private judgment (religious or editorial)—are analogous. See Bezanson, *The New Free Press Guarantee*, *supra* note 10, 731; M. Nimmer, *Introduction—Is Freedom of the Press a Redundancy: What Does It Add to Freedom of Speech?*, 26 Hastings L.J. 639 (1975); Stewart, *supra* note 10, 631; W. Van Alstyne, *The Hazards to the Press of Claiming a "Preferred Position,"* 28 Hastings L.J. (1977).

[113]283 N.W.2d 289 (Iowa 1989), cert. denied, 445 U.S. 904 (1980).

[114]Bernard Roshko, *Newsmaking* 55 (1975).

[115]*Des Moines Register,* 8A, col. 3 (February 15, 1976), reprinted in App. 61–64, *Howard v. Des Moines Register & Tribune Co.,* 283 N.W.2d 289 (Iowa 1989), cert. denied, 445 U.S. 904 (1980).

[116]*Ibid.*

[117]*Ibid.*

[118]The trial court's decision was reported at 3 *Media L. Rptr.* 2304 (Iowa District Court 1978), aff'd, *Howard v. Des Moines Register & Tribune Co.,* 283 N.W.2d 289 (1979), cert. denied, 445 U.S. 904 (1980).

[119]Walter Lippmann, *Public Opinion* 358 (reprinted 1945).

[120]*See* Randall Bezanson, *The Right to Privacy Revisited: Privacy, News, and Social Change, 1890–1990,* 80 Calif. L. Rev. 1133, 1151–1172 (1992) [hereafter Bezanson, *The Right to Privacy Revisited*].

[121]As Jim Carey has put it: "Social life is, after all, the succession of great metaphors. The metaphor which has governed our understanding of journalism in this century has run into trouble…. The ethics of journalism will not move forward until we actually re-think, re-describe, re-interpret what journalism is: not the science or information of our culture but instead its poetry and conversation." James Carey, *Journalists Just Leave: The Ethics of an Anomalous Profession, in Ethics and the Media* 19 (Maile-Gene Sagen, ed., 1987).

[122]Bernard Roshko, *Newsmaking* 55 (1975).

[123]For information on the frequency of privacy claims against the press, their success (or lack of success), and the reasons for this, see Bezanson, Cranberg, & Soloski, *Libel Law and The Press: Myth and Reality* 107–11, 115–17 (1988); Bezanson, *The Right to Privacy Revisited, supra* note 120, 169–172.

[124]Michael Schudson argues that objectivity, grounded in process or mode of performance, is a product of detachment effected through professional norms and standardized process. Michael Schudson, *Discovering the News: A Social History of American Newspapers* 6, 7–9 (1978).

[125]These matters are developed at much greater length in Bezanson, *The Right to Privacy Revisited, supra* note 120.

[126]*Ibid.* An interesting example of statutory approaches based on control and confidentiality is the Model Health Information Disclosure Act, a proposed statute drafted by students in a seminar at the Iowa Law School and published in 25 *Journal of Corporation Law* 119–135 (1999).

[127]*CBS v. Democratic Nat'l Comm.,* 412 U.S. 94, at 124 (1973).

[128]The press' basic claim is analogous, in its broadest articulation, to a claim of civil disobedience. Civil disobedients, however, recognize the illegality of their actions, engage in them to foster awareness and social change, and generally accept the law's sanction—indeed, some would argue that they must accept it in order for the act to be morally correct—in order to publicly express their act of moral conscience and thus foster social change. See Martin Luther King, Jr., "Letter From Birmingham Jail," *Why We Can't Wait* 84 (1963); Bruce Ledewitz, *Civil Disobedience, Injunctions, and the First Amendment,* 19 Hofstra L. Rev. 67 (1990); Steven M. Bauer & Peter Eckerstrom, *The State Made Me Do It: The Applicability of the Necessity Defense to Civil Disobedience,* 39 Stan. L. Rev. 1173 (1987).

[129]See, for example, *ibid.*; Student Note, *And Forgive Them Their Trespasses: Applying the Defense of Necessity to the Criminal Conduct of the Newsgatherer,* 103 Harv. L. Rev. 890 (1990).

[130]See James Cavallaro, Jr., *The Demise of the Political Necessity Defense: Indirect Civil Disobedience and United States v. Schoon,* 81 Calif. L. Rev. 351 (1993) (Casenote); Laura

Schulkind, *Applying the Necessity Defense to Civil Disobedience Cases*, 64 N.Y.U. L. Rev. 79 (1989); Bauer & Eckerstrom, *supra* note 192.

[131]*Ibid.*, 1175, citing *United States v. Bailey*, 444 U.S. 394, 409–15 (1980), *United States v. Dorrell*, 758 F.2d 427 (9th Cir. 1985); W. Lafave & A. Scott, *Criminal Law* 385–88 (1972).

[132]The risk of harm to wildlife, of course, was likely to diminish because of the search (assuming the facts about the Bergers were true); CNN's participation in the search would not further reduce that risk of harm, and therefore the marginal contribution of CNN's illegal conduct (violation of the Bergers' constitutional rights, trespass, invasion of privacy) toward eliminating any harm was zero. Some might argue that CNN's illegal behavior was justified by the greater impact the filmed footage would have in generating political pressure to protect wildlife in the future. This, of course, is both conclusory and speculative. More basically, however, to accept such an argument would be to open the necessity defense so wide as to effectively create a news exemption from trespass and other law under a different name only.

[133]See Connor Cruise O'Brien, *Great Melody: A Thematic Biography and Commented Anthology of Edmund Burke* (1992). Alexander Bickel put the point thus:

> Another sort of limit on civil disobedience has to do with means. Violence must be a monopoly of the state. In private hands, whatever its possible misuses by the state, it is always an unjust weapon. *** [W]hen the interference [of civil disobedience] is massive, when it is not civil, when it borders on violence or threatens it, when it is coercive not in its ultimate intent—as all civil disobedience is, but in its immediate impact ... then it is unacceptable.
>
> —Alexander Bickel, *The Morality of Consent* 113 (1975).

[134]Jerry Thomas, "Jackson Arrested During Protest at Science Museum," *Chicago Tribune* 3 (Metro Section) (February 11, 1997).

[135]Phillip Kurland, *Of Church and State and the Supreme Court*, 29 U. Chi. L. Rev. 1, 6 (1961) (stating that "the religion clauses of the first amendment ... should be read as a single precept that government cannot utilize religion as a standard for action or inaction because these clauses prohibit classification in terms of religion either to confer a benefit or to impose a burden").

[136]Bezanson, *Taxes on Knowledge in America, supra* note 102, 252–285.

[137]See, e.g., *Berger v. Hanlon*, 129 F.3d 505, at 508 (9th Cir. 1997).

PART II

Journalism and Privacy

3

The Right to Be Let Alone

Anthony Lewis
Columbia University

The subject of privacy is a profoundly important concern in contemporary society—important and easily overridden in our rush for gossip, entertainment, and profit.

I have taken the title of this chapter, as many readers will recognize, from Louis D. Brandeis. Brandeis and his law partner, Samuel Warren, used the phrase "the right to be let alone" in the article that invented the legal theory of privacy: "The Right to Privacy," published in 1890 in the *Harvard Law Review*.[1] But that was not the end of the matter for Brandeis. He was a man of strong and lasting convictions. Thirty-eight years later, in 1928, when a majority of the Supreme Court held that wiretapping was not a search subject to the Fourth Amendment to the Constitution, Justice Brandeis disagreed.

> "The makers of our Constitution," he wrote in his dissenting opinion: "recognized the significance of man's spiritual nature, of his feelings and his intellect. They knew that only a part of the pain, pleasure and satisfactions of life are to be found in material things. They sought to protect Americans in their beliefs, their thoughts, their emotions and their sensations. They conferred, as against the government, the right to be let alone—the most comprehensive of rights and the right most valued by civilized men."[2]

Brandeis said that when the Fourth Amendment was adopted in 1791, the government could obtain a person's "papers and articles incident to his private life" only by breaking and entry. But by 1928, he said, "subtler and more far-reaching means of invading privacy have become available to the government. Discovery and invention have made it possible for the government, by means far more effective than stretching upon the rack, to obtain disclosure in court of what is whispered in the closet."[3] He went on to warn that the development of invasive technology was "not likely to stop with wiretapping. Ways may some day be developed," he said, "by which the government, without removing papers from secret drawers, can reproduce them in court, and by which it will be enabled to expose to a jury the most intimate occurrences of the home."[4]

We have come a long way down the path that Brandeis foresaw in 1928. Instead of private papers in a drawer, most of us now confide private thoughts to a computer, where they are not at all safe from prying eyes. Kenneth Starr printed out from Monica Lewinsky's computer her unsent love letters and emotional jottings, and he published them all in the material he sent to the House of Representatives. The National Security Agency, with its enormous eavesdropping capacity, intercepts millions of telephone conversations around the world. A novice in the computer game can rather quickly find out unlisted telephone numbers. Bank accounts and other financial data are no longer secret from anyone who really wants to know.

Jeffrey Rosen, associate professor at the George Washington University Law School and a legal commentator for *The New Republic*, not long ago wrote a book called *The Unwanted Gaze*, and it compellingly describes what Rosen subtitles his book, "The destruction of privacy in America." Rosen cites the lawsuit by Paula Jones as an example of how sexual harassment law has been perverted into a destroyer of privacy. By accusing President Clinton of an offensive sexual advance years before, Jones was able to compel him and others to describe their consensual, private sexual activities in testimony that inevitably became public. Monica Lewinsky was asked by Jones' lawyers to hand over her diaries, address books, letters, notes, and so on. Rosen asks, "How could the law permit such unreasonable searches, in which the investigation of the offense seemed more invasive than the offense itself?"[5]

Monica resented more than anything Kenneth Starr's subpoena demanding that a Washington bookstore produce a record of all the books she had bought there. "I felt like I wasn't a citizen of this country anymore,"[6] she said. But Starr said courts had upheld a subpoena for records of books read by Timothy McVeigh, the Oklahoma City bomber, so they should do the same for him. That a prosecutor would advance so absurd an analogy shows how the interest of privacy has been devalued in the legal mind.

On April 5, 2000, *The New York Times* ran a story about one manifestation of technology's destruction of privacy: software that allows a company manager to read every e-mail sent or received by every one of his or her employees. The one redeeming feature of this depressing story was that the manager who was interviewed said he had qualms about learning so much about employees' private lives.

This volume considers privacy in two contexts, the First Amendment and the profession of journalism. So let me describe a case that brings out some of the difficult—I would say painful—tensions of this subject. It is the case of William James Sidis, one that I dare say is familiar to some readers. I take that risk because it is such a wonderful example of our subject.

Born in 1898, Sidis was a boy genius. His father, Boris, a psychotherapist, set out almost from William's birth to develop the boy's faculties. William was said to have read *The New York Times* by the age of 18 months. By the time he started school, he knew not only English but German, French, Russian, and Hebrew. Boris relentlessly trained his son, and issued bulletins to the press. At the age of 11, William entered Harvard, and *The Times* described him as the "wonderfully successful result of a scientific forcing experiment."[7] The press followed William and praised his father's theories. But as any of us might predict, William did not enjoy life in a goldfish bowl. After college and incomplete attempts at graduate school, he sought obscurity. Working variously as a clerk and a translator, Sidis dropped out of the public eye until 1937, when *The New Yorker* published an article by Jared L. Manley about Sidis. It was headed "Where Are They Now?"[8] Under that was the line "April Fool," a play on the fact that Sidis was born on April 1.

The article described Sidis as living a lonely life in "a hall bedroom in Boston's shabby South End."[9] It spoke of his "curious laugh," his collection of streetcar transfers, and his interest in the lore of the Okamakamesset Indians. It was, as a judge said later, a "merciless" exposure of a man who desperately wanted to be let alone.

Sidis sued for violation of his privacy. The case was decided in 1940 by the United States Court of Appeals for the Second Circuit. Judge Charles Clark, a former dean of the Yale Law School, expressed sympathy for the plaintiff. Sidis claimed that *The New Yorker* article had held him up to "public scorn, ridicule and contempt," causing him "grievous mental anguish [and] humiliation."[10] There is no reason to doubt the accuracy of those claims. But Judge Clark found for the defendants, the publishers of *The New Yorker*. He did not apply the First Amendment to protect the magazine—the Supreme Court had not yet brought libel and privacy within the ambit of the Amendment. Instead, he simply balanced the interests and said the court was not disposed "to afford to all the intimate details of private life an absolute immunity from the prying of the press."[11] Brandeis to the contrary notwithstanding, Judge Clark allowed "limited scrutiny of the 'private' life of any person who has achieved, or has had thrust upon him, the questionable and indefinable status of a 'public figure.'"[12]

The phrase "thrust upon him" is what did it for William Sidis. Unfair as it may have been to make him suffer for the fame that his father thrust upon him and that he could not resist as a child, it would have been strange—in a country devoted to free expression—to bar the press from taking a continuing interest in someone who had been a publicized boy genius. That is even clearer now, in light of subsequent interpretation of the First Amendment.

But that still leaves the question of journalism. Was the Jared Manley article good journalism? Was it professionally right? Was it decent of *The New Yorker* to publish it? When I teach the Sidis case, I ask my students whether they have read anything else by Jared Manley. It is a trick question, because he did not exist—Jared Manley was a pseudonym used by James Thurber. And another thing: Thurber evidently did not meet William Sidis. The article said a woman had "recently succeeded in interviewing him."[13] Did she disclose her purpose, or did she pose as a new friend to the lonely Sidis when she visited his hall bedroom and inspected his collection of streetcar transfers? We cannot be sure, but it smacks to me of the slippery methods of British tabloids. What I am suggesting is that a piece of journalism prying into someone's private life may not give the victim a right to damages, but it may be indecent nonetheless. It may violate the standards that we as journalists ought to have.

William James Sidis—by the way, William James was his godfather—lived just 4 more years after the Second Circuit decision. He died of a cerebral hemorrhage, unemployed and destitute.

Here is another unhappy story, this one engaging the First Amendment. In 1952, three escaped convicts took over the home of James Hill and his family in a Philadelphia suburb. The Hills and their five children were held hostage for 19 hours but were treated gently and respectfully by the convicts, who left and were caught 10 days later. The press covered the story intensely, to the distress of the family and especially of Mrs. Hill, who was a very private person. To escape from the glare of publicity, the Hills moved to Connecticut and sought obscurity. Two years later, a play called *The Desperate Hours* opened on Broadway. It depicted a 2-day reign of terror by escaped convicts in a home they invaded: sexual assault, brutality, and general menace. The play was set in Indianapolis; but *Life* magazine, doing a feature on the opening, decided to photograph the actors in the former home of the Hills near Philadelphia and to describe the play, with all its terror, as a reenactment of what had happened to the Hills. The *Life* story was devastating to the Hill family. Mrs. Hill suffered a psychiatric breakdown. Mr. Hill said he could not understand how *Life* could publish such a story without at least telephoning him to check its truth. "It was just like we didn't exist," he said, "like we were dirt."[14]

The Hills sued Time Inc. for invasion of privacy under New York law. A jury awarded Mr. Hill $50,000 compensatory and $25,000 punitive damages. After appeals and a second trial fixing damages at $30,000, Time Inc. eventually took the case to the Supreme Court of the United States where, as it happens, Mr. Hill was represented by Richard M. Nixon. After the argument the justices voted 6 to 3 to affirm the modest judgment awarded Mr. Hill. The opinion was assigned to Justice Abe Fortas. He began with a stinging attack on *Life*'s handling of the story. "Needless, heedless, wanton and deliberate injury of the sort inflicted by Life's picture story," he wrote, "is not an essential instrument of responsible journalism. Magazine writers and editors are not, by reason of their high office, relieved of the common obligation to avoid deliberately inflicting wanton and unnecessary injury. The prerogatives of the press—essential to our liberty—do not preclude responsible care.... "

Justice Fortas spoke—I think movingly—of the constitutional dimensions of privacy. "It is not only the right to be secure in one's person, house, papers, and effects," he said. "It is more than the specific right to be secure against the Peeping Tom or the intrusion of electronic espionage.... The right of privacy reaches beyond any of its specifics. It is, simply stated, the right to be let alone; to live one's life as one chooses, free from assault, intrusion or invasion except as they can be justified by the clear needs of community living under a government of law."[15]

But you will not find those words in the reports of the Supreme Court. At the passionate urging of Justice Black, the Court set the case for reargument the following fall. Then, by a vote of 5 to 4, it reversed the judgment for Mr. Hill.[16] In the opinion of the court, by Justice Brennan, the key factor was the recent decision in *New York Times v. Sullivan*. In that case the Court, in a notable opinion by Justice Brennan, held that a public official could not recover libel damages for a false statement about him or her unless he or she proved that the statement was published with knowledge of its falsity or in reckless disregard of the truth. *Life* had not falsified the Hills' story knowingly or recklessly, Justice Brennan said, so Mr. Hill lost.

Unlike most press lawyers, I think the case of *Time Inc. v. Hill* was wrongly decided. James Hill was not a public official of the kind for whom the Sullivan rule was imposed—a person who should have stayed out of the kitchen if he could not stand the heat. He and his family were obscure, private individuals who were caught up in public attention for reasons beyond their control, and they did all they could to escape that attention. I do not think the James Hills of this world should have to jump such high hurdles in order to make a modest legal point about their privacy.

Now think of the Hill case in terms not of law, but of journalism ethics. Justice Fortas's criticism of *Life*—"needless, heedless, wanton injury"—was hyperbolic. But does he not have a point in suggesting that responsible journalists have a duty of reasonable care, not least toward powerless private individuals like the Hill family?

Leonard Garment, who was a law partner of Richard Nixon, wrote a fascinating article on the Hill case. He disclosed, with Mr. Hill's permission, something we had not known. Two eminent psychiatrists found, as Mr. Garment put it, that Mrs. Hill "had come through the original hostage incident well but had fallen apart when the *Life* article brought back her memories transformed into her worst nightmares and presented them to the world as reality.... In August 1971 Mrs. Hill took her life."[17]

The factors of law and journalistic professionalism must always both be considered. Twenty years ago, two Minnesota television stations asked a court to give them copies of videotapes that had been used as evidence in a criminal trial. A kidnapper and rapist had recorded his victim, bound and blindfolded, before raping her. The judge rejected the request, finding that broadcast of the tapes would violate the woman's right to privacy "without proper public purpose," merely for commercial exploitation of prurient interest. Whatever the answer in law, were the television stations right to ask to broadcast those tapes?[18]

I have been writing about the claims of privacy for people who have not sought fame. However, I need hardly say that an acute question of our time is whether the famous and powerful have any right to privacy.

Press attitudes on that question have changed drastically. When Franklin Roosevelt was president, reporters and photographers effectively hid from the public the fact that he spent most of his time in a wheelchair. When a new photographer at the White House took a picture of him in the wheelchair, colleagues removed the film from his camera. Judge Charles Clark, in the opinion rejecting William Sidis' lawsuit, said that he could envision situations when what he called "public characters" could protect their privacy by law. "Revelations," he said, "may be so intimate and so unwarranted in view of the victim's position as to outrage the community's notions of decency."[19]

Nowadays it is hard to imagine any revelation that the press would consider too intimate to publish. Anything that shows a politician in a bad light, especially a president, is fair game. And of course sex is best of all. We can date the change to the moment a *Washington Post* reporter asked Gary Hart at a press conference, "Senator, have you ever committed adultery?"

We are obsessed with the sex life of politicians, yet I have never seen any evidence that sexual purity produces wiser leadership. When a Linda Tripp comes along with her tales and her tapes, I think a mainstream newspaper editor or broadcast producer should tell her to peddle them to a supermarket tabloid. That is what a French editor would certainly do, but the French equivalent of supermarket tabloids would not be interested. Sex? What else is new? Only in the United States and Britain does the press go mad over straying politicians. Is it something about the Anglo-Saxons, as the French call us? Or does it have to do with the increasing competitiveness of communication? If we do not publish it, some bottom-dwelling slug will put it on his or her Web site. (I took that phrase from Joseph Alsop, who used it in the McCarthy years.) Well, I think the new competitiveness has produced something like Gresham's Law, with everyone in the news business rushing to the bottom.

When President Clinton made his television remarks after testifying about Monica Lewinsky, most commentators condemned him for criticizing Kenneth Starr's attacks on privacy. He should have stuck to being contrite, they said. But the public showed no signs of feeling that way. The President's ratings remained high after the broadcast. I think the public understood what the Starr crusade was doing to privacy and didn't like it.

The public is a two-faced beast: It deplores television reporters who exploit tragedy, poking microphones at the mothers of crash victims; but people watch the programs. I think there is a feeling of shame at our prurient interest in sex and sorrow. Privacy has suffered grievously in our society, but Americans have not lost their sense of its value.

Think about the journalistic ethics in the following story. Ruth Shulman was driving on a Los Angeles freeway when her car was hit by another and rolled down an embankment. She was gravely injured, ending up a paraplegic. A rescue helicopter came to the scene of the accident and flew Ms. Shulman to a hospital. What she did not know was that an attendant in the helicopter was secretly filming her in agony, and the nurse talking with her had a hidden microphone. It was all broadcast on a so-called "reality TV" program that looked like news but was in fact created by an entertainment company. Do we need to do that under the mantle of the First Amendment?[20]

Or think about Charles and Geraldine Wilson of Rockville, Maryland. They were still in bed early one morning; their 9-year-old granddaughter was up and waiting for the school bus. They heard her open the door to someone. Mr. Wilson, wearing only shorts, went out to look. Three policemen with guns drawn ordered him to the floor. A photographer took a picture of him with an officer's knee on his back and gun at his head. Mrs. Wilson came in wearing a negligee.

The photographer worked for the *Washington Post*, and a reporter was there with him. They were working together with the police to record something called "Operation Gunsmoke," a search for wanted felons. The Wilson's adult son was wanted on charges of violating probation. He was not there, and in due course the police left. The Wilsons sued the police, claiming that their right to be secure in their house—as the Fourth Amendment puts it—had been violated. In this and a companion case, the Supreme Court held that the joint raids indeed violated the Fourth Amendment.[21]

Some leading press organizations, including my newspaper, *The New York Times*, filed a brief in the Supreme Court defending such press ride-alongs, as they are called. "They afford the public," the brief said, "a unique window through which to observe the conduct of those officials … and the social conditions they confront."[22] Does that persuade you? Not me—I do not think we need to find out about social conditions by having reporters and photographers burst into homes with armed policemen.

What I have written may not be what you expected. I was a reporter and a columnist for a long time, and I believe with all my heart in the First Amendment. If the press is to do its job, it must pry into some closed areas of life and society. It could hardly be effective in holding power accountable if it had to ask the permission of those who hold power before investigating them. I believe, as Judge Murray Gurfein put it in the Pentagon Papers case, in "a cantankerous press, an obstinate press, a ubiquitous press."

However, none of that requires us to treat the interest of privacy with contempt and disregard. Privacy is essential to all of us, as individuals and as a society. The reasons were beautifully stated recently by Thomas Nagel, professor of philosophy and law at New York University: "Each of our inner lives is such a jungle of thoughts, feelings, fantasies and impulses," Professor Nagel said, "that civilization would be impossible if we expressed them all, or if we could all read each other's minds, just as social life would be impossible if we expressed all our lustful, aggressive, greedy, anxious or self-possessed feelings, and private behavior could be safely exposed to public view."[23]

Professor Nagel made a telling point about our obsession with the sexual lives of presidents and other politicians. "We can't limit the choice of political figures," he said, "to those whose peculiar inner constitution enables them to withstand outrageous exposure, or those whose sexual lives are simon-pure."

We are in the age of exposure nowadays—self-exposure on Oprah Winfrey and the like, and exposure of others by gossip-mongers and the press. When I watched the talking heads on television piously condemning President Clinton, I wondered how they would like to have their sex lives displayed to the world.

Secrecy is a red flag to journalists, including me. Governments use it to hide corruption and incompetence. But in another sense, secrecy is an essential component of life. Why? I end with the words of the Czech novelist Milan Kundera, spoken while he was in exile in 1985:

> For me, indiscretion is a capital sin. Anyone who reveals someone else's intimate life deserves to be whipped. We live in an age when private life is being destroyed. The po-

lice destroy it in Communist countries, journalists threaten it in democratic countries, and little by little the people lose their taste for private life and their sense of it.

Life when one can't hide from the eyes of others—that is hell. Those who have lived in totalitarian countries know it; but that system only brings out, like a magnifying glass, the tendencies of all modern society. Without secrecy, nothing is possible—not love, not friendship.[24]

NOTES

[1]Louis D. Brandeis & Samuel D. Warren, *The Right to Privacy*, 4 Harvard Law Review 193 (1890).

[2]*Olmstead v. United States*, 277 U.S. 438 (1928), at 478.

[3]*Ibid.*, at 473.

[4]*Ibid.*, at 474.

[5]Jeffrey Rosen, *The Unwanted Gaze*, Random House 4 (2000).

[6]Andrew Morton, *Monica's Story*, St. Martin's Press 215 (1999).

[7]"Sidis Could Read at Two Years Old," *New York Times* 7 (October 18, 1909).

[8]*The New Yorker* 22 (August 14, 1937).

[9]*Sidis v. F-R Publishing*, 113 F2d 806 (2nd Cir., 1940), at 807.

[10]Sissela Bok, *Secrets*, Vintage Books 251 (1984).

[11]*Sidis v. F-R Publishing*, op cit., at 809.

[12]*Ibid.*

[13]*The New Yorker,* op. cit., at 25.

[14]Bernard Schwartz, *Unpublished Opinions of the Warren Court*, Oxford University Press 249 (1985).

[15]Schwartz, op. cit., at 243.

[16]*Time, Inc. v. Hill*, 385 U.S. 374 (1967).

[17]Leonard Garment, "Annals of Law: The Hill Case," *The New Yorker* 90, 109 (April 17, 1989).

[18]*In re Application of KSTP Television v. Ming Sen Shiue*, 504 F. Supp. 360 (1980).

[19]*Sidis v. F-R Publishing*, 113 F2d at 809.

[20]See *Shulman v. Group W Productions, Inc.*, 955 P2d 469 (Cal. 1998).

[21]See *Wilson v. Layne*, 526 U.S. 603 (1999); *Berger v. Hanlon*, 520 U.S. 808 (1999).

[22]Brief Amici Curiae of ABC, Inc. et al., in support of petitioners in Hanlon v. Berger, Supreme Court 2 (October Term, 1998).

[23]Thomas Nagel, "The shredding of public privacy," *Times Literary Supplement* 15,13 (August 14, 1998).

[24]"A Talk With Milan Kundera," *New York Times Magazine* 72, 85 (May 19, 1985).

4

Why Journalists Can't Protect Privacy

Anita L. Allen
University of Pennsylvania Law School

The professional standards of print and broadcast journalism have often called for respect for privacy. For example, the Code of Ethics promulgated by the Society of Professional Journalists in 1996 exhorts members "absent an overriding public need" to avoid "intrusion into anyone's privacy."[1] The Associated Press Managing Editors' Code of Ethics, updated in 1995, urges newspapers to "respect the individual's right to privacy."[2] In the 1920s, the American Society of Newspaper Editors (ASNE), in its Canons of Journalism, affirmed that "[a] newspaper should not involve private rights or feeling without sure warrant of public right as distinguished from public curiosity."[3]

Although privacy has been on the ethical radar screen for some time, professional journalists are notorious for reaching into other people's personal lives to gather information of potential interest to the general public. Moreover, some would argue that the twin demands of the public's right to know and the First Amendment entail that robust privacy protection cannot be the legal or moral responsibility of journalists. Any limit on news coverage, whether legal or ethical, risks reducing the press' power to inform the public and to right wrongs. That includes privacy law.[4] The First Amendment protects speech about "daily life matters" as well as political matters, and one scholar has argued that "in a free speech regime, others' definitions of me should primarily be molded by their own judgments, rather than by my using legal coercion to keep them in the dark."[5]

Quite apart from lofty principles, there are matters of practicality that count against journalistic regard for privacy. Shouldering the burden of respecting privacy grows increasingly impractical as the information demands of our complex society multiply and as diverse, pluralistic conceptions of 'private' flourish. Notions of privacy vary from cultural group to cultural group and from individual to individual. A cultural group's consensus on what is private may be obtainable from community leaders or ethnographers, but these may err, innocently or otherwise, and it may be difficult to determine their relevance to a particular news subject. Ascertaining an individual's view, however, may require invading his/her privacy to find out what he/she considers private. Once a journalist knows a subject's conception of privacy, a new problem arises. Respecting an individual's or group's notion of privacy may entail a kind of "discrimination" against those with less restrictive norms. If the onus is placed on the news subject to assert his/her privacy expectations, two more problems are created: A wrongdoer may invent privacy claims to shield his/her wrongs, and an unsophisticated news source may be unable to effectively communicate privacy concerns to journalists who are listening for specific privacy-claiming words.

The burdens of impracticality and principle might be thought to justify journalism's abandonment of privacy values, both in theory and in practice. Some professional journalists have already jettisoned privacy even as a hortatory ethical ideal. The guidelines for ethical news gathering that were adopted in 1999 by the Gannett Company, publishers of *USA Today* and numerous local newspapers, express a commitment to "[s]eeking and reporting the truth in a truthful way" and in the public interest, and "uphold[ing] First Amendment principles," but do not even mention the word *privacy*.[6]

Is respect for privacy a dead letter as an ethical imperative for journalists? Should future codes of journalism ethics formally preserve the troublesome mandate to gather and report the news in a manner consistent with respect for others' personal privacy? Or should future codes openly jettison privacy in favor of free expression, truth, and accountability? Appropriately respecting valued and valuable forms of personal privacy would ideally remain an ethical consideration, among others, for journalists. Yet it is plain that respecting privacy will be neither a priority nor a pragmatic, costless consideration for journalism in the current cultural, commercial, and constitutional environment.

REPORTING PRIVATE FACTS

In recent years, a range of controversies in the United States and abroad has reflected the conflicting values of journalistic freedom and privacy. One such controversy took place in Israel. Ofra Haza was a Sephardic Jew whose family emigrated from Yemen to Israel. She grew up in poverty but went on to become an internationally recognized singer. Haza contracted AIDS. Although rumors of the nature of her illness eventually abounded, Haza wanted to conceal her disease. She managed to keep the fact a secret from the general public until her death from complications of AIDS. One week after she died, however, the Israeli daily newspaper *Ha'aretz* reported the cause of death. As quoted in *The New York Times*, *Ha'aretz* explained that "it felt compelled to ... lift 'the fragile tissue of silence, stretched tenuously over a fervor of rumors.'"[7] *Ha'aretz* felt an obligation to report the whole, true story of the star's death, in the face of pervasive gossip and rumor. Truth and completeness are indeed *desiderata* of journalistic reporting, but medical privacy is a *desideratum* of respect for persons potentially harmed by the vulnerability, embarrassment, and stigma that can follow unwanted health disclosures.

In the course of the 2000 presidential campaign, then-vice presidential candidate Dick Cheney was less than completely forthcoming about his heart condition. Shortly after the election, doctors on his case at the George Washington University Hospital spoke of "minimally elevated" enzymes when the candidate had in fact suffered a heart attack. Debate over Cheney's medical privacy continued into the new administration. Although some nonjournalists sympathized with Cheney's desire for medical privacy,[8] editorial boards were unanimous, or virtually so, in demanding more openness.[9] Even *The New York Times* columnist William Safire, a Republican who has argued for privacy in other contexts, wrote that "an appointee especially one with a finger on or near the nuclear button must expect to give up a private citizen's right to privacy."[10]

Revealing (and relentless) television coverage followed the plane crash that killed John F. Kennedy, Jr., his wife, and his sister-in-law. Much of the television news coverage appropriately focused on government efforts to determine the cause of the crash, and to recover the victims' bodies and plane wreckage. Additional news coverage focused on the lives of the deceased crash victims. That coverage paid special attention to Kennedy's legacy as the force behind *George* magazine and to his mystique as a Kennedy—the handsome, charming grandson of Joseph Kennedy, the son of the assassinated President John F. Kennedy and icon Jacqueline Kennedy Onassis, and the nephew of both the slain former Attorney General Robert F. Kennedy and senior United States Senator Edward Kennedy. Many people criticized the amount of coverage given to the Kennedy plane crash.

Among the controversial news overkill was the coverage of Caroline Kennedy Schlossberg's response to the deaths. Schlossberg is John F. Kennedy, Jr.'s older sister and is now the last surviving embodiment of the Kennedys' mythic Camelot. American journalists have reason to be aware of the importance of privacy to Caroline Kennedy Schlossberg, a serious, reserved woman who takes pains to avoid the press and who is the co-author of a well-received book about the value of privacy. Schlossberg learned to esteem and expect privacy, despite fame, from her mother, who took paparazzi photographer Ronald E. Galella to court to keep him at a safe distance from her children and herself. Yet Schlossberg did not get the privacy she is known to have wanted and that she, like anyone, deserves while in mourning. On the contrary, for days after her brother's death, the press tracked her every move and sought to capture her every facial expression on camera. Television journalists gestured oddly at respect for her privacy. They did not turn off their cameras to respect privacy in a meaningful way. Instead, they used whispered and reverent-seeming tones while addressing their viewing audiences with remarks like, "She is a very private person" and "Here she is returning to her home on her bicycle after a bit of exercise with her husband to relieve some of the stress she must be experiencing after the loss of her brother." Not allowed inside the Manhattan church during the celebration of the funeral Mass, the press pointed its frustrated cameras at the outside church door, inviting us to join them in hours of idle speculation about the thoughts and feelings of Caroline and the black-clad Kennedy family and friends arriving at and leaving the service.

Another example of the conflict between the desire for privacy and desire for publication is *Food Lion, Inc. v. Capital Cities/ABC, Inc.*[11] Employees of ABC News'
Prime Time Live lied on applications they submitted to obtain jobs at Food Lion su-
permarkets for the purpose of undercover investigation of charges concerning the
adulteration and mislabeling of food products. Hidden cameras revealed Food Lion
employees engaging in questionable practices mandated by store management, such
as putting new sell-by dates on old meat and deli products. Although Food Lion initially won a large monetary judgment in a lawsuit for fraud and trespass, the interest
in public health and information seemed to outweigh the privacy preferences of Food
Lion management and individual employees. The courts ultimately reduced Food
Lion's damage award to $2. In a similar case, *Desnick v. ABC,*[12] a federal court held
valid the fraudulently obtained consent that *Prime Time Live* used to gain access to
the offices of two eye surgeons who had performed more than 10,000 cataract operations in a single year. Although ABC promised the doctors they would not be subjected to ambush journalism or undercover surveillance, it sent agents disguised as
patients and carrying concealed cameras to see the doctors. When ABC broadcast a
program suggesting that the doctors were performing unnecessary surgery, the doctors unsuccessfully sued for privacy intrusion and trespass.

Sometimes there is no desire for privacy expressed by the object of journalistic
attention, but segments of the public believe ethical journalism would dictate privacy. Elian Gonzalez' fate became a political cause when he survived an accident at
sea that took the lives of his mother and others seeking to escape from Cuba to Miami. Elian was was brought alone to the South Florida shore by an exiled Cuban
fisherman on Thanksgiving Day. After Elian was released to his uncle Lazaro, the
Cuban exile movement in Miami rallied around Lazaro in his conflict with Fidel
Castro and Elian's father, Juan Miguel. The conflict concerned whether Elian, who
took on symbolic and even religious significance to both parties seeking to control
him, would remain in the United States. Too young to have distinct views and understandings about personal privacy, Elian was often before the eye of the camera in
situations orchestrated by his family, the press, and, eventually, the federal government. Many people were happy that his dramatic and violent "rescue" from his uncle's home was caught on film. Many others rejected as misleading and invasive of
the boy's privacy interests photographs published in newspapers across the world
and in a video in which the child pleaded with his father, perhaps under coercion, to
let him remain in the United States.

PRACTICAL MATTERS: NEGOTIATING NORMS

It has grown increasingly impractical for working journalists to respect privacy,
even when they would like to. First, respecting privacy can be impractical because
success in the marketplace goes to media that regularly serve up data about personal
life. To be economically viable, major news organizations had to train cameras on
Caroline Kennedy Schlossberg after her brother's death and had to broadcast the
scandalous video of Elian Gonzalez pleading with his father not to return him to

Cuba. (CBS declined to intensely cover Gary Condit, the former California Congressman, about his affair with a young intern reported missing by her family. This decision is a rare exception, possibly a principled one, and appears not to have greatly hurt the network.)

Ironically, at the same time that "protect privacy" has become a battle cry of ethicists and consumer advocates, there has been an explosion in the market for information about the sexual, medical, familial, and financial lives of other people, celebrities and unknowns alike. The appetite for personal information is so great that most media organs—shielded by the First Amendment freedom of the press—would be at a distinct economic disadvantage were they to refuse to profit from the public's codependent exhibitionism and voyeurism. Very often it seems as though it is not so much a question of whether the media will serve up privacies, but how. It may be done through frank interviews by veteran mainstream journalists, like Barbara Walters, or it may be done through campy "reality" television. But it will be done.

Second, respecting privacy is impractical because it is difficult for journalists acting in good faith to comprehend what respecting privacy is supposed to entail concerning individuals in a diverse population. Just what is personal; what is private? Some people would say that there is nothing private about Food Lion employees at work, but others would argue that people at work have reasonable expectations of privacy, including that they will not be surreptitiously filmed for major media without their consent. Some would say that a pop diva or a daughter of a U.S. president cannot expect privacy in ill health and grief, others that such expectations are entirely reasonable and understandable. Some would say that criminally fraudulent physicians have no "privacy" in their offices; others would say that norms of medical privacy and confidentiality, and an office worker's or caregiver's privacy expectations, are not extinguished by professionals' malfeasance.

Once fairly uniformly deemed personal and private, today sexual matters, medical matters, family matters, finances, and criminal histories are commonly shared with mass-media audiences. The new openness about medical conditions is especially striking. People who share medical information point out the benefits to individual and public health of shedding traditional shame and modesty about illness. In the new cultural environment of mutual self-disclosure, it is difficult to know whether a particular person will be or should be especially offended by journalistic investigation and publicity. Our de facto openness may have as its result de facto accountability in those instances when we would rather have privacy.

Furthermore, the scope of politics has expanded. If "the personal is political," it is also newsworthy. Sexuality is on the political table not only in scandals but also in debates over reproductive autonomy, gay rights, Internet filtering, sex education, and AIDS prevention, among other issues. Can these stories be covered properly without violating privacy? The issue of gay rights, for example, may look different to a people whose image of homosexuality is defined by the often flamboyant pageantry of gay pride parades than it does to people who have just been informed that their favorite athlete, whom they have long admired without knowing anything about his or her life off-camera, is gay.

Making the situation even more difficult for journalists trying to respect privacy, many people value privacy inconsistently or idiosyncratically. People expect what they consider privacy and yet embrace certain kinds of mass publicity. A journalist who wants to be sensitive to the actual privacy expectations of subjects will have to know more about that individual's preferences and needs than he or she generally will know. For example, for many years a man I know who was infected with HIV kept the fact a secret from most people, even his girlfriend's family, with whom he frequently socialized. Yet this same man voluntarily appeared on a local news program in a major city in which he identified himself as HIV-positive and as a volunteer for an AIDS advocacy group. After the broadcast—viewed by hundreds of thousands—his secret was out, but he resumed his previous level of reserve. As far as he was concerned, his health was still a private matter. To take another example, the cohost of a popular nationally broadcast morning television program, citing a desire for privacy for her children, announced on the air her plans to leave the show after more than a decade in which she openly discussed the details of her pregnancies and her children's developmental milestones.

What would it mean for a journalist now to respect the privacy of the HIV-infected man or the television host? The desire of the infected man and the television host to carve out a private domain around their health or families is understandable, yet the boundaries they drew were arguably unclear, idiosyncratic, or unreasonable. Would it be unethical for a news reporter to contact the HIV-positive man, who is not a public official or public figure, for subsequent news or perspectives about HIV and AIDS, or to attempt to speak to his family and friends about "living with AIDS"? Lawyers might try to answer the question by classifying the man as a limited public figure for HIV- and AIDS-related issues, on the ground that he voluntarily inserted himself into the public debate on that issue. However, that characterization of the facts distorts the man's true intent. The television host is, as a matter of constitutional law, a public figure whose subjective expectations of privacy merit less protection. Still, after her announcement that she was seeking privacy, an ethical journalist might conclude that it would be wrong to ask the host questions about her children, and wrong for a magazine to seek or publish photographs of the woman and her children that were taken without their consent.

Ascribed the unprecedented duty of ascertaining actual privacy preferences, the community of journalists could quickly grow weary of the vexatious, expensive, and self-contradictory task of respecting individuals' privacy individually. The task is self-contradictory because a journalist would have to know a subject very well to respect his/her actual privacy needs and preferences, when getting to know the subject that well would require detailed information gathering that many people deem offensive privacy intrusion. It is all too convenient for journalists, eager for lucrative stories, to claim that they do not know what respecting privacy entails; and yet, given cultural diversity, pluralism, and recent social change, they may be right.

MATTERS OF PRINCIPLE: THE PUBLIC'S RIGHT TO KNOW

Some principled journalists may feel trapped between conflicting responsibilities of protecting uncertain privacies and publishing in the public interest. Other principled journalists do not feel trapped because they are strongly inclined toward publicity. The latter category of journalists has the advantage. In this confusing climate, expansive interpretations of the principles of freedom of the press, freedom of information, and the public's right to know function as comfortable philosophical shelters for aggressive, privacy-indifferent journalists. Although the complex contours of First Amendment law may elude most practicing journalists, the political ideal we call the "right to know" is accessible to all.

The right to know is society's or the press' obligation to channel useful and important information to the general public through laws and practices tending toward maximum dissemination of information. The right to know is a powerful and broad normative ideal that greatly influences journalistic practice and public policy. As generally understood today, the public's right to know is actually a collection of several distinct rights to know. They include:

- The right to monitor the government.
- The right to monitor the conduct of officials and candidates, and, further, a right to know enough about candidates to make an informed vote.
- The right to inspect or obtain copies of government records.
- The right to learn important news and relevant history.
- The right to hear debate among members of the public.
- The right to be informed about the conduct of public figures.
- The right to monitor businesses' and nonprofits' use of public funds and impact on the public welfare.

A free press—along with freedom of information statutes, public schools, public libraries, and consumer advocacy groups—fulfills societal obligations implied by the public's right to know. Journalists have assumed the professional responsibility of channeling news and information to the general public, which has grown reliant on their newspapers, radio stations, television stations, and computer services to provide information. Journalists seeking justification for privacy intrusions can turn to the right to know as a defense against almost any condemnation for invasion of privacy.

The ideas of press freedom and the right to know have important roles in liberal democratic theory. There is no shortage of scholarship discussing and debating the details of their roles. In a democratic society, citizens must be free and self-governing. There is a wide consensus that access to information enables each person to make reliable, independent judgments about matters of personal and collective concern that are required by responsible citizenship. Access to information also enables citizens effectively to evaluate and criticize government and the other institutions that affect public well-being.

However, the demands of liberal democracy do not require that information gathering and dissemination be utterly unconstrained by concern for privacy. On the contrary, the demands of liberal democracy seem to require protection of various forms of privacy, notwithstanding individual and societal information needs. The liberal democratic theoretical framework that famously provides an argument for press freedom and the right to know also provides an analogous argument for individual privacy. Opportunities for physical, informational, and decisional privacy are preconditions for the kind of individuality—moral independence—and repose presupposed by free, meaningful participation in civic life.

Although an effective citizenry of healthy, independent minds requires both information and privacy, not all journalists have the respect for privacy seeking that they have for information seeking. This may be due, in part, to the fortuity that although the Supreme Court has repeatedly held that privacy is a value of constitutional importance, freedom of speech and press (but not privacy) are expressly enshrined in the Bill of Rights. Privacy claims can seem less grounded. More profoundly, in a society in which people constantly choose to forgo opportunities for privacy, some have come to doubt the lofty claims made by liberal philosophers about the vital importance of privacy to the formation of persons, intimate bonds, and liberal social order. Furthermore, journalists are self-selected. Individuals with a strong preference for the free flow of information may be more likely to be drawn to that profession than are individuals who are passionate about privacy.

JOURNALISM FOR PRIVACY

It is important to emphasize that journalism does not stand, either in theory or in practice, in complete opposition to privacy values. Journalists can and do respect privacy in a number of important contexts. Indeed, practicing journalists, whose core responsibilities are to research and report information about others, sometimes go out of their way to protect personal privacy. Consider the widespread journalistic practice of granting anonymity to juveniles accused of crimes and to rape victims. The policy of *The New York Times*, for example, calls for such anonymity in many cases, although a high-ranking editor is to be involved in the decision in each case.[13] Consider that journalists who travel with political candidates routinely treat some of what they learn about the personal habits and mannerisms of our political leaders as "off the record."[14] Finally, consider that journalists commonly protect the confidentiality, and in that sense, the privacy, of news sources averse to public mention, a commitment that ASNE's Statement of Principles renders in strong language: "Pledges of confidentiality to news sources must be honored at all costs, and therefore should not be given lightly."[15] Likewise, even information in a reporter's notes that the reporter will use if he/she deems it newsworthy is widely viewed as confidential unless it is published, although the issue is not discussed by widely used codes of ethics. The privacy of sources, then, can be and is protected; it is the subject who is not a source whose privacy is disregarded.

Journalists have even become champions of privacy values. In recent years, journalists have published articles or broadcast news stories that cast a critical eye on governments, employers, traditional businesses, and e-commerce for jeopardizing personal privacy needlessly, self-interestedly, or unjustly. *The New York Times* columnist William Safire, for example, has made privacy a major theme, promising his readers that "harangues on this issue will continue ... while apostles of efficiency, in bureaucracies public and private, try to pooh-pooh concerns of newly energized asserters of privacy."[16] Journalist and law professor Jeffrey Rosen has published several proprivacy articles in major newspapers and magazines.[17] Responding to the call for greater surveillance that followed the events of September 11, 2001, Rosen stressed that: "When we say we are fighting for an open society, we don't mean a transparent society.... We mean a society open to the possibility that people can redefine and reinvent themselves every day; a society in which people can travel from place to place without showing their papers and being encumbered by their past; a society that respects privacy and constantly reshuffles social hierarchy."[18]

Journalists have sought to inform the public about measures they can take to protect their privacy on the Internet and at work. Journalists criticize one another when they fail to acknowledge legitimate privacy interests,[19] and they have even begun to criticize the public for neglecting its own privacy needs. Newspaper and magazine commentaries by professional journalists have chided Americans for devaluing their own privacy. Is it really necessary to live in front of the Webcam or to tell all to prurient television audiences and tabloids; to deliver your baby, have your surgery, or lose your virginity live over the Internet? One woman broadcast her mastectomy in a live Webcast.[20] The Learning Channel devoted two weekly shows to "simulcast" births.

The privacy-protective aspects of journalistic practice just mentioned are consonant with the privacy-protective ideals of some corners of the profession, reflected in the Society of Professional Journalists' (SPJ) hortatory Code of Ethics. Although the present Code was adopted in 1996, its precursors date back to the 1920s, when SPJ's predecessor, Sigma Delta Chi, adopted the American Society of Newspaper Editors' Canons of Journalism. The Preamble of the Code names "public enlightenment" as the "forerunner of justice and the foundation of democracy."[21] The Preamble states that the duty of "[c]onscientious" journalists from "all media and specialities" is to further the ends of justice and democracy by "providing a fair and comprehensive account of events and issues" with "thoroughness and honesty."[22]

The four main imperatives set forth in the Code are: seek truth and report, minimize harm, act independently, and be accountable. Each of these four commands potentially conflicts with the goal of respecting privacy. The first conflicts because the truth one is obligated to seek and report may be about personal matters deemed private. The second calls for minimizing harm, noting that "[e]thical journalists treat sources, subjects and colleagues as human being deserving of respect."[23] Although respecting privacy is certainly one way to respect people as human beings, there will be situations in which refusing to investigate or report supposedly private matters can lead to serious emotional or physical injury. The third imperative clashes with privacy because acting independently may lead a journalist to report personal information that others deem private and have urged the journalist to withhold. Finally, being accountable under the fourth directive may require disclosing information to persons to whom one is answerable even though the information relates to someone else's intimate life.

The Code's privacy-protective dimensions are, however, distinct. Its general imperative to minimize harm is accompanied by eight specific harm-minimization requirements. These implicitly and explicitly acknowledge privacy intrusion as a harm. Thus, the Code asks journalists to "[r]ecognize that gathering and reporting information may cause harm or discomfort."[24] This type of ethical recognition of responsibility may have caused the Israeli press to initially hesitate about publishing the cause of death of Ofra Haza. The interest in privacy of persons like Caroline Kennedy Schlossberg or Elian Gonzalez, who lost his mother at sea, is recognized in the requirement that a journalist "[b]e sensitive when seeking or using interviews or photographs of those affected by tragedy or grief."[25]

The Code contains one express privacy protection provision. After an instruction that journalists "[r]ecognize that private people have a greater right to control information about themselves than do public officials and others who seek power, influence or attention," the Code observes that "[o]nly an overriding public need can justify intrusion into anyone's privacy."[26] This statement implies that journalists must give presumptive priority to protecting privacy. The ethical issue for journalists thus posed by the *Food Lion* case against *Prime Time Live* was whether the public interest in knowledge of Food Lion's adulteration practices overrode the presumptive privacy interests of Food Lion employees who were subjected to surreptitious surveillance. The eye surgeons' case against *Prime Time Live* raised the same ethical issue: whether the public health and the safety interests of persons seeking health care overrode any claims the doctors may have had to the privacy of their professional relationships and offices.

The Code recognizes privacy-related interests in anonymity. Journalists are asked to "[b]e cautious about identifying juvenile suspects or victims of sex crimes."[27] The Code tolerates the use of anonymous news sources, but is skeptical about anonymity. Privacy can be a tool of abuse. The general imperative to "Seek Truth and Report It" is followed by a specific imperative to "[a]lways question sources' motives before promising anonymity."[28] The Code is also skeptical of government demands for bureaucratic concealment, beseeching journalists to "recognize a special obligation to ensure that the public's business is conducted in the open and that government records are open to inspection."[29] Nevertheless, the Code recognizes that secrecy and deception may have value to journalists in gathering the news and uncovering truth, but urges avoidance: "Avoid undercover or other surreptitious methods of gathering information except when traditional open methods will not yield information vital to the public."[30] The Code thus provides a potential ethical justification for the conduct of the journalists in the *Prime Time Live* cases. Traditional methods would not have yielded irrefutable visual evidence of meat repackaging.

JOURNALISM FOR ACCOUNTABILITY

Although some notable journalistic ethics, practices, and news or editorial concerns suggest that privacy is a key value for responsible journalists, a great many others do not. The 2000 Radio–Television News Directors Association Code of Ethics and Standards, predecessors of which commanded that privacy be respected, now asks broadcasters only to "give children greater privacy protection than adults."[31] The word *privacy* is missing from the ASNE Statement of Principles, adopted in 1975, which commands that freedom of the press "be defended against encroachment or assault from any quarter, public or private."[32]

The current direction of journalistic privacy ethics is perhaps better represented by the Gannett Company's 1999 ethical guidelines for news gathering and reporting than by the Society of Professional Journalism's four-pronged 1996 Code. The Gannett code reflects a commitment to "[s]erving the public interest" by "[s]eeking and reporting the truth in a truthful way."[33] The public's right to know is at the heart of Gannett's conception of the public interest. Gannett's commitment to serve the public interest includes pledges to "uphold First Amendment principles to serve the democratic process," "be vigilant watchdogs of government and institutions that affect the public," "provide the news and information that people need to function as effective citizens," "seek solutions as well as expose problems and wrongdoing," "provide a public forum for diverse people and views," "reflect and encourage understanding of the diverse segments of our community," "provide editorial and community leadership," and finally, "seek to promote understanding of complex issues."[34]

Gannett's guidelines include ethical standards for managing confidentiality requests from news sources, including an option for an agreement not to reveal a source except under court order and an option to promise to protect the source's identity "under any circumstances."[35] However, it requires that sources be warned that such agreements will not be honored "if the sources have lied or misled the newspaper."[36] In a section concerning the ethics of investigative journalism, where one might expect to see some mention of privacy, there is none. On the contrary, the core commitment to finding and reporting truth is the sole theme: "Aggressive, hard-hitting reporting is honorable and often courageous in fulfilling the press' First Amendment responsibilities, and it is encouraged."[37] The Gannett code contains no explicit commitment to protecting privacy. To be fair, however, such a commitment might be inferred from the promise to "treat people with dignity, respect and compassion."[38] A commitment to privacy protection might also be inferred from general pledges to "act honorably and ethically in dealing with news sources," to "obey the law," to "observe common standards of decency," and to "try to do the right thing."[39] The laws that must be obeyed include the privacy laws. Privacy norms may be included among common standards of decency, and respecting privacy can be, on occasion, the right thing. Although these inferences are possible, it is plain enough that Gannett sought to avoid elevating the public's privacy interests to the same level of importance as the public's interest in access to information.

The fact that Gannett left privacy protection in the shadows suggests a conscious effort to stand tall for the public right to know and the freedom of the press in the face of the factors that prompted its statement of ethical guidelines. Quoting Gannett's press release, those factors included "public distrust of the media" and "a need to address the increase in lawsuits focusing on newsgathering methods and not on the truth of stories."[40] It is clear that Gannett is troubled by the idea that the press should ever be liable for publishing what is true, even if doing so is highly offensive to a person's privacy and even if the facts were obtained through methods that violate privacy expectations.

A long trail of litigation in which media organizations have sought to escape liability for privacy invasion reflects the subordination of privacy to the right to know and First Amendment freedoms. In well-known privacy law cases too numerous to mention, the media has positioned itself as a foe of privacy rather than a friend. For example, in *Shulman v. Group W Productions, Inc.*,[41] media defendants fought charges that they violated the common law privacy rights against intrusion and disclosure of accident victims whose injuries and medical rescues were graphically broadcast on television. In *United States Department of Justice v. Reporters Committee for Freedom of the Press*,[42] journalists fought a decision under privacy exceptions to the Freedom of Information Act to deny them access to government "rap" sheets. In *Berger v. Hanlon*,[43] the United States Court of Appeals for the Ninth Circuit deemed media defendants to be joint actors with government agents for purposes of a civil rights claim based on a "ride along" with law enforcement, and in *Wilson v. Layne*,[44] the Supreme Court held that police violated the Fourth Amendment by bringing journalists with them when executing a search warrant in a house. In these cases and others involving the common law, statutes, and the Constitution, the media asserted freedom-of-the-press, freedom-of-information, and right-to-know values over and against privacy values.

Although the media lost these particular cases, they are often the victors in their battles against privacy. Outstanding victories include *Sidis v. F-R Publishing Corp.*,[45] in which an unfulfilled genius was unsuccessful in claiming invasion of privacy after an article and cartoon about his misfortunes appeared in the *New Yorker* magazine; *Cox Broadcasting Corp. v. Cohn*,[46] in which a lawsuit by the family of a deceased rape victim was thwarted by the Supreme Court's finding that the First and Fourteenth amendments barred liability under state law for broadcasting the identity of a rape victim when that identity had been made available in public court documents; and *Lerman v. Flynt Distributing Co.*,[47] in which a woman who could not prove the publisher acted with actual malice lost on appeal a $10 million judgment won at trial against publishers of a misleading and exceedingly distasteful magazine story.

HOW TO BEHAVE

Professional journalists, print or broadcast, are no more likely to be consciously guided on a daily basis by the ethical codes of their profession than lawyers, physicians, stock analysts, real estate brokers, or engineers are guided by theirs. Nevertheless, it is interesting to understand the extent to which journalists are (or are not) being urged by their employers and professional organizations to avoid privacy intrusions. The Society of Professional Journalists' Code of Ethics and the contrasting Gannett code approach the privacy problem in distinctly different ways, at least on the level of overt rhetoric. Yet the basic, general guidance both would give to a young journalist is the same.

Suppose an uninitiated novice journalist went to the codes in search of answers to these three questions: First, should I ever report a true fact about a person when I know that the person prefers privacy respecting that fact? Second, should I ever engage in open surveillance of the private conduct of a person I know prefers privacy with respect to that conduct? And third, should I ever engage in covert surveillance to uncover immoral, unlawful, or unhealthful practices? Both codes would give novice journalists affirmative answers to these questions. The more interesting and revealing set of inquiries from a novice would be about when a journalist ethically ought not report true personal facts, ought not engage in unwanted open surveillance, and ought not undertake covert surveillance or investigation. The wording and context of the Gannett code suggests that it should be read to recognize fewer restraints on journalists than the Society of Professional Journalists' Code, yet the privacy-loving public cannot find total comfort in the provisions of the SPJ Code or their likely interpretation by practicing journalists.

REPORTING TRUTH

Should a journalist ever report a true fact about a person when the journalist knows the person prefers privacy respecting that fact? The answer to this question is clearly yes. We should be more accountable than we want to be. Unwanted exposure is sometimes a privacy intrusion justified, in the words of the SPJ Code, by "an overriding public need."[48] Even where there is no overwhelming public need the Code seems to permit privacy intrusion where someone has sought "power, influence or attention."[49] This latter aspect of journalistic ethics is more problematic than the first, because public figures and officials are not without legitimate privacy interests. A man like General Electric's Jack Welch has privacy interests even though he was a famous CEO. A man like Jesse Jackson has privacy interests, even though he once ran for president.

Having legitimate privacy interests does not entail immunity from public accountability. Congressman Gary Condit's legitimate privacy interests should not have kept the press from probing into the precise nature of his relationship with intern Chandra Levy. Yet once he had cooperated with police and admitted a sexual affair, hounding him for details was indefensible. It is debatable whether the public needed to know the Israeli singer Haza's exact cause of death. One could argue that *Ha'aretz* had an overriding obligation to honor the wishes of the star for medical privacy. Medical privacy is indeed important. On the other hand, Haza was plainly someone whose privacy entitlements were affected both by both her high-risk conduct and her status as a person who had sought power, influence, or attention.

In defense of publication in Ms. Haza's case, I would adduce two needs: the need to quell rumor and innuendo, and the need to educate the public about a major public health concern. Mass rumor and innuendo can be damaging to the quality of public discussion and debate. *Ha'aretz* did its country a favor by quieting rumors and allowing the public so focused on Haza's death and the implications of AIDS to focus on facts about these important matters. Journalists have a responsibility to inform and thereby to educate the public about the demographics and reach of a terrifying public health threat. Although the press is not entitled to make particular private citizens into "poster children" for tragic diseases, *Ha'aretz* argued that two factors militated in favor of disclosures specific to Haza: First, she utilized public resources when she used the emergency room of the local hospital seeking care for acute AIDS-related illness, reportedly without disclosing her HIV status to unsuspecting medical staff. Second, she was deceased by the time of the newspaper's disclosure, so, at least to some minds, her subjective feelings and sensibilities fall from the equation. (In American tort law, for example, privacy rights do not survive the death of the right holder.)

The press appropriately concludes in some cases that it cannot give individuals the privacy they want and still fulfill its obligations to the public. Journalists could not offer Monica Lewinsky all the privacy she wanted once the independent counsel's pornographic report implicating the president of the United States in crimes went to Congress. *Ha'aretz* arguably did the right thing when it published facts about the death of a popular public figure from a wrongly stigmatized illness that is one of the great international public health problems of our time. A newspaper's printing of the cause of death of a public figure suffering from an epidemic disease is a proper discharge of ethical responsibility in journalism.

Notice that there is nothing in this argument to suggest that a public figure should never be permitted to conceal a medical condition. I believe our society is not well served by the Code-supported and popular notion that the medical, health, and family privacy of public officials and public figures merits no protection and concern. The notion confers a carte blanche to the press to reveal, dwell on, and sensationalize aspects of persons' lives that the persons deem intimate or about which they are deeply modest, embarrassed, or ashamed. It encourages deception, evasion, and lies on the part of public figures and officials, and it can discourage participation in public life by those whom we would like to participate. Attempts to legislate privacy for public persons have been common in the aftermath of the death of Princess Diana of Wales. California recently adopted a law aimed at paparazzi that makes it unlawful to photograph persons, including public figures and officials, engaging in private "family" activities on private property.[50]

OPEN SURVEILLANCE

Should a journalist engage in open surveillance of the private conduct of a person whom the journalist knows prefers privacy with respect to that conduct? Sometimes such surveillance is justifiable. Presidential candidate Gary Hart wanted a free-wheeling, Clintonesque personal life, but (bizarrely) challenged the media to come up with evidence of his alleged infidelities. I do not think Mr. Hart believed anyone would take up the challenge. The media promptly responded to open season on Gary Hart with the famous "Monkey Business" shots of Donna Rice on his lap.

But sometimes open surveillance of private conduct is not justifiable, even when the person is a public figure or public official, and even when the press keeps its physical distance. How proper is broadcasting live images of a privacy-loving public figure in grief after the unexpected deaths of his/her closest relatives? As previously observed, the Code expressly recognizes the privacy needs of grieving persons. Press coverage of Caroline Kennedy Schlossberg violated her privacy wishes and the ethics of journalism, all without good reason. The Israeli press might have been open to criticism had it deferred to the privacy wishes of Haza. Would the American press have been open to criticism if it had respected the privacy wishes of Kennedy Schlossberg? Suppose the press had simply stayed away from her home. Would the response have been that the press violated its obligation to report the news? Suppose the press had broadcast images of the general public crowded in the streets around the church, but not the grieving churchgoers? Would it be open to criticisms of inadequate news coverage and abridging the public's right to know? I believe the answer to these questions is plausibly "No." The exercise of taste and civility might have been applauded. The public might have said: "We know we don't need or have a right to what we have been accustomed getting from aggressive, competitive, market-oriented news organizations, namely, morbid, sentimental, lurid, tragic, joyous details of other people's private lives. We know the Kennedy family is not really our family."

COVERT SURVEILLANCE

Should a journalist ever engage in covert surveillance to uncover immoral, unlawful, or unhealthful practices? Again, the answer is surely yes. We sometimes use privacy to thwart beneficial forms of accountability, including criminal sanctions, but there are limits. Journalists have been criticized both for "ambush" tactics and for "tag along" practices in which they arrogate the government's Fourth Amendment powers to themselves, but for commercial rather than law enforcement purposes. Ambush and undercover tactics are consistent with journalists' ethical responsibilities so long as the covert and deceptive tactics are necessary and reasonably calculated to increase public awareness of important news and issues. The *Prime Time Live* tactics in the *Food Lion* and *Desnick* cases pass ethical muster.

In *Dietemann v. Time, Inc.*,[51] journalists breached legal limits because they used deception to enter someone's home. Did they also behave unethically? In this situation, *Life* magazine used deception to get two employees posing as patients into the home of an uneducated man who claimed he had the capacity to diagnose and heal illnesses. Photos of the man taken in his home and a story exposing him as a quack appeared in the magazine. The man, who informed one of the *Life* employees that she had a lump in her breast caused by eating rancid butter exactly "11 years, 9 months and 7 days prior,"[52] was prosecuted for the unlicensed practice of medicine, but then sued the magazine for invasion of privacy. In announcing its decision in the civil suit, the court said, "[w]e have little difficulty in concluding that clandestine photography of the plaintiff in his den and the recordation and transmission of his conversation without his consent resulting in emotional distress warrants recovery for invasion of privacy."[53] The court stressed that the plaintiff cloaked himself in privacy. He had no phone, he did not advertise, he locked his gate.

Medical quackery of the sort practiced by the plaintiff in *Dietemann* is a public health menace. As an ethical matter, I side with the press in this case. Ambush-style press investigation was warranted by the ineffectiveness of traditional overt means of investigation combined with the importance and magnitude of the risks to the public of the plaintiff's unlawful conduct. Courts are ambivalent about deception, but several have sided with the press when covert tactics are used in commercial or professional offices rather than homes. The case law seems to imply that quackery or other misconduct in an office suite may be more aggressively and deceptively investigated than quackery in someone's home. The distinction between home and office is a meaningful one in many instances and for many purposes, but it should not be treated in every instance as a distinction that makes a difference. (I am writing this from my home; my spouse's criminal defense law practice is run out of an adjoining home office. Are we at home or at work? Are we in a private space or a professional space?) That misconduct occurs in the home may create a legitimate presumption against deception-aided entry, but should not rule it out. Imagine that a quack is feeding arsenic to patients as "medicine" for headaches; he/she needs to be exposed whether the quackery is happening in a home or a shopping mall. On the other hand, deceptive entry by the press to follow up on a hot tip that a person has 55 unpaid parking tickets on top of his kitchen table seems ethically unwarranted.

CONCLUSION

Can journalists respect privacy? I have posed this question to many people and have received a variety of interesting answers. I recently posed it to a former research assistant, Alexander Cohen, whose experience in print and online journalism is impressive for a man of 25. In formulating his answer, Cohen distinguished between "duty" stories and "option" stories. He argued that when it comes to reporting stories that journalists must report to fulfill duties correlative to the public's right to know, privacy must take the back seat. But when it comes to stories whose coverage is optional, journalism ought to show respect for privacy. In the case of Bill Clinton, the duties of reporting outweighed most of the former president's privacy interests in his extramarital affairs. However, reporting the surviving sister's grief following John F. Kennedy, Jr.'s plane crash was largely optional, and deference to privacy would have been appropriate. Cohen made it clear that he was not suggesting that journalists are required to be nice to people. Yet, he said, "I think it plausible to suggest that journalists ought not to use their power to make people miserable just because other people will enjoy it." He continued: "Some measure of *noblesse oblige* may apply. If nothing else, reporting that is no more than voyeurism makes reading and watching the news a guilty pleasure, which undermines the public's trust in the Fourth Estate."

Journalists do indeed have special power. They can make, break, and shape a man or woman's reputation. They can make special times less special and bad times worse. Professional journalists should understand that their power ought to be wielded with a keen sense of moral responsibility. Of course, there are profits to be earned in guilty pleasures, be they gourmet ice creams or sensational privacy-invading press reports. As individuals in a competitive profession accountable to corporate interests and a truth-hungry public, it would be self-defeating for journalists to consider privacy protection a priority, a concern coequal to the right to know and First Amendment freedoms. But although privacy protection should not be a priority, it would not be completely impractical to make (or retain) privacy protection as a constraint. I say this persuaded that opportunities for solitude and seclusion, secrecy and confidentiality, anonymity and reserve have not lost their importance for the healthy and happy persons presupposed by pervasive concepts of moral agency, autonomy, intimacy, and social participation.

Mainstream journalists will need to do just enough right by privacy to maintain a degree of public trust in "the Fourth Estate." However, journalists should begin or continue to consider privacy interests, because protecting privacy is often the right thing to do. In addition, journalists have an educative role to play in helping to preserve privacy as a value in a society in which the taste for privacy and the expectation of privacy may be rapidly, and regrettably, diminishing below acceptable levels.[54] To respect and shore up privacy values, journalists could use the set of traditional conceptions of privacy and private places as a flexible, presumptive framework. They would need to listen to people's expressed privacy preferences, recognizing that traditional conceptions are changing and that there is diversity in privacy norms. They would have to set aside commercial interests more than they have in the past to respect meaningfully and seriously the personal privacy needs they should presuppose that public and private persons share. They should discourage exhibitionism unrelated to news and genuine collective concerns. Figuring out how and when to protect privacy and how to bear the costs of doing so is an ethical and financial challenge, but any profession worth the name and worthy of its own ethical code must embrace the ethical challenges that come within the purview of its responsibilities.

NOTES

[1]*Society of Professional Journalists' Code of Ethics*, available at <http://www.spj.org/spj ethics code.asp> (last visited May 1, 2002).

[2]*American Society of Newspaper Editors' Statement of Principles* available at <http://www.asne.org/kiosk/archive/principl.htm> (last visited May 1, 2002).

[3]*American Society of Newspaper Editors' Canons of Journalism* (superceded by ASNE Statement of Principles) available at <http://www.iit.edu/departments/csep/PublicWWW/codes/coe/American%20Societ%20of%20Newspaper%20Editors%2023.html> (last visited May 1, 2002).

[4]John H. Fuson, *Comment: Protecting the Press From Privacy*, 148 University of Pennsylvania Law Review 629–671 (1999).

[5]Eugene Volokh, *Freedom of Speech and Information Privacy: The Troubling Implications of a Right to Stop People From Speaking About You*, 52 Stanford Law Review 1049–1124, 1093 (2000).

[6]*Gannett Newspaper Division Principles of Ethical Conduct for Newsrooms,* "Protecting the Principles," "Reinforcing the Principles" and press release available at <http:// www.gannett.com/ go/press/pr061499.htm> (last visited May 1, 2002).

[7]Deborah Sontag, "A Pop Diva, a Case of AIDS and an Israeli Storm," *The New York Times* A6 (February 29, 2000).

[8]Jeffrey Kahn, "Avoid Medical Voyeurism," *USA Today* A12 (March 7, 2001).

[9]"Mr. Cheney's Heart Attack," *The New York Times* A18 (November 25, 2000).

[10]William Safire, "The Telltale Heart," *The New York Times* A35 (November 30, 2000).

[11]*Food Lion, Inc. v. Capital Cities/ABC, Inc.*, 194 F.3d 505 (4th Cir. 1999).

[12]*Desnick v. ABC*, 44 F.3d 1345 (7th Cir. 1995).

[13]Allan M. Siegal & William G. Connolly, eds., *The New York Times Manual of Style and Usage* 178, 282 (1999).

[14]Brent Cunningham, *A Journalist's Life: A Compulsion to Know*, Columbia Journalism Review 48 (July/August 2000); see Howard Kurtz, *When the Press Outclasses the Public* Columbia Journalism Review 31, 34 (May/June 1994).

[15]*American Society of Newspaper Editors Statement of Principles* available at <http:// www.asne.org/kiosk/archive/principl.htm> (last visited May 1, 2002).

[16]William Safire, "Stop Cookie-Pushers," *The New York Times* A27 (June 15, 2000).

[17]Jeffrey Rosen, "Indecent Exposure," *New Republic* 24, 26 (November 8, 1999); see Rosen, "The Eroded Self," *The New York Times Magazine* 46 53, 68, 129 (April 30, 2000).

[18]Jeffrey Rosen, "The Watchful State," *The New York Times Magazine* 38 (October 7, 2001).

[19]Lisa de Moraes, "ABC News Draws Flak for Elian Interview," *Washington Post* C1 (March 30, 2000); see Hal Boedeker, "Family's Grief 'Unspeakable' TV News Unbearable," *Orlando Sentinel* A12 (July 23, 1999).

[20]PR Newswire, *As Part of Breast Cancer Awareness Month, the Health Network Will Webcast Live Mastectomy and Breast Reconstruction Surgery* (October 13, 1999).

[21]*Society of Professional Journalists Code of Ethics, supra* note 1.

[22]*Ibid.*

[23]*Ibid.*

[24]*Ibid.*

[25]*Ibid.*

[26]*Ibid.*

[27]*Ibid.*

[28]*Ibid.*

[29]*Ibid.*

[30]*Ibid.*

[31]*Radio and Television News Directors Association* (current and old) available at <http:// web.missouri.edu/~jourvs/rtcodes.html> (last visited May 1, 2002).

[32]*American Society of Newspaper Editors Statement of Principles supra* note 15.

[33]*Gannett Newspaper Division Principles of Ethical Conduct for Newsrooms, supra* note 6.

[34]*Ibid.*

[35]*Ibid.*

[36]*Ibid.*

[37]*Ibid.*

[38]*Ibid.*

[39]*Ibid.*

[40]*Ibid.*

[41]*Shulman v. Group W Productions, Inc.*, 955 P.2d 469 (Cal. 1998).

[42]*United States Department of Justice v. Reporters Committee for Freedom of the Press,* 489 U.S. 749 (1989).

[43]*Berger v. Hanlon*, 129 F.3d 505 (9th Cir. 1997), vac'd on other grounds, 526 U.S. 808 (1999).

[44]*Wilson v. Layne*, 526 U.S. 603 (1999).

[45]*Sidis v. F-R Publishing Corp.*, 113 F.2d 806 (2d Cir. 1940).

[46]*Cox Broadcasting Corp. v. Cohn*, 420 U.S. 469 (1975).

[47]*Lerman v. Flynt Distributing Co.*, 745 F.2d 123 (2d Cir. 1984).

[48]*Society of Professional Journalists Code of Ethics*, *supra* note 1.

[49]*Ibid.*

[50]See Cal. Civ. Code 1708.8 (West 1998).

[51]*Dietemann v. Time, Inc.*, 449 F.2d 245, 248 (9th Cir. 1971).

[52]*Ibid.*, at 246.

[53]*Ibid.*, at 248.

[54]Anita L. Allen, *Coercing Privacy*, 40 William and Mary Law Review 723 (2000).

5

Law Breaking and Truth Telling: Formal Legal Doctrine and the Imbalance Between Intrusion and Revelation Claims

Rodney Smolla
T. C. Williams School of Law, University of Richmond

In this chapter I examine two strains of American privacy law in relation to First Amendment rights of free speech and press. The first involves claims of "intrusion." The second involves claims of "revelation." For the purposes of this chapter, when I discuss intrusion-style privacy claims I do not intend to limit the analysis to the common-law tort of intrusion, but rather mean to include the broad family of "intrusion-related" torts and crimes. Some of these are the product of the common law and some were created by statute, but all in one way or another seek to impose liability for invasive *conduct* of some kind, divorced from any information that might have been gathered and subsequently disseminated as a result of the invasion. When used against the media, these are commonly described as "news-gathering torts," in the sense that they focus on actions antecedent to any publication or broadcast of material. "Revelation" privacy claims may similarly involve tort or criminal law actions broader than the common-law tort of "publication of private facts," although that tort is probably the legal doctrine most famously associated with the revelation strain of privacy.

I begin with the supposition that there is a striking imbalance in the formal legal doctrines applicable to intrusion and revelation privacy claims. The law is quite generous and sympathetic to plaintiffs who bring intrusion claims. Conversely, legal doctrine is curmudgeonly and hostile to revelation claims. To make the same point from the mirror perspective of the First Amendment, the law is inhospitable to the introduction of free speech or free press defenses to intrusion, yet it is inviting, virtually to the point of slavish submission, to the free speech and free press defenses to revelation.

The law, in the words of Oliver Wendell Holmes, is "the witness and external deposit of our moral life."[1] In privacy law, there appears to be a disconnection between the moral deposit and the legal balance sheet. If it is true that the moral intuitions and sensibilities of many in our society about the propriety of intrusion and revelation are far more balanced and complex than the one-sided legal doctrines that currently exist, the questions become why this is the case, and whether it ought to be.[2] My hypothesis is that this extreme imbalance is unsound. I want to explore this imbalance from a variety of cultural and legal perspectives, attempt to account for it, and then critique it.

To the extent that one might hope or expect that the law would be a moral distillation of public sensibility on these issues, one would be disappointed. The law appears out of alignment. I understand, of course, that such a hope or expectation might itself be wrong. But for now, simply to describe the misalignment, the law appears out of synch with society in this way: Legal doctrine strongly supports recovery for intrusion, to the point of providing plaintiffs too much protection. Conversely, legal doctrine weakly supports recovery for revelation, to the point of providing plaintiffs too little protection. I next wish to ruminate on these results by considering some of the factors that might help account for the one-sided quality of existing doctrines, and for the far less one-sided array of public opinion.

In my view, intrusion claims are doctrinally generous to plaintiffs, for many reasons. First, intrusion claims partake of a strong common-law solicitude for the protection of interests that can be conceptualized in relatively definite contours. The notion of an "intrusion" connotes some act of invasion or penetration of some *barrier*, some border, some line, or wall, or place. Although intrusion claims are not strictly spatial, and not strictly limited to such property notions as physical trespass (if they were, we would only need the law of trespass to contend with them), they are largely wrapped up in the sense that the defendant has entered some forbidden *space*.[3] It is quite striking, for example, how almost all successful intrusion claims *do* involve some invasion of some nonpublic residential or business space. Intrusion in a public space, or even *from* a public space (e.g., a street or sidewalk outside a home) done without some technological enhancement device is rarely held actionable. The space may be literally "spatial," or may be defined more in terms of personal or psychic space, but the imagery of property invasion, of metes and bounds, of breach of one's individual integument, runs strong and deep in the tradition of this style of tort.

Second, defendants have an enormous difficulty getting any First Amendment defense jump-started when it comes to intrusion-style claims, because they usually find themselves overwhelmed by the dichotomy between content-based and content-neutral regulation of speech. At most, the argument goes, intrusion claims rely on laws that are passed to vindicate interests unrelated to the suppression of free expression, and only incidentally impact freedom of speech. Thus, some people argue, intrusion-style privacy claims are based on content-neutral laws and should, at *most*, be subject to the type of intermediate scrutiny commonly applied to content-neutral speech regulation. When intermediate First Amendment scrutiny is applied, privacy interests tend to trump speech and press claims, because they rather easily satisfy the modest doctrinal limits imposed by intermediate level judicial review.[4]

Third, intrusion cases arguably do not impact free expression at all. Intrusion claims, if conceptualized as penalizing only conduct and not speech, are merely content-neutral regulations of speech and press deserving of only intermediate scrutiny under the First Amendment. They are claims that do not implicate regulation of speech or the press in any sense, and in turn merit *zero* First Amendment scrutiny. This idea is most famously expressed through the aphorism that the First Amendment does not protect the press against generally applicable laws. The First Amendment provides no license to trespass, engage in fraud, or breach contracts. Thus, the Supreme Court's well-known decision in *Cohen v. Cowles Media Company*[5] held that the First Amendment did not prevent Minnesota from using its law of contracts and promissory estoppel in a suit against the press brought by a source for breach of a reporter's promise of confidentiality. The press, in short, must obey the law, like everyone else.[6] Just as First Amendment doctrine is generally unsympathetic to claims for wholesale exceptions from generally applicable laws for religious enterprises,[7] it is hostile to such claims when they come from the press.[8]

What about revelation claims? What accounts for the relatively lopsided law here? One reason is the converse of the "definable contours" element of intrusion claims. Although it is relatively easy for the law to get its hands around the notion of intrusion, and give contours and definition to the personal space of the individual that is being protected, it is not so easy to give clear definition to a private fact about one's life. This is not to say that such definition is impossible, but in the absence of the literal or metaphorical parallel to spatial invasions that intrusion claims have, it is quite difficult.[9]

Second, and most powerfully, revelation claims by hypothesis reveal truth. In the world of The First Church of the People's Right to Know, the truth will set you free. Strong First Amendment doctrines presumptively protect the right of the press to publish truthful information, lawfully obtained.[10] Thus, unless the revelation claim can be *coupled* with an intrusion claim, so that the argument can be pushed that the truthful information was *not* lawfully obtained, the press may invoke this very formidable doctrinal tradition. Thus, whereas the First Amendment enters the law of intrusion only meekly (through intermediate scrutiny), and perhaps not at all (through the notion that it does not protect against generally applicable laws), the First Amendment comes thundering into revelation on the high white horse of truth.

The Supreme Court addressed this recently in *Bartnicki v. Vopper*,[11] holding that federal and state statutes prohibiting the disclosure of information obtained through illegal interception of cellular phone messages were unconstitutional as applied to certain media and nonmedia defendants who received tape recordings of the intercepted messages from anonymous sources and then disclosed them to others.

Third, any attempt to fashion some legal doctrine that would at once give contour to the notion of a "private fact" and cabin the presumption favoring unfettered publication of truth must contend with a second powerful First Amendment norm, the strong reluctance of courts to craft doctrines that effectively second-guess editorial judgment on what is or is not newsworthy.[12] Virtually by definition, if a journalist prints a fact, the journalist must have thought it newsworthy. If the law is to punish the journalist for such printing, either through a criminal penalty or by holding the journalist accountable in tort, the law must be willing to reject the journalist's decision on newsworthiness. Either the law must say that the invasion of privacy was so severe that it deserves punishment even if the law accepts that the truth printed was newsworthy, or the law must say that the journalist was simply wrong in judging the material as being newsworthy. The First Amendment tradition that argues against permitting judges and juries to substitute their editorial judgment for that of journalists and editors heavily weakens the legal strength of revelation claims, rendering them virtually impotent in current doctrine. As the Supreme Court put the matter in *Miami Herald Publishing Co. v. Tornillo.*[13]

> A newspaper is more than a passive receptacle or conduit for news, comment, and advertising. The choice of material to go into a newspaper, and the decisions made as to limitations on the size and content of the paper, and treatment of public issues and public officials—whether fair or unfair—constitute the exercise of editorial control and judgment. It has yet to be demonstrated how governmental regulation of this crucial process can be exercised consistent with First Amendment guarantees of a free press as they have evolved to this time.[14]

If these are some (although admittedly not all) of the doctrinal factors that appear to influence the current state of the law, how might they be critiqued? One starting point is to take stock of the competing speech and privacy interests in light of several of the philosophical justifications that have classically been advanced to explain and justify heightened protection for speech and for privacy. Heightened constitutional protection for freedom of speech, for example, is often justified on the basis of the importance of speech to democratic self-governance,[15] for the value it serves to enlighten society in the ongoing quest for truth through the operation of an open marketplace of ideas,[16] or for the integral role it plays in individual self-fulfillment and realization.[17] The legitimacy and persuasiveness of these classic rationales are themselves the subject of constant and intense debate. For the purposes of this chapter, however, I need not go "behind them," if you will, or even choose among them.[18] It is enough now simply to accept them all as possible justifications for freedom of speech, separately or collectively, and then attempt to take some measure of how they operate in relation to privacy claims for intrusion and revelation. By the same token, it may be useful to attempt to assess the conflict between speech and privacy against the backdrop of several of the philosophical justifications for protecting privacy, such as the enhancement of human dignity, autonomy, personal solitude, identity, or intimacy.

To put all of this in extremely simple terms for a moment, we might imagine putting our privacy-invading journalist on the witness stand, and asking the journalist these questions on cross-examination:

Why did you intrude?

Why did you reveal?

Can you connect these actions to the enhancement of self-governance?

Can you connect these actions to enlightenment, and service to the marketplace of ideas?

Can you connect these actions to individual fulfillment and self-realization, either your own or that of the people who will receive the information?

Let's let our journalist answer, and see how persuasive those answers are.

What goes around comes around, however, and our invaded privacy plaintiff must also take the stand. On cross-examination, the plaintiff will be asked, in effect, why are you whining? Specifically, we can easily imagine our rough and ruthless lawyer asking such questions as:

In what respect do you claim that this intrusion or revelation diminished your human dignity?

Your autonomy?

Your solitude?

Your identity?

Your exercise of intimacy?

In sorting through answers to these questions (from both sides), a preliminary point worth making is that First Amendment defenses to intrusion claims, unlike defenses to revelation claims, will always have a derivative quality. In revelation claims, the First Amendment is directly served by the revelation, because the act of revealing, itself an act of expression, is at once the gravamen of the offense and the soul of the defense. However, there is no defending the act of intrusion itself, for its own sake. The act is just an act, no better than a vandal's violence or violation. It is only the motivation for the act that can possibly save it, and in the contest between privacy and speech, only a motivation linked to speech can suffice. Thus, the intruder is always in the immediately awkward derivative position of attempting to interpose a revelation-style defense to prevent liability for an intrusion-style offense.

Hence, the question becomes: What were you trying to reveal, and why? Attempts to justify acts of intrusion that involve law breaking on the grounds that the intrusion will reveal information essential to democratic self-governance are likely to be singularly unpersuasive.[19] Law-breaking intrusions thus seem to reduce themselves to the assertion that the ends justify the means. Yet, the ideal of democratic self-governance will normally include some conception of the rule of law.[20] This means that in the case of intrusion, the ends of a law-abiding society are supposedly being served by the means of law breaking. There is a manifest perversion in this. The break-in of the Democratic Headquarters at the Watergate complex that ultimately led to the downfall of President Richard Nixon was arguably, from the perspective of the burglars, an exercise in illegal means to pursue altruistic political ends. It was, in a sense, the quintessential political intrusion. What mattered, however, was that the break-in was an affront to the rule of law, and to the notion that only agents of the state, restrained by such constitutional requirements as warrants and probable cause, are authorized to engage in such intrusions.

This calculus is not persuasively changed by altering the identity of the burglars. If it had been reporters from *The Washington Post* who had committed the burglaries, the claim that the *Post* was engaged in excusable law breaking would not have been taken seriously, even if the *Post* were able to demonstrate convincingly that what it had unearthed in its burglary was information important to voters in a pending election.

This is not to say that law-breaking intrusions may never be morally justifiable on democratic self-governance grounds, it is only to say that the moral justification will not be legally convincing. A break-in accomplished to expose illegal behavior, tyranny, or corruption may, in the eyes of the criminal journalist, be the lesser of two evils and thus morally justifiable. In such cases, however, the journalist is engaged in civil disobedience. Such civil disobedience may well be morally defensible, but classically it is not legally excusable. The civil disobedient goes to jail.

Would intrusions that are not criminal, but are tortious instead, fare better? On one level, this may well be a false dichotomy, or at least a contrived one, because the argument might be advanced that if conduct can be made tortious, it can also always be made criminal. Yet, we can easily imagine a gap between the two systems, either temporary or permanent, in which certain news gathering techniques might well be judged appropriate for the imposition of civil liability, even though no existing criminal statute has been violated. Now we may be faced with a sort of "buyout" variant of civil disobedience. The journalist might be understood as having a moral justification for the intrusion, but no civil excuse from paying damages. If the journalist undertakes the act of intrusion, the journalist must "buy" the easement, if you will, by compensating the victim. The journalist who commits an intrusion crime is a civil disobedient who pays the penalty of jail. The journalist who commits an intrusion tort is a civil disobedient who pays the price of monetary damages.

Imagine, however, that someone else perpetrates the break-in, and hands the fruit of the poisonous tree to the journalist, who finds it newsworthy and meriting publication. Existing law will treat this handing over of the material not as an act of intrusion by the journalist, directly or vicariously, and will not treat the stolen material as "privacy contraband" (the possession of which may itself be penalized); rather existing law will view this as entirely a revelation paradigm, if the material is published. Because the interests of self-governance can be brought to bear to justify publication, and the journalist's passive receipt of information does not raise the equal and opposite interest in preserving the rule of law, existing doctrine is likely to immunize the journalist from any responsibility, even though the acceptance and publication of the material arguably created a market for the goods that encouraged the act of law breaking by the original intruder.[21] It may be argued, of course, that no new market is created if the source is not paid, but this puts too much emphasis on monetary exchange as the measure of a market. Certainly, the widespread broadcast of material may in many circumstances create an incentive for privacy invasions undertaken for some other agenda—such as political, economic, or personal motive to embarrass the victim. This was true in *Bartnicki v. Vopper*, for example, where the motive was almost certainly to embarrass the teachers' union in a labor dispute.[22] (*Bartnicki* is discussed in greater depth, later in this chapter.)

What of intrusions cannot be connected in any persuasive way to self-governance, but are nonetheless defended on grounds that they serve the enlightenment function and contribute to the marketplace of ideas? Imagine, for example, that a journalist breaks into the home of a movie star to plant a hidden camera in the house to catch the star in a lesbian relationship, so that the journalist can reveal the star's sexual preference to the world and thus expose her "hypocrisy" as an apparently straight person. In defending this act, the journalist explains that he/she did not think of this as related to self-governance in any direct sense, but did think it was a highly important contribution to enlightenment concerning the human condition and the marketplace of ideas. Human sexuality and mores about lesbianism are clearly matters of public interest and concern, the journalist claims, and the act of intrusion was done in the service of that ongoing discussion.

There are multiple reasons why this style of argument is not likely to be deemed persuasive to many people. Perhaps the most obvious is that it seems to prove too much, and thus prove too little. On a most elemental level, a basic datum of human existence is that nothing is what it seems. More poignantly, nobody is who he or she seems. Every person projects a persona to the world that is not entirely authentic. Even if we could entirely know our own selves, it is doubtful that we would be much good at accurately revealing those selves. Just think about how much difficulty most of us routinely have explaining and expressing our most complex feelings, when we are *trying* to be honest. Almost none of us, however, are trying to be honest all the time, or revealing our innermost feelings all the time. All of us live, more or less, behind masks—masks that disguise to greater or lesser degrees our real selves.

This basic fact of human existence makes any exposure of what is behind another person's mask *intrinsically* interesting. Stripping away some part of the human mask is one of the major enterprises of life—of art, music, literature, and of course, of journalism. When someone is shown to be something more or less than what he/she appears to be, the revelation is indeed often intriguing, striking, shocking, arresting, or compelling. The revelation may reveal matters profound, matters universal.

All of this sounds good from the perspective of our journalist, but is it truly convincing? This is, it must be remembered, the act of intrusion we are attempting to defend. To the extent that a journalist claims that intrusions are justifiable because they penetrate a person's mask, the journalist is really saying that all intrusions are inherently justifiable, because all intrusions penetrate. This becomes penetration for the sake of penetration, the breaking of masks because there *are* masks.

This leads to the final justification for free speech, the self-fulfillment of the speaker. In essence, the claim would now be that the self-realization that the journalist gains from the penetration of the mask justifies the invasion, because there is artistic or intellectual fulfillment in exposing that all is not what it seems. There is no question that this self-realization may be real and realized. The difficulty is that the individuality of the invading defendant is being vindicated here at the expense of the individuality of the invaded plaintiff. Some hedging may be called for here, because there are human dignity values on both sides of the equation. The plaintiff is being asked to surrender a measure of personhood to subsidize the personhood of the defendant. There is an inherently exploitative and predatory quality to this bargain, at once paparazzitic and parasitic.

The conduct of the plaintiff is yet another factor that is likely to influence our intuitions on the speech/privacy trade-off. Whether the legal claim is intrusion based or revelation based, the credibility that we are willing to give to the responses of our privacy-invading defendant and our privacy-invaded plaintiff will undoubtedly be colored by what the plaintiff was doing at the time. Imagine, for example, that the intrusion and the revelation both involve misconduct on the part of the plaintiff. The plaintiff may be committing murder, abusing animals, engaging in unhealthy and unsanitary practices in the preparation of food in a grocery store, bilking medical patients, carrying on an illicit adulterous liaison, smoking marijuana, engaging in gay or lesbian sex in a state that makes such conduct criminal, assisting a terminally ill patient in suicide, or any number of a thousand other activities that are arguably wrong.

I intentionally include a wide range of arguable misconduct. Some of the acts, like murder, are universally condemned. Other acts on the list may be technically criminal, but are either widely practiced and countenanced or subject to widely divergent views regarding their moral propriety. In our society, police have an ongoing mandate, subject to constitutional restraints, to "intrude" and to "reveal" misconduct that is criminal. The jurisdictional divide that in effect sets the privacy border is the criminal law itself. With rare exception, there is no privacy right to commit crimes in public. (This does not mean that the law of crimes is indifferent to the public or private setting of an act. There are things that are criminal if done in public, but not criminal if done in private, such as walking nude.[23])

When the assertion of a right to intrude or reveal is made by the journalist, however, reliance on the criminal law as the jurisdictional divide is troublesome, because this appears to place the journalist in the position of the police—sex police, drug police, whatever police. Once again, the notion of the rule of law is implicated. A traditional component of the rule of law is that it is the ruler who enforces the law. Acts of private justice—at least private intrusion and private punishment— are normally considered acts that affront law's rule.

I next turn the tables somewhat and look at the philosophical justifications that may be advanced from the privacy side, focusing first on intrusion. If the tort of intrusion was constructed merely to preserve corporeal interests, there would be no conspicuous reason for its existence.[24] Bodily integrity is already safeguarded by the criminal and tort law, through such concepts as assault and battery. The same is true of property protection—torts such as trespass or conversion, and crimes such as theft, will do the trick. What about protection of psychological well-being? Again, there are already torts suited for the task, such as the tort of intentional infliction of emotional distress.

Why, then, have the tort of intrusion at all? What social value does it add to the array of torts already in existence? The beginning of the answer may lie in looking more carefully at the concept of seclusion. As in Fourth Amendment search and seizure jurisprudence, intrusion cases may trigger courts to ask whether the plaintiff had a "reasonable expectation of privacy" in the seclusion that has allegedly been invaded. The notion of a reasonable expectation of privacy is, of course, a social construct. The judgment that a particular plaintiff's expectation was or was not reasonable in a particular set of circumstances inevitably implicates issues relating to physical space, personal and professional relationships, human intimacy, psychological peace, and personal culpability.

Spatial concepts often play into analysis at the threshold. Courts are usually unwilling to hold that an "intrusion" can exist when, for example, a person is photographed in a place open to the public.[25] Contrast these holdings with quintessentially private spaces, such as one's residence. As our tradition goes, one's home is one's castle:

> A man can still control a small part of his environment, his house; he can retreat thence from outsiders, secure in the knowledge that they cannot get at him without disobeying the Constitution. That is still a sizable hunk of liberty—worth protecting from encroachment. A sane, decent, civilized society must provide some such oasis, some shelter from public scrutiny, some insulated enclosure, some enclave, some inviolate place which is a man's castle.[26]

The integrity of the home as castle has been reinforced by the Supreme Court's holdings in the ride-along cases, in which the Supreme Court held that a criminal suspect's civil rights are violated when the press accompany police while the police execute search or arrest warrants in the home.[27]

Other physical spaces treated in our society as presumptively private acquire that gloss because of a combination of the attributes of the space itself and the nature of the human activity that typically occurs in the space. We treat hospital rooms as private because of the intimate nature of the medical treatment that occurs there, and because of the sense that a patient is at least transiently "resident" in the room.[28] The hospital room is seemingly more private than a mere hotel room because we attach privacy interests to the medical care the patient is receiving.[29]

It is easy enough to say that intrusion claims are weakest in public spaces and strongest in private spaces. However, there are many spaces that have a hybrid quality, and thus defy glib characterization. How should we treat an ambulance, for example, or a rescue helicopter? Should it make a difference whether the door to the ambulance or helicopter is open or shut? A recent California case, wrestling with these concerns, held that a viable intrusion claim did exist in a case in which a news cameraman filmed an accident victim's conversations with medical rescue workers while she was inside a rescue helicopter.[30]

Because privacy is a social construct, our social and legal views of privacy are also influenced by its connection to the web of personal, civic, religious, and business relationships that define social existence. In traditional legal theory, defamation is often described as a "relational" tort, in that at its core it exists to protect a construct we call "reputation." In its orthodox conception, defamation is an injury to one's personal, social, family, or business relationships.[31] Privacy is typically conceptualized as somewhat less "relational," on the theory that privacy law is oriented inward, at the harm a privacy invasion may visit on an individual's tranquility or psychological remove.[32]

In fact, however, both defamation and privacy torts more commonly perform double duty, looking at once outward and inward. In most jurisdictions a mere surface showing of damage to reputation will open the door to recovery by plaintiffs of recompense for emotional distress.[33] In theory the emotional distress reward is parasitic, riding on the back of the reputational claim, but this is largely legal fiction. Indeed, some jurisdictions have dispensed with the fiction, and the plaintiff is allowed to recover for personal anguish without even demonstrating reputational harm, a rule that all but abandons any principled distinction between libel and privacy damages.[34] By the same token, causes of action for invasion of privacy at times work to protect personal and professional relationships, such as the confidentiality shared in a professional setting or with one's intimate partner.[35] Thus, eavesdropping on the conversation of an attorney with his/her client, or a priest and his penitent, may well be deemed more of an invasion than eavesdropping on an animal trainer's conversations with his/her monkeys.[36] A major ongoing battleground for intrusion is whether entry into a place of business or commerce constitutes an entry into a space sufficiently imbued with privacy interests to merit protection under the intrusion tort.[37] The legal landscape on these issues is likely to be heavily influenced in the future by the Supreme Court's recent decision in *Bartnicki v. Vopper.*[38] In *Bartnicki*, the Court examined statutory prohibitions against the intentional disclosure of illegally intercepted communication that the disclosing party knows or should know was illegally obtained. In an opinion by Justice Stevens, the Court ruled that these statutes were content-neutral laws of general applicability, but that application of those provisions against media defendants violated their free speech rights, at least in a context in which the purloined conversations involved topics that the Court deemed to be matters of public concern, and on the assumption that the defendants had played no part in the illegal interception.

The case involved an intercepted conversation between two persons actively involved in a labor dispute, Gloria Bartnicki and Anthony Kane. Gloria Bartnicki was a principal labor negotiator for a teachers' union in Pennsylvania, the Pennsylvania State Education Association. Anthony Kane, a high school teacher at Wyoming Valley West High School, was president of the union. In May 1993, Bartnicki and Kane had a telephone conversation concerning the ongoing labor negotiations with a local school board. Kane was speaking from a land phone at his house. Bartnicki was talking from her car, using her cellular phone. Strategies and tactics were discussed, including the possibility of a teacher strike. The talk was candid, and included some blunt down-and-dirty characterizations of their opponents in the labor controversy, which at times got personal. One of the school district's representatives was described as "too nice," another as a "nitwit," and still others as "rabble rousers." Among the opposition tactics that raised the ire of Bartnicki and Kane was the perceived proclivity of the school district to negotiate through the newspaper. The papers had reported that the school district was not going to agree to anything more than a pay raise of 3%. As they discussed this position, Kane stated, "If they're not gonna move for three percent, we're gonna have to go to their, their homes ... [t]o blow off their front porches, we'll have to do some work on some of those guys."[39]

An unknown person, presumably using a scanner that picked up the cell phone transmissions, intercepted and recorded the conversation on a cassette tape. An unknown person proceeded to place the tape in the mailbox of the president of a local taxpayers group that was opposed to the teachers' union and its bargaining positions, a man named Jack Yocum. Yocum listened to the tape, recognized the voices of Bartnicki and Kane, and took the tape to a local radio station talk show host, Frederick Vopper.[40] Yocum, who first received the tape, and Vopper, who played it on the radio, both realized that it had been intercepted from a cell phone, and that a scanner had probably been used to make the intercept. Vopper received the tape in the spring of 1993, but waited until September 30 to broadcast it, which he did a number of times. At first, Vopper broadcast a part of the tape that revealed Bartnicki's phone numbers. She began to receive menacing calls, and was forced to change her numbers. The tape later was warped so that the numbers would be indistinguishable when it was played on the air. Other media outlets, including a newspaper in Wilkes-Barre, also received copies of the tape, but no other broadcaster or publisher played the tape or disclosed its contents until after Vopper broadcast the material on the tape. Once Vopper broke the story, however, secondary coverage of the events, including the contents of the tape, appeared in other media outlets. Invoking a federal statute and a very similar Pennsylvania law, Bartnicki and Kane sued Yocum, Vopper, and the radio stations that carried Vopper's show, for using and disclosing the contents of their intercepted telephone conversation.

The Court in *Bartnicki* emphasized that it was not answering the ultimate question of whether the media may ever be held liable for punishing truthful information lawfully obtained, but was rather addressing what it described as "a narrower version of that still-open question,"[41] which it put as: "Where the publisher of information has obtained the information in question in a manner lawful in itself but from a source who has obtained it unlawfully, may the government punish the ensuing publication of that information based on the defect in a chain?"[42] The purpose of the law, the Court explained, was to protect the privacy of wire, electronic, and oral communications, and it singles out such communications by virtue of the fact that they were illegally intercepted—by virtue of the source rather than the subject matter.[43]

Nevertheless, the Court found the prohibition against disclosures was still fairly characterized as a regulation of speech.[44] The Court held that the first interest identified by the government in support of the law—removing an incentive for parties to intercept private conversations—could not justify the statute. "The normal method of deterring unlawful conduct," the Court argued, is to punish the person engaging in it, and it would be "remarkable," the Court claimed, "to hold that speech by a law-abiding possessor of information can be suppressed in order to deter conduct by a non-law-abiding third party."[45]

The government's second interest—minimizing the harm to persons whose conversations have been illegally intercepted—was in the view of the Court considerably stronger. Privacy of communication, the Court accepted, is an important interest.[46] Nevertheless, the Court reasoned, because the statements made by Bartnicki and Kane would have been matters of "public concern" had they been made in a public arena, they were also matters of concern when made in private conversation.[47] Invoking the long line of precedents granting the media a First Amendment right to print truthful information on matters of public concern that is "lawfully obtained,"[48] the Court held that the newsworthiness of the information revealed trumped the privacy rights of the parties to the conversation.[49] Significantly, Justice Breyer, in a concurring opinion joined by Justice O'Connor,[50] took a much narrower view of matters, heavily emphasizing the fact that the conversation between Bartnicki and Kane appeared to contemplate violent and illegal action.[51] In the views of those two concurring Justices, it was only this added element of illegality that provided the special circumstances that warranted application of a newsworthiness defense to the disclosure of the intercepted conversation.[52] Chief Justice Rehnquist, joined by Justices Scalia and Thomas, dissented.[53] The laws at issue, he argued, were content neutral, they sought to restrict only the disclosure of information that was illegally obtained in the first instance, they placed no restrictions on republication of material already in the public domain, they did not single out the media for especially disfavorable treatment, they utilized a scienter requirement to avoid trapping the unwary, and they promoted both the privacy interests and the free speech interests of those using devices such as cellular telephones.[54]

The *Bartnicki* decision is far from a ringing endorsement of the right of the press to trump privacy concerns any time the subject matter of the ostensibly private facts that are revealed is a "matter of public concern." Rather, given the far more limited understanding of the Court's ruling expressed by concurring Justices Breyer and O'Connor, a better interpretation of *Bartnicki* is to treat the expansive remarks of Justice Stevens, writing for the nominal majority, as really expressing only the views of a four-Justice plurality. The pivotal concurring opinion of Justice Breyer was in many respects more in philosophical tune with Chief Justice Rehnquist's dissent than with the opinion of Justice Stevens. Most importantly, Justice Breyer's concurrence made it clear that he was only applying "intermediate scrutiny" to the statute,[55] and that he believed in many cases—such as those not implicating speech that posed the specter of criminal violence—he would be willing to sustain the types of disclosure limits created by eavesdropping laws.[56]

In short, when one takes the moderate concurring opinion of Justices Breyer and O'Connor and combines that opinion with the dissenting views of Chief Justice Rehnquist and Justices Scalia and Thomas, it appears that the last word from the Supreme Court in *Barnicki* is far from the final word, and that the conflict between privacy and expression addressed by the Court still has a long way to go before it is resolved.

NOTES

[1] Oliver Wendell Holmes, *Natural Law*, 32 Harvard Law Rev 40 (1918).

[2] See Amitai Etzioni, *The Limits of Privacy* 2 (1999): "Public opinion polls show that Americans are appropriately agitated" about invasions of privacy, citing *1996 Equifax/Harris Consumer Privacy Survey* 20–29, available at <http://www.equifax.com/consumer/parchive/svry96/docs/summary.html>; 1997 *Monday* magazine poll, cited in Barnet D. Wolf, "Computers' Spread Heightens Consumer Privacy Concerns," *Columbus Dispatch* 1H (September 7, 1997); 1997 Harris-Westin survey for the Center for Social Legal Research, cited in Lawrence A. Ponemon, *Privacy Needs Protection*, 23 Journal of Commerce 7A (1998); Alan Westin, *1998 Harris-Westin Survey on Privacy, and the Elements of Self-Regulation*, paper presented at Department of Commerce Privacy Conference, Washington, DC (June 23, 1998). See also Jennifer Lambe, *Dimensions of Censorship: Reconceptualizing Public Willingness to Censor*, 7 Communications Law and Policy 187 (2002), which analyzed public attitudes toward censorship in light of numerous variables, including privacy. See, generally, Ellen Alderman & Caroline Kennedy, *The Right to Privacy* (1995); Jeffrey Rothfelden, *Privacy for Sale* (1992).

[3] See Rodney A. Smolla, *Privacy and the First Amendment Right to Gather News*, 67 George Wash. L. Rev. 1097, 1121–22 (1999).

[4] In constitutional law, variants of "intermediate scrutiny" are often employed to impose demanding standards of review considerably more rigorous than the highly deferential reasonableness or rational basis tests applied to ordinary economic and social legislation, yet not as demanding as such extremely high standards as "strict scrutiny," or "clear and present danger." The requirements that the government demonstrate "important" or "substantial" justifications for its actions, "narrowly tailor" ends to means, and leave open ample alternative means of communication are the touchstones of intermediate review. Intermediate scrutiny tests, varying slightly in their exact formulation as doctrinal contexts change, have thus been employed to impose significant protection against the abridgement of constitutional norms across the expanse of constitutional adjudication. See, for example, *Central Hudson Gas & Electric Corp. v. Public Service Commission of New York*, 447 U.S. 557, at 566 (1980), adopting an intermediate-level commercial speech standard requiring, among other things, that the regulation be supported by a "substantial" governmental interest and be "not more extensive than necessary" to serve that interest.

[5] 501 U.S. 663 (1991).

[6] See, for example, *Citizen Publishing Co. v. United States*, 394 U.S. 131 (1969), sustaining application of antitrust laws to the press; *Associated Press v. United States*, 326 U.S. 1 (1945), also sustaining application of antitrust laws to the press; *Associated Press v. NLRB*, 301 U.S. 103 (1937), sustaining application of National Labor Relations Act to the press; *Oklahoma Press Publishing Co. v. Walling*, 327 U.S. 186 (1946), sustaining application of Fair Labor Standards Act to the press. *Konigsberg v. State Bar*, 366 U.S. 36, at 50–51 (1961): "[G]eneral regulatory statutes, not intended to control the content of speech but incidentally limiting its unfettered exercise, have not been regarded as the type of law the First or Fourteenth Amendment forbade Congress or the States to pass, when they have been found justified by subordinating valid governmental interests."

[7]See *Jimmy Swaggart Ministries v. Board of Equalization*, 493 U.S. 378 (1990), sustaining generally applicable tax laws as applied to religious institution.

[8]See *Citizen Publishing Co. v. United States*, (1969); *Associated Press v. United States*, 326 U.S. 1 (1945); *Associated Press v. NLRB*, 301 U.S. 103 (1937); *Oklahoma Press Publishing Co. v. Walling*, 327 U.S. 186 (1946).

[9]See *Florida Star v. B.J.F.*, 491 U.S. 524 (1989), holding unconstitutional an attempt to hold newspaper liable for identifying name of rape victim inadvertently released in a police document. See, generally, Diane L. Zimmerman, *Requiem for a Heavyweight: A Farewell to Warren and Brandeis' Privacy Tort*, 68 Cornell L. Rev. 291, 351 (1983); Geoff Dendy, *The Newsworthiness Defense to the Public Disclosure Tort*, 85 Ky. L.J. 147, 148 (1997): "But the general case is that many courts provide media with the extraordinarily broad newsworthiness defense, leaving the public disclosure tort effectively impotent."

[10]See, for example, *Cox Broadcasting Corp. v. Cohn*, 420 U.S. 469 (1975), holding unconstitutional a civil damages award entered against a television station for broadcasting the name of a rape-murder victim obtained from public courthouse records; *Florida Star v. B.J.F.* (1989), holding unconstitutional the imposition of liability against a newspaper for publishing the name of a rape victim in contravention of a Florida statute prohibiting such publication in circumstances in which a police department inadvertently released the victim's name; *Smith v. Daily Mail Publishing Co.*, 443 U.S. 97, 104 (1979), finding unconstitutional the indictment of two newspapers for violating a state statute forbidding newspapers to publish, without written approval of the juvenile court, the name of any youth charged as a juvenile offender, where the newspapers obtained the name of the alleged juvenile assailant from witnesses, the police, and a local prosecutor, stating that the "magnitude of the State's interest in this statute is not sufficient to justify application of a criminal penalty"; *Landmark Communications, Inc. v. Virginia*, 435 U.S. 829 (1978), overturning criminal sanctions against a newspaper for publishing information from confidential judicial disciplinary proceedings leaked to the paper; *Butterworth v. Smith*, 494 U.S. 624 (1990), refusing to enforce the traditional veil of secrecy surrounding grand jury proceedings against a reporter who wished to disclose the substance of his own testimony after the grand jury had terminated, holding the restriction inconsistent with the First Amendment principle protecting disclosure of truthful information.

[11]121 S.Ct. 1753 (2001).

[12]See Dendy, 148.

[13]418 U.S. 241 (1974).

[14]*Ibid.* at 258. See also Steven Helle, *The News-Gathering/Publication Dichotomy and Government Expression*, 1 Duke Law J. (1982), "Of course, 'the Press is free to try to uncover, and if it succeeds it is free to publish' the information that the government attempts to conceal," quoting Louis Henkin, *The Right to Know and the Duty to Withhold: The Case of the Pentagon Papers*, 120 U. Pa. L. Rev. 271, 278 (1971). As Justice Potter Stewart elaborated, "[t]he primary purpose of the constitutional guarantee of a free press was ... to create a fourth institution outside the Government as an additional check on the three official branches," Potter Stewart, *Or of the Press*, 26 Hastings L.J. 631, 634 (1975).

[15]See Alexander Meiklejohn, *Free Speech in Its Relation to Self-Government*, (1948); Robert Bork, *Neutral Principles and Some First Amendment Problems*, 47 Ind. L. Rev. 1 (1971).

[16]See Stanley Ingber, *The Marketplace of Ideas: A Legitimizing Myth*, 1984 Duke L. J. 1.

[17]See Rodney A. Smolla, *Free Speech in an Open Society* 12–17 (1992).

[18]Steven Shiffrin, *Liberalism, Radicalism, and Legal Scholarship*, 30 U.C.L.A. L. Rev. 1103, 1197–98 (1983).

[19]See, for example, *Harper & Row, Publishers, Inc. v. Nation Enterprises*, 471 U.S. 539, at 559 (1985), holding that President Gerald Ford and his publisher had valid copyright infringement claim for "scoop" publication in *Nation* magazine of Ford's memoirs, notwithstanding the news value of the material, rejecting a fair use defense.

[20]See Randall Bezanson, *Means and Ends and Food Lion: The Tension Between an Exemption and Independence in Newsgathering by the Press*, 47 Emory L.J. 895 (1995).

[21]See *McNally v. Pulitzer Publishing Co.*, 532 F.2d 69, at 79, n. 14 (8th Cir. 1976): "Moreover, although the manner in which information is obtained may be relevant in assessing whether the privacy tort of intrusion has been committed, the law in this developing area seems to be that a newspaper does not commit intrusion by its mere receipt of tortiously obtained private facts, even when the newspaper has actual knowledge of such impropriety"; *Pearson v. Dodd*, 410 F.2d 701, 703–05 (D.C. Cir. 1969), refusing to permit a common-law intrusion claim against journalists who had received and published the contents of documents stolen from a United States Senator's office by third parties, cert. denied, 395 U.S. 947 (1969).

[22]See *Bartnicki v. Vopper*, 532 U.S. 514 (2001).

[23]See *City of Erie v. Pap's A.M.*, 529 U.S. 277 (2000), sustaining a ban on nude dancing at public establishments; *Barnes v. Glen Theatre, Inc.*, 501 U.S. 560 (1991), also sustaining a ban on nude dancing at public establishments.

[24]See Smolla, *Privacy and the First Amendment Right to Gather News*, at 1121–22.

[25]See, for example, *Oklahoma Publishing Co. v. District Court*, 430 U.S. 308 (1977), determining that a photograph of an 11-year-old boy taken in connection with juvenile proceeding involving that child and attended by reporters was not private; *Ault v. Hustler Magazine*, 860 F.2d 877, at 883 (9th Circuit 1988), cert. denied, 489 U.S. 1080 (1989), asserting that when a person agrees to be photographed for a newspaper, the photograph is not a private concern; *Heath v. Playboy Enterprises, Inc.*, 732 F. Supp. 1145, at 1148 (S.D. Fla. 1990): "A photograph taken in a public place is not private"; *Jackson v. Playboy Enterprises, Inc.*, 574 F. Supp. 10, at 11 (S.D. Ohio 1983), maintaining that photographs of three minor boys and a policewoman on city sidewalk in plain view of the public eye were not "purely private activity"; *Cape Publications, Inc. v. Bridges*, 423 So.2d 426, at 427 (5th DCA 1982), review denied, 431 So.2d 988 (1983), cert. denied, 464 U.S. 893 (1983), determining that a photograph of a woman clutching a dish towel to her body to conceal her nudity as she was escorted to police car after kidnaping was "in full public view."

[26]*United States v. On Lee*, 193 F.2d 306, at 315–16 (2nd Circuit, 1951) (Frank, J., dissenting).

[27]See *Wilson v. Layne*, 119 S.Ct. 1692 (1999); *Hanlon v. Berger*, 119 S.Ct. 1706 (1999).

[28]See *Noble v. Sears, Roebuck & Co.*, 33 Cal. App.3d 654, 109 Cal. Rptr. 269 (1973).

[29]See *Green v. Chicago Tribune Co.* 286 Ill. App.3d 1, 221 Ill. Dec. 342, 675 N.E.2d 249, at 255–256 (1996); *Barber v. Time, Inc.* 348 Mo. 1199, 159 S.W.2d 291, at 295 (1942): "Certainly, if there is any right of privacy at all, it should include the right to obtain medical treatment at home or in a hospital … without personal publicity."

[30]*Shulman v. Group W Productions, Inc.*, 18 Cal. 4th 200, 74 Cal. Rpt. 2d 843, 955 P.2d 469 (1998).

[31]See Rodney Smolla, *Law of Defamation* Sec. 1.06[1] (1986, 1998 Supp.).

[32]*Ibid.* at Section 10.01.

[33]See, for example, *Little Rock Newspapers v. Dodrill*, 281 Ark. 25, 660 S.W.2d 936 (1983).

[34]See *Time Inc., v. Firestone*, 424 U.S. 448 (1976).

[35]See David Elder, *The Law of Privacy*, Sec. 2.7 at 50 (1991).

[36]See *People for the Ethical Treatment of Animals v. Bobby Berosini, Ltd.* 111 Nev. 615, 895 P.2d 1269, at 1280–1281 (1995), rejecting an intrusion claim by an animal trainer who allegedly engaged in abuse of monkeys in a backstage preparation area.

[37]The California Supreme Court recently accepted review in a case involving an undercover camera story by ABC in a business context. See *Sanders v. American Broadcasting Companies*, 52 Cal. App. 4th 543, 60 Cal. Rpt. 2d 595, review granted, 64 Cal. Rpt. 2d 399 (1997). See also *Sundheim v. Board of County Commissioners*, 904 P.2d 1337, at 1351 (Colo. App. 1995), aff'd, 926 P.2d 545 (Colo. 1996): in a nonmedia case, the court observed that "[b]usiness premises are protected from unreasonable searches but they are open to intrusions that would not be permissible in purely private circumstances. A commercial establishment enjoys a diminished expectation of privacy in those areas which are open to the public," citing *G.M. Leasing Corp. v. United States*, 429 U.S. 338 (1977).

[38]121 S.Ct. 1753 (2001).

[39]*Ibid.*, at 1757.

[40]The host of the show was named Frederick Vopper, though he appeared on the air under the name "Fred Williams."

[41]*Ibid.*, at 1755.

[42]*Ibid.*, at 1762, quoting *Boehner v. McDermott*, 191 F.3d 463, at 484–85 (D.C. Cir. 1999) (Sentelle, J., dissenting). The Court observed that its unwillingness to construe the question before it any more broadly was consistent with the "Court's repeated refusal to answer categorically whether truthful publication may ever be punished consistent with the First Amendment." *Bartnicki*, 121 S.Ct., at 1762.

[43]*Ibid.*, at 1761.

[44]*Ibid.*

> "On the other hand, the naked prohibition against disclosures is fairly characterized as a regulation of pure speech. Unlike the prohibition against the 'use' of the contents of an illegal interception in Sec. 2511(1)(d), subsection (c) is not a regulation of conduct. It is true that the delivery of a tape recording might be regarded as conduct, but given that the purpose of such a delivery is to provide the recipient with the text of recorded statements, it is like the delivery of a handbill or a pamphlet, and as such, it is the kind of 'speech' that the First Amendment protects. As the majority below put it, '[i]f the acts of 'disclosing' and 'publishing' information do not constitute speech, it is hard to imagine what does fall within that category, as distinct from the category of expressive conduct'" (internal citations omitted).

[45]*Ibid.*, at 1762: "The normal method of deterring unlawful conduct is to impose an appropriate punishment on the person who engages in it. If the sanctions that presently attach to a violation of Sec. 2511(1)(a) do not provide sufficient deterrence, perhaps those sanctions should be made more severe. But it would be quite remarkable to hold that speech by a law-abiding possessor of information can be suppressed in order to deter conduct by a non-law-abiding third party."

[46]*Ibid.*, at 1764, citing *Harper & Row, Publishers, Inc. v. Nation Enterprises*, 471 U.S. 539, at 559, 105 S.Ct. 2218, 85 L.Ed.2d 588 (1985).

[47]*Bartnicki*, 121 S.Ct. at 1760.

[48]See, for example, *Smith v. Daily Mail Publishing Co.*, (1979): "state action to punish the publication of truthful information seldom can satisfy constitutional standards"; *Florida Star v. B.J.F.*, (1989); *Landmark Communications, Inc. v. Virginia*, (1978); *New York Times Co. v. United States*, 403 U.S. 713, 91 S.Ct. 2140, 29 L.Ed.2d 822 (1971) (per curiam).

[49]*Bartnicki*, 121 S.Ct. at 1760.

[50]Ibid., at 1766 (Breyer, J., concurring).

[51]Ibid. at 1767 (Breyer, J. concurring): "The speakers had little or no *legitimate* interest in maintaining the privacy of the particular conversation. That conversation involved a suggestion about 'blow[ing] off ... front porches' and 'do[ing] some work on some of these guys,' ... thereby raising a significant concern for the safety of others" (emphasis in original).

[52]*Ibid.*

[53]*Ibid.*, at 1768 (Rehnquist, C.J., dissenting).

[54]*Ibid.*, at 1772.

[55]*Ibid.*, at 1766 (Breyer, J., concurring):

> I would ask whether the statutes strike a reasonable balance between their speech-restricting and speech-enhancing consequences. Or do they instead impose restrictions on speech that are disproportionate when measured against their corresponding privacy and speech-related benefits, taking into account the kind, the importance, and the extent of these benefits, as well as the need for the restrictions in order to secure those benefits? What this Court has called "strict scrutiny"—with its strong presumption against constitutionality—is normally out of place where, as here, important competing constitutional interests are implicated.

[56]*Ibid.*, at 1767 (Breyer, J., concurring: "As a general matter, despite the statutes' direct restrictions on speech, the Federal Constitution must tolerate laws of this kind because of the importance of these privacy and speech-related objectives.... Rather than broadly forbid this kind of legislative enactment, the Constitution demands legislative efforts to tailor the laws in order reasonably to reconcile media freedom with personal, speech-related privacy," citing Samuel Warren & Louis Brandeis, *The Right to Privacy*, 4 Harv. L. Rev. 193 (1890); *Restatement (Second) of Torts* Sec. 652D (1977); *Katz v. United States*, 389 U.S. 347, at 350–351; 88 S.Ct. 507, 19 L.Ed.2d 576 (1967): "[T]he protection of a person's general right to privacy—his right to be let alone by other people—is, like the protection of his property and of his very life, left largely to the law of the individual States."

6

What's in a Name? Privacy, Property Rights, and Free Expression in the New Communications Media*

Jane E. Kirtley
School of Journalism and Mass Communication, University of Minnesota

Reflecting either America's entrepreneurial spirit or perhaps its obsession with litigation as the solution to all society's problems, whether real or imagined, Ram Avrahami devised a plan to get a cut of the profits from the proliferation of mass-marketing and address-swapping schemes in which many companies engage.[1] Beginning in 1991, Avrahami altered the spelling of his name in 19 different ways when ordering goods and services from various direct marketers.[2] For example, Avrahami purposefully misspelled his name on his subscription application to *U.S. News and World Report* by replacing the *m* in his name with an *n*.[3]

Avrahami's usual practice was to contact the mail-order companies he ordered from and to ask them not to include his name in mailing lists.[4] He also contacted the Mail Preference Service (MPS), a free service that helps individuals "opt out" of direct marketing.[5] However, Avrahami forgot to contact MPS again with his new personal information after he moved from Virginia to Kansas.

Like many companies, *U.S. News* offered its subscribers' mailing lists for sale, charging approximately $80 per 1,000 subscribers.[6] Before a sale, *U.S. News* would have MPS compare its "opt out" list against the magazine's list and suppress any subscribers' names and addresses who appeared on the MPS list.[7] Mail Preference Service's case-sensitive matching program did not suppress Avrahami's name because the names and addresses on each list were different. Avrahami subsequently received solicitations for "Ram Avrahani" from the *Smithsonian Magazine*, the American Heart Association, the Missions Group, and the Gospel Mission.[8]

---

*The author gratefully acknowledges the research assistance of Oliver Kim, J.D. 2000, University of Minnesota, and Kirsten Murphy, J.D. candidate 2003, University of Minnesota.

Avrahami sued the magazine in state court, alleging a violation of a Virginia statute[9] that prohibits the commercial use of an individual's name or likeness without that person's consent.[10] However, the trial court ruled that "[t]he inclusion of an individual name as part of a mailing list constitutes neither a use for an advertising purpose nor a use for the purpose of trade."[11] There was no real "value" in the use of Avrahami's name alone, the court found. Rather, Avrahami's name was only valuable to mass marketers when it was included in a list of tens of thousands of names.[12]

In the several years since Avrahami filed his suit against *U.S. News and World Report*, the collection and exchange of personal information has exploded into a public policy issue as we reconsider what uses should be considered a violation of personal privacy. As Justice William Brennan once observed, "The central storage and easy accessibility of computerized data vastly increase the potential for abuse of that information, and I am not prepared to say that future developments will not demonstrate the necessity of some curb on such technology."[13] As information technology continues to advance, some fear that Justice Brennan's pre-"cyberage" concerns have come true.

More than ever before, personal information—ranging from an individual's name, address, and phone number to his/her purchasing preferences—is available with a click of a mouse. Consumer purchases, whether made over the counter or over the Internet, can provide sophisticated mass marketers with a detailed profile on virtually any individual. Well-publicized problems with Internet security[14] and privacy protocols[15] have spurred both federal and state legislatures to consider how much, if any, personal data should be available to the public.[16]

The fight to defeat federal and state proposals to restrict the use of personal information[17] is being led by mass marketers who, fairly or not, have garnered the lion's share of the public's animus and hysteria over the collection and dissemination of personal information. The Supreme Court recently attempted to balance access to publicly held information against purported personal privacy concerns. In striking the balance in favor of privacy, the Court implicitly suggested that personal information, at least when compiled into a database, ceases to be merely intangible but instead metamorphoses into an actual economic commodity, perhaps a form of personal property.

This chapter discusses how this eruption of privacy initiatives, promoted by both domestic and international pressures, poses serious problems for the free press. First, giving personally identifiable information the status of a pseudo-commodity may open up both the news media and government agencies to possible economic liability if the data are somehow released accidentally into the public domain. Second, if a state or federal agency with limited resources is faced with the Hobson's choice of either expending those resources to develop and enforce a complicated dissemination policy or simply closing its records altogether, one can assume that the agency will opt for secrecy.

The first part of this chapter briefly discusses U.S. judicial interpretations of the competing interests of privacy and individuals' access to public information. Then,

I address two recent Supreme Court decisions reexamining these concepts. Next, I consider domestic and international proposals to increase privacy protection. Finally, I explore the potential ramifications such proposals may have on the news media's investigative function.

JUDICIAL CONSTRUCTIONS OF PRIVACY AND ACCESS

To most privacy absolutists, privacy and access are diametrically opposed. In their view, granting access to personal information without first seeking the consent of the record subject necessarily results in an invasion of that individual's privacy. By contrast, access absolutists contend that publicly held information must be fully open to inspection, copying, and subsequent use at the requester's sole discretion, and they consider the invocation of privacy as the basis for denying access to be, at best, opportunistic. But although neither concept is explicitly mentioned in the Constitution, the Supreme Court has recognized the core values of both privacy and access, and has attempted to balance these competing interests in numerous cases.

The Right to Privacy

The Supreme Court has never recognized an absolute, fundamental right to privacy,[18] but instead has recognized valid privacy interests in certain circumstances. Courts have drawn on federal and state statutes, common law tort law, the Fourth Amendment, and the due process clauses in the Fifth and Fourteenth Amendments as the basis for formulating various privacy interests that may or may not outweigh other competing interests.[19] However, the legal theories used to justify recognition of the asserted privacy interests have been vastly different, leading some courts to question whether a concept as nebulous as privacy can even be satisfactorily defined.[20]

By the same token, establishing privacy as a fundamental right could undermine accountability in government.[21] Scholars have noted that the free flow of information and ideas is a core value of the First Amendment, as well as fundamental to both democracy and a capitalist marketplace.[22]

Much of our privacy jurisprudence developed from tort law.[23] The common law recognizes four types of general "privacy" torts:[24] intrusion into an individual's seclusion;[25] public disclosure of facts that are not "newsworthy";[26] portrayal of an individual in a false light;[27] and misappropriation of a person's name or likeness.[28] These torts raise significant First Amendment concerns because the fear of tort liability can lead to self-censorship, crippling the news media's ability to investigate and report on many important issues of public concern.[29]

Nevertheless, courts generally place First Amendment rights above privacy when a speaker or publisher has *lawfully* obtained truthful information about an individual, particularly if the information is arguably newsworthy.[30] For example, in *Florida Star v. B.J.F.*, a rape victim sued the *Florida Star* for invasion of privacy after it published her name in a crime summary, claiming that the weekly newspaper had negligently violated a state statute[31] prohibiting the news media from disseminating the name of a victim of a sexual offense.[32]

The Court stated that sanctioning only the media for publishing truthful information about sexual assault victims not only failed to protect victims' privacy interests, but was an unconstitutional intrusion into press freedom, "where the government's mishandling of sensitive misinformation leads to its dissemination."[33] Instead, the blame, and liability, rested with the sheriff's department, because it had improperly released the information in the first place and moreover had the ability to "classify certain information, establish and enforce procedures ensuring its redacted release."[34] Although the Court recognized privacy as an important concept, it noted that "it is highly anomalous to sanction persons other than the source of its release."[35] In other words, once the government had released information into the public domain, whether intentionally or accidentally, the government was responsible for the consequences.[36] The Court further found that Florida did not have a substantial state interest to justify singling out the press for punishment after it had published the information.[37]

When a newspaper obtains a secret document entrusted to public officials, the courts have held that the proper defendant is not the newspaper but the public official who neglected his/her duties. For example, in *Sheets v. Salt Lake County*,[38] the Tenth Circuit considered whether an individual had a right to privacy in his wife's diary. The plaintiff, Gary Sheets, gave police officers permission to examine the diary that had belonged to his deceased wife Kathy during the course of investigating her murder.[39] Once the case was closed, however, the diary and other information relating to the murder was archived and made available for public inspection.[40] Additionally, an investigator for the Salt Lake County Attorney's Office inadvertently lent excerpts of the diary, copied as part of his investigative file, to an author who was his personal friend.[41] Although it was unclear whether the police had in fact assured Sheets that the diary's contents would remain confidential, Sheets testified that he gave the diary to the police only because he expected it to remain private.[42] Passages from the diary were later published in three books about the incident, either as supporting materials or as direct quotations.[43]

Sheets sued Salt Lake County, several prosecutors, and police officers in federal district court, claiming invasion of privacy.[44] In affirming the jury verdict for the plaintiff, the Tenth Circuit held that "[t]he fact that [the police] could not recall whether [they] had initially assured Mr. Sheets of the diary's confidentiality does not negate … that an understanding of confidentiality did exist."[45] Moreover, even though there was a "compelling state interest" in releasing the diary to the police as part of their investigation, there was "no such compelling interest in the dissemination of Mrs. Sheets' diary" to the public at large.[46]

Privacy has also been conceptualized as the "right to be left alone,"[47] both in order to limit physical invasion of an individual's property and to prevent the government from interfering with an individual's ability to make personal decisions. Privacy has frequently been invoked to protect a person's home from unwarranted intrusion.[48] The Court has also used privacy as a driving rationale for opinions relating personal choices in family rearing[49] and reproduction.[50]

Privacy is also implicated in criminal investigations and, in that specific context, courts consider whether an intrusion is reasonable under the Fourth Amendment.[51] The courts have looked for an *expectation* of privacy, drawing on what transactions the paradigmatic "reasonable person" would expect would remain private.[52] The Fourth Amendment itself does *not* create an expectation of privacy; rather, courts must find such an expectation "by reference to concepts of real or personal property law."[53] Thus, the Court has found that having a dog sniff one's luggage[54] or being stopped by police officers on a bus about to depart[55] do not offend the Fourth Amendment's prohibition on unreasonable searches and seizures, and do not constitute unconstitutional intrusions into personal privacy.

The public's "right to know," however, may outweigh all these privacy interests, particularly in areas concerning public health and safety.[56] Indeed, this communitarian "right to know" is one of the primary rationales for granting government agencies authority to assemble giant databases containing information on numerous individuals. By assembling such a database, the theory goes, the government can better protect the community from potential threats from dangerous individuals.

Information Gathering, Privacy, and Access

Federal and state actors often have legitimate reasons for obtaining information on individuals. For example, agents of public regulatory agencies may need access to personal records to promote public health and safety[57] or to inspect a listing of campaign contributors to ensure the honesty of elected officials.[58] Stockpiling information in an electronic database can make a government bureaucrat's life much easier by reducing paper and storage costs and increasing efficiency by making information more readily available.[59]

But electronic databases, whether held by public or private entities, are often perceived as posing significant threats to privacy for several reasons. First, many databases contain numerous pieces of information on individuals, including such personal "identifiers" as name, race, gender, birth date, or Social Security number. Many privately held databases also contain information relating to an individual's personal preferences. For example, a database maintained by a compact disc vendor might include information on what CDs a customer has purchased before or how much he/she typically orders. Second, an individual may have little say in what information is collected or how it is done. Once the information is in the hands of another person, the subject may have very little ability to control the future disclosure or use of that information.

Although acknowledging the Constitution does not prohibit states and the federal government from hoarding massive amounts of information,[60] the Court has suggested that personal information in public databases ought to be protected from "unwarranted" disclosure.[61] In the seminal "database" case, *Whalen v. Roe*,[62] the Supreme Court considered a challenge to the registry scheme for the New York controlled substance act.[63] The challengers argued that the statute "threaten[ed] to impair both their interest in the nondisclosure of private information and also their interest in making important decisions independently."[64] Patients feared they might be stigmatized if the registry data were released accidentally, thus revealing their medical conditions and the type and dosage of drugs they took.[65] In turn, this fear affected the decision-making process of both doctors and patients because some patients might "be reluctant to use, and some doctors reluctant to prescribe, such drugs even when their use is medically indicated."[66] In response, New York asserted that its interest in preventing creation of a black market for prescription drugs outweighed any individuals' privacy interests.[67]

The Court found that New York's concerns were legitimate, noting that the state's plan was "manifestly the product of an orderly and rational legislative decision."[68] New York had provided significant statutory safeguards to protect patient records, and none of the states that had adopted such a registry had ever improperly disclosed a patient's medical history.[69] Although the apparent adequacy of these safeguards seemed to drive much of the opinion, the Court stopped short of declaring such protections mandatory for regulatory schemes, merely recognizing a "concomitant statutory or regulatory duty to avoid unwarranted disclosures."[70]

Courts have acknowledged that the government needs to collect some personal information on individuals for the proper functioning of an orderly, efficient government.[71] To live in a modern democracy, we must give up some degree of personal privacy. At the same time, the government must assure citizens that such information will not be used to abridge their freedom and will not be arbitrarily released, potentially embarrassing or causing harm to the record subject. Although courts have adopted a balancing test to weigh these two competing interests, the balance generally has been struck in favor of allowing the government to maintain databases.[72] However, some courts have ruled for the government only when satisfied that sufficient procedural safeguards ensure that personal information remains private.[73] Government agencies may also be held to a higher standard of accountability if they fail to keep individuals' personal information private by inadvertently releasing it.[74]

However, by allowing—even urging—the government to enact such safeguards, courts have given short shrift to the reality that these often Byzantine regulatory schemes restrict the public's ability to gain access to and to review publicly held information. In the seminal case *United States Department of Justice v. Reporters Committee for Freedom of the Press*,[75] the Court considered a CBS news correspondent's Freedom of Information Act request for specific criminal histories, or "rap sheets," held by the Federal Bureau of Investigation in a centralized electronic repository.[76] The records contained information on members of the Medico family, who had been identified by the Pennsylvania Crime Commission as having connections to organized crime figures and being implicated in a government contracting scandal, and were withheld by the FBI on privacy grounds.[77] The federal Court of Appeals for the District of Columbia, two to one, agreed with the news media, finding that an individual had little privacy interest in his/her rap sheet because it contained information already available to the public.[78] The court remanded the case, suggesting that the FBI might be able to "satisfy its statutory obligation by referring [the correspondent] to" the original source of the criminal records.[79]

The Supreme Court, however, reversed, rejecting the appellate court's rationale that an individual had no privacy interest in a government record if the information in that record had been publicly disclosed elsewhere.[80] In an opinion by Justice John Paul Stevens, the Court noted that "plainly there is a vast difference between the public records that might be found after a diligent search of [public records] throughout the country and a computerized summary located in a single clearinghouse of information."[81] Merely because "an event is not wholly 'private' does not mean that an individual has no interest in limiting disclosure or dissemination of the information," it added.[82] Echoing then-Judge Kenneth Starr's dissenting opinion in the D.C. Circuit's ruling, the Court found that Congress had not intended the Freedom of Information Act to turn the federal government into a "clearinghouse for highly personal information."[83]

Concurring in the judgment, Justice Harry Blackmun, joined by Justice Brennan, nevertheless cautioned that the majority's "bright-line approach" would frustrate important uses of FOIA to obtain personally identifiable information, such as ferreting out possible corruption in government officials.[84] Whereas the majority would not necessarily require government agencies to inquire into "the purposes for which the request for information is made" in every case,[85] Blackmun advocated "a more flexible balancing approach" that would allow agencies to take into account the reason an individual, such as a journalist, might seek to obtain another person's rap sheets.[86]

A NEW TREND IN THE RIGHT OF ACCESS?

The Supreme Court recently returned to the issues of privacy and access in two cases, *Condon v. Reno* and *Los Angeles Police Department v. United Reporting Publishing Corporation*. Both opinions, authored by Chief Justice William Rehnquist, could have serious negative implications for the news media's ability to gain access to public records. In both cases, the Supreme Court seemed particularly concerned about the potential for "misuse" of information, viewing any right of access as subservient to the public's expectation that information held by the government would remain private and not be arbitrarily disseminated to third parties.

Los Angeles Police Department v. United Reporting Publishing Corporation: Controlling Subsequent Use of Information Contained in Public Databases

In *Los Angeles Police Department*,[87] the Court rejected a publisher's First Amendment challenge to a California statute forbidding individuals to obtain copies of arrest records if they intended to use the information they gleaned for commercial purposes.[88] Under an earlier version of California open records law, state and local law enforcement agencies were compelled to "make public the name, address, and occupation of every individual arrested."[89] United Reporting Publishing Corporation, a private publishing service, had routinely obtained the names and addresses of recent arrestees from law enforcement records, then sold them to attorneys, insurance companies, substance abuse clinics, and other interested parties.[90]

In 1996, the California legislature amended the California statute to restrict the subsequent use of such records. Persons requesting access to arrest records were required to sign declarations under penalty of perjury that they sought the information for one of five enumerated purposes[91] and would not reuse the information "directly or indirectly to sell a product or service."[92] Under the amended statute, United Reporting arguably could still review the arrest records for "journalistic" reasons, but the publisher could not re-release the information to its customers. Seeking injunctive relief, United Reporting argued the statute was unconstitutional under the First Amendment because it restricted the publisher's ability to speak.[93]

The Ninth Circuit affirmed the district court's finding that the statute violated United Reporting's freedom of speech under the First Amendment. As an initial matter, the Ninth Circuit concluded that United Reporting was engaged in solely commercial speech.[94] The publisher unsuccessfully argued that its speech went "beyond the mere proposal of ... a transaction and involve[d] the passing of ideas and information including ideas and information necessary to the exercise of the Sixth Amendment right to retain the assistance of counsel."[95] Although conceding that no bright-line rule existed to determine what constituted commercial speech, the Ninth Circuit found that, "in light of [the] surrounding circumstances," United Reporting was engaging in commercial speech. "United Reporting sells arrestee information to clients; nothing more. Its speech can be reduced to, 'I [United Reporting] will sell you [client] the X [names and addresses of arrestees] at the Y price,'" the court said.[96]

Despite its finding that United Reporting's speech was merely commercial speech, the Ninth Circuit agreed with the publisher that it was entitled to some protection under the First Amendment.[97] Using the four-prong *Central Hudson*[98] test, the court found that the government did have a substantial interest in protecting the arrestees' privacy, agreeing that the government could be concerned with "direct intrusion into the private lives and homes of arrestees and victims."[99] However, the court noted, the particular statutory regulation failed to advance this interest. Other individuals statutorily qualified to view the information could publish the arrestees' information in "any newspaper, article, or magazine in the country so long as the information is not used for commercial purposes," the court noted.[100] By comparison, "[h]aving one's name, crime, and address printed in the local paper is a far greater affront to privacy than receiving a letter from an attorney, substance abuse counselor, or driving school eager to help one overcome his present difficulties (for a fee, naturally)."[101]

The Supreme Court, however, rejected the argument that the statute infringed on United Reporting's First Amendment rights at all. Rather, Chief Justice Rehnquist framed the issue before the Court as "nothing more than a governmental denial of access to information in its possession."[102] As operator of the database, California has considerable leeway in deciding whether to limit or to extend access to information it has collected, the high court said.[103] Indeed, the Court went further, finding that California could decide not to give out this information at all without violating the First Amendment.[104]

However, several Justices observed that the statute was the equivalent of the state granting favored status to certain legal uses over others. In her concurrence, Justice Ruth Bader Ginsburg agreed that the state statute was "a restriction on access to government information, not ... a restriction on protected speech,"[105] arguing that a grant of access amounts to a type of subsidy that California could give to certain groups so long as "the award of the subsidy is not based on an illegitimate criterion such as viewpoint" or political party affiliation.[106] Ginsburg cautioned the Court to avoid pushing states into a position in which they could only choose between keeping records open to the entire public or closing them completely.[107] Rather, the Court should give states leeway in ensuring accessibility of records to guarantee the flow of at least some information.[108]

Justice Antonin Scalia argued that the Court should have adopted a narrower holding because United Reporting had not raised an "as-applied" challenge but instead had broadly challenged the statute as being unconstitutional on its face.[109] In his concurrence, which was joined by Justice Clarence Thomas, Scalia noted "[a] law that is formally merely a restriction upon access to information subjects no speaker to the risk of prosecution, and hence there is no need to protect such speakers by allowing someone else to raise their challenges to the law."[110] But Justice Scalia argued that the Court had not determined whether the California statute created "a restriction upon access that allows access to the press (which in effect makes the information part of the public domain), but at the same time denies access to persons who wish to use the information for certain speech purposes."[111] In his opinion, such a restriction would be an unconstitutional "restriction upon speech."[112]

Justice Stevens, who had delivered the majority opinion in *Reporters Committee*, dissented here. Joined by Justice Anthony Kennedy, Stevens agreed with much of the majority's reasoning, conceding that California could constitutionally restrict the arrestee data in its entirety, or even "release the information on a selective basis to a limited group of users who have a special, and legitimate, need for the information."[113] But Stevens found that the state's scheme—making the information available to scholars, news media, politicians, and others, while denying access to a narrow category of persons *solely* because they intend to use the information for a constitutionally protected purpose[114]—was a form of unconstitutional discrimination.

Los Angeles Police Department is troubling, because it holds that the government can set conditions on access based on the subsequent use of any information gleaned from the databases. Yet, unlike in the *Reporters Committee* opinion, the Court failed to address the underlying privacy interest that had been the rationale California had asserted before the Ninth Circuit. As the Ninth Circuit held and Justice Stevens argued in his dissent, the majority opinion grants states virtually unlimited deference, allowing them to set arguably irrational conditions before granting access to public data.[115] Here, there was no rational link between protecting privacy and the statutory regulation: The information could be published in one source but not another.[116]

Condon v. Reno: Information as a Commodity

In *Condon v. Reno*,[117] the Court unanimously rejected a Tenth Amendment challenge by the state of South Carolina to a federal regulatory scheme affecting state motor vehicle databases. The federal Driver's Privacy Protection Act (DPPA) required all state agencies responsible for maintaining drivers and motor vehicle records to prohibit the indiscriminate release of such information to the general public no later than September 14, 1997.[118] The statute, however, allowed certain public and private actors such as courts,[119] law enforcement officers,[120] insurance companies,[121] tow-truck operators,[122] and commercial trucking employers[123] to continue to have access to motor vehicle records. By a subsequent amendment, DPPA also prohibited states from disclosing records to mass marketers unless citizens had consented to "opt in" such mass distributions.[124] Finally, the statute authorized the U.S. Attorney General to impose fines on states that improperly disseminated driver or vehicle records to an unauthorized party,[125] and gave individuals the right to sue authorized recipients who released personal information contained in the records to unauthorized third parties.[126]

State governments reacted differently to the enactment of DPPA. Whereas some states welcomed DPPA as a means of reducing administrative workload,[127] others feared that DPPA compliance would impose significant financial burdens.[128] Many states would be compelled to enact conforming legislation to comply with DPPA because driving and motor vehicle records had generally been considered public information under their open records laws.[129] A few states had sold these records to commercial requesters, providing a steady source of income that often netted millions of dollars annually.[130] Rather than incur huge expenses and sustain the loss of significant revenue, several states challenged this regulatory scheme as unconstitutional under the Tenth Amendment.[131]

In defending these cases, the federal government had advanced two arguments on the constitutionality of DPPA. First, the government argued that under the Fourteenth Amendment Congress can remedy state abuses of civil rights; here, DPPA enforced a constitutional right of privacy that "automobile owners and operators [reasonably expected in] their names, addresses, and phone numbers."[132] The Seventh and Tenth Circuits did not even reach this question,[133] and the Fourth and Eleventh Circuits categorically rebuffed this argument,[134] consistent with prior Supreme Court rulings rejecting such an expansive reading of the Fourteenth Amendment.[135] The Fourth Circuit noted as an initial matter that "there is no general right to privacy" guaranteed by the Constitution.[136] The Supreme Court had recognized a right to privacy only in such intimate areas as reproduction, contraception, and marriage, the court said.[137] These areas generally concern the sanctity of the home, thus carrying a corresponding "reasonable expectation of privacy."[138] No such expectation exists in the personal information contained in a motor vehicle

record, because individuals routinely provide identical information in daily transactions. Moreover, driving is a highly regulated field, and motor vehicle records
have generally been considered public.[139]

Similarly, the Eleventh Circuit held, without significant comment, that DPPA
was not constitutional under the Fourteenth Amendment.[140] Although the court
conceded a "right to confidentiality" in personal information, it did not find that
such a right extended to information contained in DMV records.[141]

The federal government relied solely on its second argument—that DPPA was a
constitutional exercise of congressional power under the Commerce Clause—in
defending the constitutionality of the statute before the Supreme Court.[142] The
Court agreed with this Commerce Clause argument, finding that DPPA did not violate the Tenth Amendment. Distinguishing its rulings in earlier Tenth Amendment
challenges, the Court found that DPPA "regulate[d] state activities, rather than
seek[ing] to control or influence the manner in which States regulate private parties."[143] The Court conceded that many states might have to amend their statutes and
administrative regulations, but such changes were "an inevitable consequence of
regulating a state activity."[144]

The Court ruled that the South Carolina driver and vehicle registry was not a
unique state function, finding no discernible distinction between a state or a company
owning and operating a database. Although South Carolina argued that the federal
government was commandeering its administrative functions, the Court rejected this
contention, noting that the federal government had the power to regulate a
state-owned public database just as it could regulate a database owned by a private
company. To the *Condon* Court, personal information is a mere commodity, susceptible to federal regulation in the stream of commerce just like any other "widget." Concluding that DPPA is a "generally applicable law," the federal government "regulates
the universe of entities that participate as suppliers to the market for motor vehicle information—the States as initial suppliers of the information in interstate commerce
and private resellers or redisclosers of that information in commerce."[145] Thus, states
lose their unique status as sovereign owners and operators of databases and can be
regulated by the federal government as any other holder of information would be.

In the wake of the *Condon* decision, many commentators remarked that the decision was a rare victory for the federal government over states' rights. Few focused
on the underlying First Amendment issues that had yet to be addressed. Perhaps because the federal government chose not to raise a Fourteenth Amendment argument
before the high court, the *Condon* opinion is extremely short, and fails to say very
much about how to balance the competing interests of privacy and access.[146]

THE PUSH FOR PRIVACY

The *Condon* and *Los Angeles Police Department* decisions suggest that the Supreme Court is willing to grant both federal and state governments considerable autonomy in regulating the storage and collection of personal information, as well as
its subsequent dissemination, without much concern for the First Amendment im-

plications of those regulations. These decisions may encourage legislatures to close off all government-held information to the public rather than attempt to initiate a complicated and potentially expensive regulatory scheme.[147]

Furthermore, *Condon*, as well as the lower courts' decisions upholding DPPA, implicitly recognize that the federal government enjoys considerable power under the Commerce Clause to regulate privately held databases.[148] However, until comparatively recently the federal government has been reluctant to adopt regulations governing data held by private companies,[149] prompting privacy advocates on both the domestic and international fronts to criticize to this purported lack of statutory safeguards as an infringement on individual privacy.

The difference between the American and European concepts of privacy is profound. Whereas the Supreme Court has not recognized privacy as a fundamental right, Europeans regard privacy as a basic human right.[150] As a consequence of elevating privacy to this fundamental status, European nations have severely curtailed the "freedom of expression and the activities of the press and other authors and artists."[151] Where the First Amendment in the United States recognizes the necessity and importance of free expression, even over other interests such as privacy, Europeans would argue that individuals cannot truly engage in free expression if someone else is collecting information on them without their knowledge and consent.[152] In fact, Europeans had established privacy laws long before Brandeis and Warren wrote their influential law review article calling for privacy torts.[153] European nations were among the first to pass stringent privacy protections[154] delegating to government bureaucracies massive regulatory power.[155] Such privacy regulations also shift an enormous financial burden onto both the private and public sector.[156] At least one commentator has suggested that Europeans' heightened concerns regarding data privacy and government databases stem from the massive human rights violations that accompanied Nazi occupation in the 1930s and 1940s.[157]

By contrast, the United States' approach to privacy regulation has generally been sectoral, even within the government itself.[158] For example, there is no federal oversight commission to monitor the databases kept by various federal agencies; each agency is expected to police itself.[159] Although President Carter advocated the creation of a privacy commission,[160] subsequent administrations either gave short shrift to privacy concerns[161] or actively opposed initiatives to regulate the private sector.[162] Instead, the United States has favored allowing companies to freely collect and trade consumer data.[163] American companies, particularly those involved in e-commerce, argue that consumers ultimately benefit from such exchanges because the free flow of information allows companies to provide consumers with personalized services according to their preferences.[164]

These striking differences have created a major obstacle in international trade negotiations between the European Union and the United States. It is well known that many American companies routinely collect, store, and even trade data on customers, including names, addresses, and preferences.[165] However, American companies operating in Europe or trading with European companies were recently threatened with severe limitations on their data-collection practices by the EU Data Protection Directive.[166]

The Directive supersedes member nations' own approaches to addressing privacy concerns to create a common scheme binding on the entire European Union.[167] The Directive defines "personal information" as any data that identifies an individual, including such common identifiers as names, telephone numbers, and addresses.[168] Individuals or companies that use, disclose "by transmission," disseminate, or "otherwise mak[e] available" personal information about others are subject to government regulation.[169] Individuals who wish to obtain records containing personal information must explain their purpose for obtaining such information.[170] The subject of the record has the right to be notified, to approve the use of his/her information, and to impose conditions on using that information.[171] These conditions apply not only to the individual making the initial request but also are binding on any subsequent recipients of the information.[172]

After the passage of the Data Directive, the Clinton Administration urged the European Union to accept a government-created "safe-harbor" principle that would allow American companies to continue to voluntarily "self-regulate."[173] European officials had long worried that "self-regulation was some kind of fox guarding the chicken coop."[174] Nevertheless, by March 2000 it appeared a rapprochement would be reached. Despite a resolution adopted by the European Parliament on July 5, 2000, that questioned the adequacy of the provisions,[175] the European Commission approved the Safe Harbor Privacy Principles on July 27, 2000.[176]

Under the Safe Harbor agreement, a company in the United States may choose one of four means of complying with the Directive: subjecting itself to the authority of one of the European Union members' data protection agencies; demonstrating that it is subject to federal privacy laws that are similar to the Directive; agreeing to be monitored by a self-regulatory organization that is under the oversight of the Federal Trade Commission, or agreeing to have privacy disputes heard by European regulators.[177]

A qualifying organization may disclose personal information to third parties only if it has notified individuals "about the purposes for which it collects and uses information about them, how to contact the organization with any inquiries or complaints, the types of third parties to which it discloses the information, and the choices and means the organization offers individuals for limiting its use and disclosure."[178] But even if the organization has not provided individuals with a choice, it can still release information to a third party provided that the third party also qualifies under the "safe harbor" provision, is subject to the Directive, or "enters into a written agreement with such third party requiring that the third party provide at least the same level of privacy protection as is required by the relevant principles."[179] The organization must also give an individual the right to access, review, and correct any information it holds on him/her unless "the burden or expense of providing access would be disproportionate to the risks to the individual's privacy in the case in question, or where the rights of persons other than the individual would be violated."[180]

On February 13, 2002, the European Commission released a Staff Working Paper on the implementation of the Safe Harbor Agreement.[181] The report, although noting that few complaints have been filed, states that a "substantial number" of U.S. companies have failed to comply with the transparency requirement of the Safe Harbor principles. Moreover, the report finds that very few American companies are participating in the Safe Harbor agreement. Nevertheless, the report demonstrates that the EU is reluctant to confront the United States over privacy issues. Despite the major deficiencies found in implementation, the report attributes the lapses to "teething problems."[182]

Although privacy as defined by the federal judiciary and the Clinton administration may be at odds with the European concept, contemporary American social views on privacy are moving very much in alignment with the European Directive. As more and more Americans want to use the Internet,[183] they are voicing concerns on how Internet use is being monitored.[184] Facing investigations by state and federal regulators and sharp criticism by privacy advocates,[185] Internet analyst Doubleclick.net bowed to public pressure and agreed to abandon its plans to adopt technology that would allow it to match Web surfers against personal identifiers.[186]

Even if privacy may not be the top political issue at the federal level, many state legislatures and attorney generals have jumped on the privacy bandwagon.[187] For example, New York Attorney General Eliot Spitzer filed privacy suits against Chase Manhattan[188] and Doubleclick.net,[189] and in 1999 Minnesota Attorney General Mike Hatch settled a case against US Bank for illegally selling customer data to third parties.[190] As a political issue, privacy as a concept seems as unassailable as motherhood and apple pie, yet some commentators have suggested that it may nevertheless suffer from the "free rider" syndrome. Because it is such an amorphous and diffuse concept, they contend, few people are really willing to lobby for it.[191]

PRIVACY POSES PROBLEMS FOR NEWS GATHERING IN THE UNITED STATES

When the Supreme Court first began to consider privacy in the context of competing access rights for journalists, it seemed to suggest: "Do your own homework." In other words, although not inclined to give journalists a free pass into government databases, even though they contained information assembled from documents accessible to everyone, journalists would still be free to assemble the raw data themselves. But *Condon* and *Los Angeles Police Department,* coupled with increasing pressure to comply with the EU Data Directive, pose a serious threat to database journalism, and indeed to any kind of investigative journalism based on gaining access to public records containing personally identifiable information. Tapping into such data has become much more problematic. If databases—even those compiled and maintained by states and the federal government, and containing information that formerly was wholly public—are simply another type of commercial property, then data custodians can be compelled to follow complex, Byzantine regulations, lest they be shut down completely. Although the recent Supreme Court decisions address regulation of *public* databases, clearly Congress has considerable power to regulate private databases through the Commerce Clause.[192] Now that the EU Directive has been implemented, one wonders how American consumers will react when they learn that American companies grant European consumers substantially greater privacy than they do to their U.S. counterparts.[193]

Furthermore, *Condon* and *Los Angeles Police Department* essentially grant governments a way to circumvent the "legally obtained" holding of the *Florida Star* line of cases. (*Florida Star* recognized that journalists cannot be punished for the use of accidentally released information.) But *Condon* and *Los Angeles Police Department* allow databases owners to inquire into intended use, and to condition release of data based on the recipient's stated purpose. Although neither case reached the question of whether imposition of conditional access requirements can amount to unconstitutional prohibitions on core speech, the Court in *Los Angeles Police Department* upheld access restrictions that had the effect of prohibiting commercial speech, which receives lesser First Amendment protection.

Perhaps more important, these decisions raise the specter of journalists themselves facing prosecution for violating regulatory privacy schemes. In a sense, a journalist engaged in routine news gathering becomes a sort of database, and arguably, at least absent a specific exemption, would be required to follow both domestic and possibly international rules for collection, retention, storage, and dissemination of personal information. European nations have shown that they are more willing to aggressively police media outlets such as the Internet than is constitutionally possible in the United States.[194]

However, regulatory schemes such as the "safe harbor" provision do not adequately consider the needs and concerns of journalists.[195] Given the differing European perceptions of the roles of privacy and the press, perhaps it is not surprising that the Directive itself does not recognize the freedom and integrity of the media by absolutely exempting news gathering from its application. However, the American "safe harbor" does distinguish the role of the media, an institution ingrained both in American culture and constitutional jurisprudence.[196] Requiring journalists to alert the subjects of an investigation and allow them to "opt out" of a news story would impair the investigative function of the media. Frequently, journalists must gather copious amounts of data and then find the proverbial needle in a haystack of random facts and tangential information. Although the U.S. Department of Commerce has promised that "[p]ersonal information that is gathered for publication, broadcast, or other forms of public communication of journalistic material, whether used or not, as well as information found in previously published material disseminated from media archives, will not be subject to the requirements of the safe harbor principles,"[197] how this seemingly intractable conflict will ultimately be resolved remains to be seen.

NOTES

[1] See *U.S. News and World Report v. Avrahami*, 1996 WL 1065557 1 (Va. Cir. Ct) (June 13, 1996). Avrahami had been employed in several direct marketing projects for the long-distance provider Sprint.

[2]*Ibid.*, 2.

[3]See *Avrahami Trial Brief,* available at <http://www.epic.org/privacy/junk_mail/trial_brief.txt> (last visited February 8, 2002).

[4]See *U.S. News and World Report v. Avrahami*, 1996 WL 1065557, 2.

[5]*Ibid.*, 1.

[6]*Ibid.*, 2.

[7]*Ibid.*, 3.

[8]*Ibid.*, 5. These organizations had targeted him in part to information Avrahami had supplied to *U.S. News and World Report*, including his annual earnings.

[9]Va. Code Ann. Sec. 8.01-40(A) (Michie 1995).

[10]See *Avrahami Trial Brief, supra* note 3.

[11]*U.S. News & World Report v. Avrahami*, 1996 WL 1065557 p.7 (Va. Cir. Ct.) (June 13, 1996).

[12]*Ibid.*, 2.

[13]*Whalen v. Roe*, 429 U.S. 589, at 606–07 (Brennan, J., concurring).

[14]M. Wald, "Fearing Hackers, Environmental Agency Halts Access to Web Site," *The New York Times* A23 (February 18, 2000); M. Richtel, "Spread of Attacks on Web Sites Is Slowing Traffic on the Internet," *The New York Times* A1 (February 10, 2000).

[15]J. Guidera, "FTC Reviews Privacy Issues at Health Web Sites," *The Wall Street Journal* B6 (February 18, 2000); J. Clausing, "Health Web Sites Fail to Keep Personal Data Private, Study Finds," *The New York Times* A19 (February 2, 2000).

[16]See *infra* part III.

[17]See *infra* notes 183–187.

[18]See, e.g., *Whalen v. Roe*, 429 U.S. 589, at 607–608 (1989) (Stewart, J., concurring), noting "the Court made clear that although the Constitution affords protection against certain kinds of government intrusion into personal and private matters, there is no general constitutional 'right to privacy'" (quoting *Katz v. United States*, 389 U.S. 347, at 350 (1967)).

[19]Cf. *United States Dep't of Justice v. Reporters Committee for Freedom of the Press*, 489 U.S. 749, at 762 n. 13: "The question of the statutory meaning of privacy under the [Freedom of Information Act] is, of course, not the same as the question whether a tort action might lie for invasion of privacy or the question whether an individual's interest in privacy is protected by the Constitution."

[20]Compare *American Federation of Government Employees v. HUD*, 118 F.3d 786, at 791 (D.C.Cir. 1997)—"We begin our analysis by expressing our grave doubts as to the existence of a constitutional right of privacy in the nondisclosure of personal information"—with *Doe v. Southeastern Pennsylvania Trans. Auth.*, 886 F. Supp. 1186 (E.D.Pa. 1994), aff'd 72 F.3d 1133 (3d Cir. 1995), holding that government's need for an individual's personal information must be balanced against his/her privacy interests.

[21]See, e.g., David M. O'Brien, *Privacy, Law and Public Policy vii–ix* (1979), offering anecdotal examples such as the refusal of officials at the U.S. Embassy in Moscow to release the name of a visiting American citizen who died in an accident, because they believed the Privacy Act, 5 U.S.C. Sec. 552(a) (1994), prohibited them from making such a disclosure.

[22]See, e.g., R. H. Coase, *The Market for Goods and the Market for Ideas*, 64 Am. Ec. Rev. 384 (1974); Harry Kalven, Jr., *The New York Times Case: A Note on "The Central Meaning of the First Amendment,"* 1964 Sup. Ct. Rev. 191.

[23]The development of privacy tort theory owes much to an influential article written by Louis Brandeis & Samuel D. Warren, *The Right to Privacy*, 4 Harv. L. Rev. 193 (1890).

[24]Kathleen M. Sullivan & Gerald Gunther, *The First Amendment* 86 (1999).

[25]See *Restatement (Second) of Torts* Sec. 625B (1977).

[26]*Ibid.*, Sec. 652D.

[27]*Ibid.*, Sec. 652E.

[28]*Ibid.*, Sec. 652C.

[29]See *Time, Inc. v. Hill*, 385 U.S. 374 (1967); *Florida Star v. B.J.F.*, 491 U.S. 524 (1989); cf. *Hustler Magazine v. Falwell*, 485 U.S. 46 (1988).

[30]See Fred Cate, *Privacy in the Information Age* 70 (1997); Peter B. Edelman, *Free Press v. Privacy: Haunted by the Ghost of Justice Black*, 68 Tex. L. Rev. 1195, 1196–99 (1990).

[31]Fla. Stat. sec. 794.03 (1987).

[32]*Florida Star v. B.J.F.*, 491 U.S. 524, at 526 (1989). Although a trainee reporter had unknowingly recorded the information from police records, the paper violated its own internal policy by publishing the information (*ibid.*, 527–528). The Duval County Sheriff's Department, which had erroneously included the victim's full name on public reports, settled with B.J.F. prior to suit (*ibid.*, 528).

[33]*Ibid.*, 534.

[34]*Ibid.*

[35]*Ibid.*, 535.

[36]*Ibid.*, 538.

[37]*Ibid.*, 536. The Court also noted that the media had a unique role in "subjecting trials to public scrutiny and thereby helping guarantee their fairness" (*ibid.*, 532) and should be protected from regulations that would led to self-censorship (*ibid.*, 538).

[38]45 F.3d 1383 (10th Cir. 1995).

[39]*Ibid.*, 1386.

[40]*Ibid.*

[41]*Ibid.* The court noted that the "Salt Lake County Attorney's Office had an unwritten policy that permitted its employees to speak to members of the press about their cases once an investigation closed."

[42]*Ibid.*, 1386, 1388.

[43]*Ibid.*, 1386.

[44]*Ibid.*

[45]*Ibid.*, 1388.

[46]*Ibid.*, 1388–89; see *Fadjo v. Coon*, 633 F.2d 1172, at 1175 (5th Cir. 1981): "even if the information was properly obtained [by the State Attorney], the state may have invaded Fadjo's privacy in revealing it."

[47]Thomas M. Cooley, *A Treatise on the Law of Torts* 29 (2d ed. 1888).

[48]Compare *Martin v. City of Struthers*, 319 U.S. 141 (1943) (striking down an ordinance that prohibited handbilling at private residences) with *Stanley v. Georgia*, 394 U.S. 557 (1969) (pornography in the home) and *Griswold v. Connecticut*, 381 U.S. 479 (1965) (contraceptives in the home). But cf. *Bolger v. Youngs Drug Products Corp.*, 463 U.S. 60, at 72 (1983): "But we have never held that the government itself can shut off the flow of mailings to protect those recipients who might potentially be offended.... Consequently, the 'short, though regular journey from mail box to trash can ... is an acceptable burden, at least so far as the Constitution is concerned'" (citation omitted).

[49]See, for example, *Pierce v. Society of Sisters*, 268 U.S. 510 (1925); *Meyer v. Nebraska*, 262 U.S. 390 (1923).

[50]See, for example, *Griswold v. Connecticut*, 381 U.S. 479 (1965); *Roe v. Wade*, 410 U.S. 113 (1973).

[51]See *Pennsylvania v. Mimms*, 434 U.S. 106, at 108–09 (1977): "The touchstone of our analysis under the Fourth Amendment is always 'the reasonableness in all the circumstances of the particular governmental invasion of a citizen's personal security'" (quoting *Terry v. Ohio*, 392 U.S. 1, at 19 (1968)). For the purposes of this chapter, however, the Fourth Amendment is only interesting because it provides another means of analyzing how the Supreme Court treats privacy.

[52]See, for example, *Katz v. United States*, 389 U.S. 347 (1967), finding that, under the Fourth Amendment, an individual has a reasonable expectation to privacy while using a pay phone.

[53]3*Rakas v. Illinois*, 439 U.S. 128, at 143–44, n.12 (1978).

[54]See *United States v. Place*, 462 U.S. 696 (1983).

[55]See *Florida v. Bostick*, 501 U.S. 429 (1991).

[56]See, for example, *E.B. v. Verniero*, 119 F.3d 1077 (3d Cir. 1997), upholding constitutionality of Megan's law, forcing disclosure of sex offenders, cert. denied, 522 U.S. 1110 (1998); Amitai Etzioni, *The Limits of Privacy* 56–57 (1999); see *United States Dep't of Justice v. Reporters Committee for Freedom of the Press*, 489 U.S. 749, at 774 (1989), finding an individual's right to privacy in government rap sheets trumps the "public interest in anyone's criminal history" in rejecting a FOIA request for FBI criminal identification records.

[57]See *U.S. v. Westinghouse Electric Corp.*, 638 F.2d 570 (3d Cir. 1980); *U.S. v. Allis-Chalmers Corp.*, 498 F. Supp. 1027 (E.D. Wis. 1980); Hayley Rosenman, *Patients' Rights to Access Their Medical Records: An Argument for Uniform Recognition of a Right of Access in the United States and Australia,* 21 Fordham Int'l L.J. 1500 (1998).

[58]See *Walls v. City of Petersburg*, 895 F.2d 188 (2d Cir. 1990); *Fraternal Order of Police v. City of Philadelphia*, 812 F.2d 105 (3d Cir. 1987).

[59]The public sector has invested heavily in technology in hopes of reducing storage costs and promoting efficiency. See Mark E. Budnitz, *Privacy Protection for Consumer Transactions in Electronic Commerce: Why Self-Regulation Is Inadequate*, 49 S.C. L. Rev. 847, 872–74 (1998), noting the public sector's increasing reliance on "smart cards" and other technological advances to distribute benefits to individuals allows government employees greater access to personal, private information. Although such an investment may save money by reducing paper waste, "human capital," and storage costs, it is unknown whether states will take security measures to ensure the validity and security of collected information.

[60]*Reporters Committee for Freedom of the Press*, 489 U.S. at 770.

[61]*Whalen v. Roe*, 429 U.S. 589, at 605 (1977).

[62]429 U.S. 589 (1977).

[63]See N.Y. Health Law Sec. 3300 et seq. (McKinney Supp. 1976–77).

[64]*Whalen*, 429 U.S. at 600.

[65]*Ibid.* See also *ibid.*, 595 n. 16, which discusses the testimony of doctors, patients, and patients' families who feared the social stigma attached to taking prescription drugs.

[66]*Supra* note 65.

[67]*Whalen*, 429 U.S. at 591–92, attempting to find an effective means "to prevent the use of stolen or revised prescriptions, to prevent unscrupulous pharmacists from repeatedly refilling prescriptions, to prevent users from obtaining prescriptions from more than one doctor, or to prevent doctors from over-prescribing." New York had adopted a registry scheme similar to regulatory plans adopted by California and Illinois, (*ibid.*, 592).

[68]*Ibid.*, 597; see also *ibid.*, 598, declaring the state's interest "vital."

[69]*Ibid.*, 600–01.

[70]*Whalen*, 429 U.S. at 605.

[71]See *supra* notes 57–59 and accompanying text.

[72]See *Doe v. Attorney General of United States*, 941 F.2d 780 (9th Cir. 1991) (adopting a balancing approach to a nondisclosure claim) and *Tavoulareas v. Washington Post Comp.*, 724 F.2d 1010, at 1022–23 (D.C.Cir. 1984) (same); see *United States v. Westinghouse*, 638 F.2d 570, at p. 578 (3d Cir. 1980), which develops seven factors to be considered when weighing a privacy claim of disclosure. The circuits are split on the standard of review privacy claims about disclosure should receive. See *Cate*, *supra* note 30, 64, which notes that the 2nd, 3rd, 5th, and 9th Circuits review *Whalen*-type scenarios under a seemingly higher standard but that the 4th and 6th Circuits limit *Whalen* severely.

[73]See, for example, *Shoemaker v. Handel*, 795 F.2d 1136, at p. 1144 (3d Cir. 1986), determining that the New Jersey horse racing commission's testing plan adequately protected jockeys' privacy rights but "[i]f the Commission ceases to comply with the proposed confidentiality rules, the jockeys may return to court with a new lawsuit." See also Flavio L. Komuves, *We've Got Your Number: An Overview of Legislation and Decisions to Control the Use of Social Security Numbers as Personal Identifiers*, 16 J. Marshall J. Computer & Info. L. 529 (1998), discussing a growing judicial recognition of an individual's privacy in personal identifiers such as Social Security numbers, but noting a lack of judicial remedies for improper use of such identifiers.

[74]See *Mangels v. Pena*, 789 F.2d 836, at 839 (10th Cir. 1986): "Information is constitutionally protected when a legitimate expectation exists that it will remain confidential while in the state's possession." Most citizens, however, believe that information stored electronically will not remain confidential. Such a conclusion is not unreasonable, because anecdotal evidence about "hacking" and identity theft demonstrates. See *Cate*, *supra* note 30, 203, which notes that 90% of Americans surveyed by a *USA Today* poll believe that data-collecting agencies should develop and bear the expense of privacy-friendly "opt-in" systems; *Budnitz*, *supra* note 59, 874–79, which discusses problems in self-regulatory methods.

[75]489 U.S. 749 (1989).

[76]*Ibid.*, 757.

[77]*Ibid.*

[78]*Ibid.*, 759–60.

[79]*Ibid.*, 760.

[80]Much of the information in the FBI registry did not originate from federal sources but instead was originally compiled by state and local law enforcement and correctional agencies (*ibid.*, 751–52).

[81]*United States Dep't of Justice v. Reporters Committee for Freedom of the Press*, 489 U.S. 749, at 764 (1989).

[82]*Ibid.*, 770 (citation omitted).

[83]See *Reporters Committee for Freedom of the Press*, 489 U.S. at 761, quoting *United States Dep't of Justice v. Reporters Committee for Freedom of the Press*, 831 F.2d 1124, at 1130 (1987) (dissenting opinion).

[84]See *Reporters Committee for Freedom of the Press*, 489 U.S. at 780 (Blackmun, J., concurring). For example, Justice Blackmun argued that the public should have access to "a rap sheet [that] discloses a congressional candidate's conviction of tax fraud five years before" (*ibid.*). The candidate could not possibly argue that he had an expectation of privacy because, as a public figure, he would invite inquiry into his character and background.

[85]*Ibid.*, 771.

[86]*Ibid.*, 780.

[87]120 S. Ct. 483 (1999).

[88]*Ibid.* (quoting Cal. Govt. Code Sec. 6254(f)(3) (West Supp. 1999)).

[89]*Ibid.*, 486 (quoting Cal. Govt. Code Sec. 6254(f) (West 1995)).

[90]*Ibid.*

[91]The statute exempted investigative, "scholarly, journalistic, political, or governmental" purposes; Cal Government Code Sec. 6254(f)(3).

[92]*Los Angeles Police Dep't*, 120 S. Ct. at 486.

[93]See *United Reporting Publishing Corp. v. California Highway Patrol*, 146 F.3d 1133, at 1135 (9th Cir. 1998).

[94]*Ibid.*, 1136–37. The Supreme Court has recognized that commercial speech is entitled to some constitutional protection because society "may have a strong interest in the free flow of commercial information." See *Virginia Pharmacy Bd. v. Virginia Consumer Council*, 425 U.S. 748, at 764 (1975). But "commercial speech [is entitled to] less protection from governmental regulation than some other forms of expression." See *United Reporting* 146 F.3d 1133 at 1136. See also *California Highway Patrol*, 146 F.3d at 1136, relying on *United States v. Edge Broadcasting*, 509 U.S. 418 (1993); *Ohralik v. Ohio State Bar Ass'n*, 436 U.S. 447, at 455–56 (1977): "We have not discarded the 'common-sense' distinction between speech proposing a commercial transaction, which occurs in an area traditionally subject to government regulation, and other varieties of speech"; *Virginia Pharmacy Bd.*, 425 U.S. at 771, recognizing the government's interest in preventing false, misleading, or deceptive commercial speech.

[95]See *California Highway Patrol*, 146 F.3d at 1136.

[96]*Ibid.*, 1137, quoting *Virginia State Bd. of Pharmacy v. Virginia Citizens Consumer Council, Inc.*, 425 U.S. 748, at 762 (1976) (alterations in original).

[97]*Ibid.*, 1136, quoting *Zauderer v. Office of Disciplinary Counsel*, 471 U.S. 626, at 637 (1985).

[98]447 U.S. 557 (1980). The four prongs require a court to determine whether the speech concerns lawful activity and is not misleading; whether the asserted government interest is substantial; "whether the regulation directly advances the governmental interest asserted"; and whether the regulation "is not more extensive than is necessary to serve that interest." See *United Reporting*, 146 F.3d at 1137, quoting from *Central Hudson*, 447 U.S. at 566.

[99]*Ibid.*, 1139.

[100]*Ibid.*, 1140.

[101]*Ibid.*

[102]*Los Angeles Police Dep't*, 120 S. Ct. at 489.

[103]*Ibid.*, 489.

[104]*Ibid.*, 489. However, California could not prohibit United Publishing from disseminating the information if the company obtained the same information through alternate means. See also *ibid.*, 490 (Ginsburg, J., concurring): "Anyone who comes upon arrestee address information in the public domain is free to use that information as she sees fit"); *Florida Star v. B.J.F.*, 491 U.S. 524, at 541 (1989); John A. McWhirter & Jon D. Bible, *Privacy as a Constitutional Right: Sex, Drugs, and the Right to Life* 84–85 (1992). It is not entirely clear, however, if the Chief Justice meant to say that California could close off its records completely to the public. Such a statement, even in dictum, would conflict with prior judicial holdings on access to criminal records. See, for example, *Richmond Newspapers, Inc. v. Virginia*, 448 U.S. 555, at 575–76 (1980) (access to criminal proceedings and transcripts); *Press-Enterprise Co. v. Superior Court*, 464 U.S. 501 (1984); *Sheridan Newspapers, Inc. v. City of Sheridan*, 660 P.2d 785 (Wyo. 1983).

[105]*Ibid.*, 490 (Ginsburg, J., concurring).

[106]*Ibid.*, 491.

[107]*Ibid.*

[108]*Ibid.*

[109]*Ibid.*, 490 (Scalia, J., concurring).

[110]*Ibid.*

[111]*Ibid.*

[112]*Ibid.*

[113]*Ibid.*, 492 (Stevens, J., dissenting).

[114]*Ibid.*, 492 (Stevens, J., dissenting).

[115]*Ibid.*, 492–93: "By allowing such widespread access to the information, the State has eviscerated any rational basis for believing that the [amended statute] will truly protect the privacy of these persons" (relying on *Greater News Orleans Broadcasting Ass'n, Inc. v. United States*, 527 U.S. 173 (1999); *Rubin v. Coors Brewing Co.*, 514 U.S. 476 (1995)).

[116]*Ibid.* See *Florida Star v. B.J.F.*, 491 U.S. 524, at 542 (1989): "This law has every appearance of a prohibition that society is prepared to impose upon the press but not upon itself."

[117]120 S. Ct. 666 (2000.

[118]Pub. L. 103-322, Sec. 300003.

[119]18 U.S.C.A. Sec. 2721(b)(4).

[120]18 U.S.C.A. Sec. 2721(b)(1).

[121]18 U.S.C.A. Sec. 2721(b)(6).

[122]18 U.S.C.A. Sec. 2721(b)(7).

[123]18 U.S.C.A. Sec. 2721(b)(9).

[124]See Pub. L. 106-69 Sec. 350.

[125]18 U.S.C.A. Sec. 2723(b): "Any State department of motor vehicles that has a policy or practice of substantial noncompliance ... shall be subject to a civil penalty imposed by the Attorney General of not more than $5,000 a day for each day of substantial noncompliance."

[126]18 U.S.C.A. Sec. 2724(a–b): An individual whose personal information is wrongfully disseminated can bring a private cause of action against a "person who knowingly obtains, discloses or uses personal information ... for a purpose not permitted by DPPA." From 18 U.S.C.A. Sec. 2724(a). A court may award actual damages (capped at $2,500), punitive damages, reasonable attorney and other litigation fees, and any other equitable relief within the court's discretion. From 18 U.S.C.A. Sec. 2724(b).

[127]See John Yacavone, "Is Your State Prepared to Implement the Driver's Privacy Protection Act?" *Move* 22, (Spring 1997).

[128]See *Oklahoma v. United States*, 994 F. Supp. 1358, at 1362 (W.D. Okla. 1997); *Condon v. Reno*, 972 F. Supp. 977, at 981 (D.S.C. 1997), finding that "the implementation of the DPPA would impose substantial costs."

[129]See Yacavone, 22.

[130]*Ibid.*, 22–23; David Beatty, "Protect Motorists' Privacy," *USA Today* A10 (April 14, 1994): "In most states (37, to be exact) anyone can walk into a motor vehicle office with your tag number ... and get your name, address and phone number—no questions asked." John Gibeaut, *Keeping Federalism Alive: Courts Overturn Law Barring State Release of Driver Record*, A.B.A. J., 38 (January 1998).

[131]See *Pryor v. Reno*, 998 F. Supp. 1317 (M.D. Ala. 1998), holding constitutional, rev'd, 171 F.3d 1281 (11th Cir. 1999); *Travis v. Reno*, 12 F. Supp.2d 921 (W.D. Wis. 1998), holding unconstitutional, rev'd, 163 F.3d 1000 (7th Cir. 1998); *Oklahoma v. U.S.*, 994 F. Supp., 1358, rev'd, 161 F.3d 1266 (10th Cir. 1998); *Condon v. Reno*, 972 F. Supp., 977, holding unconstitutional, aff'd, 155 F.3d 453 (4th Cir. 1998), rev'd, 120 S. Ct. 666 (2000). See also *Loving v.*

U.S., 1997 U.S. App. LEXIS 23639 (10th Cir. Sept. 8, 1997), dismissing a First Amendment claim for lack of standing.

[132]See *Condon v. Reno*, 155 F.3d 453, at 464 (4th Cir. 1998) (citation omitted).

[133]See *Travis v. Reno*, 163 F.3d 1000, at 1007 (7th Cir. 1998); *Oklahoma v. United States*, 161 F.3d 1266, at 1273 n. 6 (10th Cir. 1998).

[134]See *Pryor v. Reno*, 171 F.3d 1281, at 1288 n. 10 (11th Cir. 1999); *Condon v. Reno*, 155 F.3d 453, at 464–65 (4th Cir. 1998).

[135]See *Condon*, 155 F.3d at 464, relying on *City of Boerne v. Flores*, 521 U.S. 507 (1997).

[136]*Ibid.*, 464, quoting *Whalen v. Roe*, 429 U.S. 589, at 608 (1977) (Stewart, J., concurring).

[137]*Ibid.*

[138]*Ibid.*

[139]*Ibid.*, 465.

[140]See *Pryor v. Reno*, 171 F. 3d 1281, at 1288 n. 10.

[141]*Ibid.* The Eleventh Circuit held that such a right to confidentiality existed "only for intimate personal information given to a state official in confidence," but the information contained in a driver or vehicle record was not of such an intimate nature. See *ibid.*, offering *James v. City of Douglas*, 941 F.2d 1539 (11th Cir. 1991), as an example.

[142]*Reno v. Condon*, 120 S. Ct. 666, at 671 n. 2 (2000).

[143]*Ibid.*, 672, quoting *South Carolina v. Baker*, 485 U.S. 505, 514–15 (1988).

[144]*Ibid.*, quoting *Baker*, 485 U.S. at 515.

[145]*Ibid.*, 672.

[146]Only one circuit considered a First Amendment challenge, rejecting it for lack of standing. See *Loving v. United States*, 1997 WL 572147 (10th Cir. Sept. 8, 1997).

[147]Cf. *Los Angeles Police Dep't v. United Reporting Publishing Corp.*, 120 S. Ct. 483, at p. 491 (1999) (Ginsburg, J., concurring).

[148]See *Condon v. Reno*, 120 S. Ct. 666, at 671 (2000); *Travis v. Reno*, 163 F.3d 1000, at 1005 (7th Cir. 1998): "[DPPA] affects states as owners of data, rather than as sovereigns.... [A state] is no more a regulator or law enforcer when it decides what information to release from its database than is the corner Blockbuster Video outlet" when it is subject to the Video Privacy Protection Act, 18 U.S.C. Sec. 2710 (1994).

[149]See *supra* notes 158, 162; cf. David Sanger and Jeri Clausing, "U.S. Removes More Limits on Encryption," *The New York Times* C1 (January 13, 2000), noting that privacy and technology concerns are politically sensitive as Vice President and Democratic presidential nominee Al Gore was seeking support from Silicon Valley technology companies.

[150]See *Cate*, *supra* note 30, 42–43; 1995 OJ L 281 [henceforth "Directive"], finding that "data- processing systems are designed to serve man" and "they must, whatever the nationality or residence of natural persons, respect their *fundamental* rights and freedoms, notably the right to privacy."

[151]*Ibid.*, 43.

[152]See Jane E. Kirtley, *The EU Data Protection Directive and the First Amendment: Why a 'Press Exemption' Won't Work*, 80 Iowa L. Rev. 639, 640 (1995); Paul M. Schwartz, *The Computer in German and American Constitutional Law: Towards an American Right of Informational Self-Determination*, 37 Am. J. Comp. L. 675 (1989).

[153]See Brandeis & Warren, *supra* note 23, 216 n. 1, citing an 1868 French statute that the authors used to support the proposition that "[s]ome things all men alike are entitled to keep from popular curiosity, whether in public life or not."

[154]See *Cate*, *supra* note 30, 47: "Europe is the site of the first privacy legislation, the earliest national privacy statute, and now the most comprehensive protection for information pri-

vacy in the world"; see also *ibid.*, 32, noting that 19 European nations and the European Union have legislated broad privacy protections.

[155]*Ibid.*, 33, discussing the powers of the French National Commission on Informatics and Liberties and the Swedish Data Inspection Board.

[156]*Ibid.*, 42–43, noting that the costs for banks to comply with European privacy initiatives "runs into millions."

[157]David Flaherty, *Protecting Privacy in Surveillance Societies* 373-74 (1989). Flaherty writes:

European data protection laws include the hidden agenda of discouraging a recurrence of the Nazi and Gestapo efforts to control the population, as so seek to prevent the reappearance of an oppressive bureaucracy that might use existing data for nefarious purposes. This concern is such a vital foundation of current legislation that it is rarely expressed in formal discussions. None wish to repeat the experiences endured under the Nazis during the Second World War.

[158]*Ibid., supra* note 157, 14, describing the American approach as "sector-by-sector." As implicitly suggested by *Condon*, the federal government has only stepped into the private sector to regulate the collection and dissemination of information as the need arises. See *Condon v. Reno*, 120 S. Ct. 666, at 672 (2000); *Travis v. Reno*, 163 F.3d 1000, at 1004–05 (7th Cir. 1998).

[159]*Ibid., supra* note 157, 315–16. Some limited oversight is provided by the Office of Management and Budget, congressional committees, and the judiciary; however, these agencies are generally reactive, not proactive.

[160]*Ibid.*, 319.

[161]*Ibid.*, 309, discussing the Carter Privacy Initiative, which would have regulated medical records, financial records, and news media notes and materials.

[162]*Ibid.*, discussing the Reagan administration's failure to address privacy issues in any "meaningful" way.

[163]See Glenn Simpson, "U.S., EU Negotiators Reach Agreement On Electronic-Commerce Privacy Rules," *The Wall Street Journal* B4 (March 15, 2000).

[164]See Brandon Mitchener & David Wessel, "U.S. in Tentative Pact Protecting Europeans' Privacy," *The Wall Street Journal* B6 (February 24, 2000).

[165]See, for example, Jeff Goodell, "Who Needs Privacy?" *Rolling Stone* 32 (March 30, 2000), noting how RealNetworks, an Internet music site, provided Internet users with free software to download music and then "surreptitiously" tracked and recorded their preferences.

[166]Directive, *supra* note 150.

[167]See *Cate, supra* note 30, 35–36. As noted, all the member nations have privacy statutes, but the Directive attempts to provide a uniform standard of protection.

[168]Directive, *supra* note 150, 2(a).

[169]*Ibid.*, 2(b).

[170]*Ibid.*, 18.

[171]*Ibid.*, 12.

[172]*Ibid.*, 15.

[173]See Electronic Commerce Task Force, International Trade Administration, U.S. Dep't of Commerce, Cover letter from Ambassador David L. Aaron to U.S. organizations requesting comments on the newly posted draft documents, available at <http://www.ita.doc.gov/td/ecom/aaron317.htm> (last visited March 1, 2000).

[174]Deborah Hargreaves, "Progress Made in Talks Over Data Privacy," *Financial Times* 8 (February 23, 2000).

[175]European Parliament, *Resolution on the Draft Commission Decision on the Adequacy of the Protection Provided by the Safe Harbour Privacy Principles and Related Frequently Asked Questions Issued by the U.S. Department of Commerce*, A4-0177/2000 (July 5, 2000).

[176]European Commission, *Decision Pursuant to Directive 95/26/EC of the European Parliament and of the Council on the Adequacy of the Protection Provided by the Safe Harbour Privacy Principles and Related Frequently Asked Questions Issued by the U.S. Department of Commerce* (July 27, 2000).

[177]See Electronic Commerce Task Force, International Trade Administration, U.S. Dep't of Commerce, International Safe Harbor Privacy Principles Issued by U.S. Department of Commerce, available at <http://www.export.gov/safeharbor/SHPRINCIPLESFINAL.htm> (last visited February 5, 2003).

[178]*Ibid.*

[179]*Ibid.*

[180]*Ibid.*

[181]Commission of the European Communities, Commission Staff Working Paper SEC (2002) 196, *The Application of Commission Decision 520/2000/EC of 26 July 2000 Pursuant to Directive 95/46 of the European Parliament and the Council on the Adequate Protection of Personal Data Provided by the Safe Harbour Privacy Principles and Related Frequently Asked Questions Issued by the U.S. Department of Commerce*, available at <http://www.europa.eu.int/comm/internal_market/en/dataprot/news/02-196_en.pdf>.

[182]*Ibid.*, 11.

[183]Internet access has become a major political issue: On the one hand, Democrats Bill Clinton and Al Gore pushed for ending the digital divide whereas Republican John McCain would have cut federal funding to schools and public libraries that did not install filtering programs for their public access Internet computers. Compare Marc Lacey, "Clinton Enlists Help for Plan to Increase Computer Use," *The New York Times* A25 (February 3, 2000) with K. Reed, "SC County Library Restricts Children's Access to Internet," *Freedom Forum*, available at <http://www.freedomforum.org> (last visited February 22, 2002) and Associated Press, "McCain: Libraries, Schools Should Filter Internet to Get Federal Funds," *Freedom Forum*, available at <http://www.freedomforum.org> (last visited February 22, 2002).

[184]See Jeri Clausing, "Report Rings Alarm Bells About Privacy On the Internet," *The New York Times* C10 (February 7, 2000); Glenn Simpson, "FTC Chief Says E-Commerce Industry Should Reconsider Privacy-Rules Stance," *The Wall Street Journal* B3 (February 11, 2000).

[185]See Jeri Clausing, "Privacy Advocates Fault New DoubleClick Service," *The New York Times* C2 (February 15, 2000); J. Guidera, "DoubleClick's Data-Collection Practices Are Investigated by FTC, New York," *The Wall Street Journal* B4 (February 16, 2000); B. Tedeschi, "Critics Press Legal Assault On Tracking Of Web Users," *The New York Times* C1 (February 7, 2000).

[186]See statement from Kevin O'Connor, CEO of Doubleclick, available at <http://www.doubleclick.com/us/corporate/presskit/press-releases.htm> (last visited February 22, 2002).

[187]See "Banking Customer Privacy: States Legislating Financial Privacy Before Federal Regulators Even Issue Draft," *US Law Week: Legal News* 2453 (February 8, 2000). At least 17 states are developing their own privacy rules for banks and other financial institutions through an amendment in the Gramm-Leach-Bliley Act. *Ibid*: Most states begin considering privacy proposals rather than wait to hear what federal agencies are proposing because they have short sessions during which bills can be introduced—by the time federal agencies issue

their proposals, many states may have to wait a whole year before beginning proposals. *Ibid*, but see M. Schroeder, "Groups Form to Stop States on Privacy," *The Wall Street Journal* A2 (February 10, 2000).

[188]See Jathon Sapsford, "Chase, New York Reach Accord on Privacy," *The Wall Street Journal* A4 (January 26, 2000).

[189]See *supra* note 181.

[190]See Dee DePass, "U.S. Bank's Zona Trades Volleys With Hatch Over Lawsuit," *Minneapolis Star-Tribune* 1D (June 18, 1999).

[191]See William N. Eskridge & Philip P. Frickey, *Legislation: Statutes and the Creation of Public Policy* 52-56 (1995); see also Conrad deFiebre, "Trying to Keep Your Business Their Business," *Minneapolis Star Tribune* (February 28, 2000).

[192]For examples of federal regulation on private databases, see the Fair Credit Reporting Act, 15 U.S.C. Sec. 1681b (1994) and the Video Privacy Protection Act, 18 U.S.C. Sec. 2710 (1994). See also *Condon v. Reno*, 120 S. Ct. 666, at 671 (2000), likening state databases to private databases and therefore implicitly recognizing federal power to regulate all databases.

[193]Through a delegation of authority, many states have introduced privacy bills regulating financial databases. See Gramm-Leach-Bliley Financial Modernization Act, Pub. L. No. 106-102 Sec. 509 (1999).

[194]See *Reno v. American Civil Liberties Union*, 521 U.S. 844 (1997).

[195]See Jane E. Kirtley, *The EU Data Protection Directive and the First Amendment: Why a "Press Exemption" Won't Work*, 80 Iowa L. Rev. 639 (1995).

[196]See Jane E. Kirtley, *Freedom of the Press: An Inalienable Right or a Privilege to Be Earned?* 9 U. Fla. J.L. & Pub. Policy 209 (1998).

[197]Electronic Commerce Task Force, International Trade Administration, U.S. Dep't of Commerce, available at <http://www.ita.doc.gov/td/ecom/FAQ5DPA300.htm> (last visited March 17, 2000).

7

Privacy, Property, and "Advertisements in Disguise": The First Amendment and the Right of Publicity

Craig L. LaMay
Medill School of Journalism, Northwestern University

When Florida State University student Becky Lynn Gritzke went to Mardi Gras in 2000, she was so taken by the spirit of the festival that, like thousands of other women before her, she bared her breasts on a public street in return for appreciative cheers and a fistful of beads. When she did, a cameraman captured the act on film, then sold the video to MRA Holdings LLP, the company that distributes *Girls Gone Wild* videos on late-night television infomercials. Gritzke's image was included not only in one of the company's videos, but also on the cover of the box in which it was packaged, on MRA's Web site, and on billboards all over Europe where MRA sells another video series called *American Girls*.

Gritzke sued MRA for "embarrassment, humiliation, mental pain and suffering and the invasion of her privacy," alleging that the video and the related promotional materials gave the impression that she was "willing to be associated with and participate in the risqué and sometimes pornographic displays in the videotapes."[1] Among Gritzke's privacy claims was that MRA portrayed her in a false light, and that she was unaware of the camera's presence and thus did not consent to the filming.[2] But as Gritzke conceded in her suit, "During the parade and other Mardi Gras celebrations, numerous celebrants, including plaintiff, removed their shirts or some other item of clothing."[3] It is hard to see how, in that context, Gritzke can say her self-exposure was in any way private or that its representation in the *Girls Gone Wild* video was somehow infected with falsity.

The most interesting of Gritzke's legal claims, however, was that MRA appropriated her name and likeness for a commercial purpose, and therefore that she was entitled to royalties from the sale of the tape.[4] The claim seeks damages that would be almost impossible for her to win under a publicity of private facts or false light claim; more fundamentally, Gritzke's purported injury has nothing to do with privacy, but is instead about an economic right in the use of her identity, even though, prior to and even after her notoriety, she was a virtual unknown. For noncelebrity plaintiffs in right of publicity cases, humiliation and loss of dignity can be significant components of the claim,[5] but in most such cases the plaintiffs are celebrities for whom the essential claim is economic.[6] In either instance, however, a time- honored defense is that the use of a plaintiff's name, likeness, or identity is newsworthy and thus a protected use under the First Amendment. As MRA's lawyer said of Gritzke's appropriation claim, "Clearly what she was doing was both newsworthy and of public interest."[7]

Most journalists would blanche at the argument that *Girls Gone Wild* is newsworthy, but of course in New Orleans Mardi Gras *is* news (just as spring break revelry is from Key West, Florida, to San Padre Island, Texas, where similar cases have arisen) and a local television station could easily have shot the same video and broadcast it, perhaps more discreetly than MRA did, but with similar profit motive. Allowing for sake of argument that *Girls Gone Wild* has no news value at all and that its billboards featuring Gritzke do no more than propose a commercial transaction, it is nonetheless hard to find a principled reason why such a "true" representation of her identity should give rise to liability when another "true" representation—a news story—does not. Moreover, trying to divine the nature and extent of the profit motive in the use—in short, whether there has been some kind of commercial theft—is inevitably arbitrary. So, too, is any test of "newsworthiness," a test that makes private facts tort claims all but hopeless for plaintiffs, but in right of publicity claims relies on the idea that news uses of a name or likeness can be reliably distinguished from commercial ones.[8] This notion is difficult to square with the fact that an editor or news director at an advertising-supported medium—whether *The New Yorker* or *A Current Affair*—selects and orders stories at least in some part on the basis of their appeal to audiences, and sometimes not even to audiences but to advertisers. Given these conceptual difficulties and the increasingly blurry lines between news and entertainment, the right of publicity may become a concern not only for advertisers, as it traditionally has been, but for news organizations as well.

THE RIGHT OF PUBLICITY
AND FIRST AMENDMENT TENSIONS

The right of publicity tort is also known as *appropriation*, sometimes as *misappropriation*. The *Restatement* offers little guidance, saying only that: "One who appropriates to his own use or benefit the name or likeness of another is subject to liability to the other for invasion of privacy."[9] In fact, the tort is more akin to intellectual property law than to traditional notions of privacy. Once called "copyright's upstart cousin,"[10] the right of publicity is not concerned with keeping matters private but with making them profitably public. In some jurisdictions the right is recognized only in statute, in others in both statute and common law,[11] but in every case the claim allows for liability where a publisher uses someone's name and likeness for commercial purposes without consent, and it protects two interests. The first is the loss of dignity that can result from unauthorized use of a person's identity; the second is the economic property interest that people, usually well-known people, have in that identity. Many courts have distinguished between these two interests, seeing the first as more closely aligned with the traditional notion of privacy as the "right to be let alone,"[12] and the second as a form of property that is both assignable and descendible.[13] In most jurisdictions and in most cases (but not all), courts have interpreted the first interest as protectable where the commercial interest in the publication is clear and the use of the plaintiff's name or likeness is substantial and not merely incidental. Other courts, as discussed later, have essentially equated the right of publicity with the tort of commercialization, in which unauthorized use of a name or likeness satisfies the claim without any further showing of harm.[14]

Until recently, journalists have had little reason to concern themselves with the right of publicity. In general, misappropriation has been a concern of advertisers; journalists, although they also make nonconsensual use of names and likenesses for a commercial purpose—trade in news—have nonetheless been granted broad exemption from liability under the tort because their use is not thought to be exploitive. When a magazine runs a prominent photograph of a professional athlete or celebrity on its front page, for example, the decision to print the photograph clearly reflects commercial as well as news judgment—the photo sells the publication. But so long as the use is newsworthy, even arguably so, courts have granted broad leeway under the First Amendment to media use of such material, including its use in subsequent promotions of the publication itself.[15] Only when such use suggests an endorsement or some other commercial use beyond telling, analyzing, or promoting the news has liability arisen.[16]

In the last few years, however, plaintiffs bringing right of publicity claims have questioned the newsworthiness of photographs, drawings, and other representations of themselves, characterizing them as primarily commercial uses. In many of these cases, plaintiffs are pursuing reputational damages; in some instances, but by no means all, they have also sued for libel or, where the tort is recognized, false light invasion of privacy. Celebrities and companies have also sued under the federal Lanham Act, which forbids commercial use of symbols or devices that may deceive consumers as to the true sponsorship of goods and services.[17] Corporations have sought reputational damages under the Lanham Act, raising the question of whether actual malice should apply to such claims.[18]

All these cases have been complicated by several factors, not least of them that, as other essays in this volume have documented, the bright lines that once separated editorial content from advertising are now messily blurred. In the horizontally and vertically integrated media firm of today, news is but a small part of a much larger enterprise that includes entertainment, sports, music, advertising, and direct marketing. The mixing of content and purpose puts journalism in a competitive environment in which the most privileged news content is that which can be easily leveraged across multiple media platforms, trends that have been amplified by deregulation and globalization. Miramax's now defunct magazine *Talk*, for example, was premised on the idea that every story would contain the seed of ancillary products—movies, books, music—that would yield revenues from licensing and electronic commerce.[19] Many community newspapers now run as editorial content what are in fact advertisements—tips on products or services, for example, in which the person providing the tip is a local merchant who has paid for the space.

Many of the privacy cases discussed elsewhere in this volume involve news stories that were conceived and driven as much or more by entertainment values than news values. ABC's reporting in its investigation of the Food Lion grocery chain, for example, was poor by almost any meaningful editorial standard, with the producers of the segment failing to document any of the worst abuses they claimed to exist. ABC decided to do undercover filming in Food Lion stores before doing any independent reporting, and then held for 6 months what it claimed to be a critical story about public health and safety, until the November 1992 sweeps period, when the segment would draw the largest audiences and ensure the highest advertising revenues. Similarly, CNN's contractual arrangement with the U.S. Fish and Wildlife Service for exclusive rights to coverage of the agency's raid on the Berger ranch was replete editorial compromises, not least concerning the timing of CNN's broadcast and the manner in which the agency would be portrayed. Finally, Internet publication and its potential for digital creation and manipulation of images has given added urgency to the question of where news coverage ends and commercial appropriation begins.

ORIGINS AND DEVELOPMENT OF THE RIGHT

Appropriation has an old pedigree. In their 1890 *Harvard Law Review* article "The Right to Privacy,"[20] article, Samuel Warren and Louis Brandeis theorized that the right to privacy was, among other things, akin to the property rights protected by copyright law. Just as copyright made inviolable an original work of expression, the authors argued, so too should the law protect the person who creates it; without privacy, the fruits of intellectual, artistic or spiritual expression would wither away.[21] The principles Warren and Brandeis argued for first reached a New York appellate court in 1902 in a case brought by a young woman whose picture was used in a flour advertisement without her permission. She lost because, as the court noted, "the so-called 'right of privacy' has not yet found an abiding place in our jurisprudence."[22] A year later it did, when New York passed a statue providing that "[t]he name, portrait or picture of any living person cannot be used for advertising purposes or for purposes of trade without first obtaining that person's written consent."[23] Two years later, the Georgia Supreme Court upheld a claim brought by a man whose photograph appeared in a New England Life advertisement along with his "testimonial" endorsing the company's services.[24]

The right to publicity was first articulated in 1953 by the Second Circuit Court of Appeals in *Haelen Laboratories v. Topps Chewing Gum*, a case involving a baseball player's right to control and contract for the use of his image on trading cards. Said the court: "We think that ... a man has a right in the publicity value of his photograph, i.e., the right to grant the exclusive privilege of publishing his picture ... this right might be called a right of publicity."[25] Seven years later, Dean Prosser broke privacy into its four distinct branches, one of them "appropriation."[26] For a time, it was assumed that appropriation did not occur unless a plaintiff could show that his name or likeness was actually used. But in 1983, in a case brought by comedian Johnny Carson against Here's Johnny Portable Toilets, a New York court extended the right to cover "identity." The expression "Here's Johnny!" was of course Carson's famous entry cue to the set of NBC's *Tonight Show*, associated uniquely with him. As such, the court said, "[I]f the celebrity's identity is commercially exploited, there has been an invasion of his right whether or not his 'name or likeness' is used."[27]

A year later, another New York court found that the right of publicity survived the celebrity and was descendible. Today, 16 states (including, importantly, California, which along with New York is home to the majority of national media firms) recognize a right of publicity by statute, and another 11 recognize a common law right of publicity. The right of descendibility exists in nine states, with varying requirements, but the most comprehensive post-mortem right is in California, where the right of publicity lasts for 50 years after death, whether or not the deceased sought to capitalize on the right while alive.[28] In this respect, as in many others, the right to publicity has little to do with being let alone or avoiding the public spotlight—to the contrary.

To date, the U.S. Supreme Court has heard only one misappropriation case, involving a television newscast that broadcast as part of a news story the entire 15-second performance of Hugo Zacchini, a "human cannonball."[29] Zacchini sued, claiming that the news story "showed and commercialized the film of his act without his consent" and as such was an "unlawful appropriation of [his] professional property."[30] The Ohio Supreme Court had found for the television station in an opinion that relied heavily on *Time Inc. v. Hill*,[31] a 1967 decision in which the high court had found that a play, although a commercial enterprise, was nonetheless protected by the First Amendment because the actual incident on which it based was "a matter of public interest."[32] By contrast, Justice White wrote, the issue in *Zacchini* was "closely analogous to the goals of patent and copyright law, focusing on the right of the individual to reap the reward of his endeavors.... The Constitution no more prevents a state from requiring respondent to compensate petitioner for broadcasting his act on television than it would privilege respondent to film and broadcast a copyrighted dramatic work without liability to the copyright owner."[33]

The reasons for this conclusion were many, White said, but centered on the damage the broadcast did to the economic value of the performance, which, once broadcast in its entirety, greatly reduced the likelihood that the public would pay to see it. Writing in dissent, Justice Powell argued that:

> When a film is used, as here, for a routine portion of a regular news program, I would
> hold that the First Amendment protects the station from a "right of publicity" or "appropriation" suit, absent a strong showing by the plaintiff that the news broadcast

was a subterfuge or cover for private or commercial exploitation.… [t]he plaintiff
does not complain about the fact of exposure to the public, but rather about its timing
or manner. He welcomes publicity, but seeks to retain control over means and manner as a way to maximize for himself the monetary benefits that flow from such publication. But having made the matter public—having chosen, in essence, to make it
newsworthy—he cannot, consistent with the First Amendment, complain of routine
news reportage.[34]

The Court's conceptual difficulty in *Zacchini*—was the broadcast commercial exploitation or news—was not, as White noted, of the kind that usually accompanies
unauthorized commercial uses of names and likenesses, but rather concerned a performance, a context in which the Court's analogizing to intellectual property law
made sense.[35] More recently, however, plaintiffs bringing right of publicity claims
have in effect made the argument that they have an economic property right in *all* uses
of their name, likeness, and "identity," including uses that are merely suggestive and
that, if brought under copyright law, would likely fail. In 1992, for example, singer
Tom Waits won $2.5 million in damages from Frito-Lay after it used in an advertise-
ment a singer whose voice and delivery strongly resembled Waits' gravelly style.[36] A
few years earlier, the Ninth Circuit allowed singer Bette Midler to sue the Ford Motor
Company for an advertisement that featured a singer who sounded like Midler and
who sang a Midler song, "Do You Wanna Dance," to which Ford's advertising
agency, Young & Rubicam, had secured the rights. Midler herself had rejected the offer to do the commercial, and contended that the ad suggested she endorsed Ford
products.[37] She eventually won $400,000 at trial. In another Ninth Circuit case, the
court allowed actor George Wendt of *Cheers* television fame to sue a company whose
restaurants featured robots resembling the characters Norm and Cliff, both regular
patrons of the television program's namesake bar. Although the restaurant chain obtained a license from the company that owned the copyright to the program, Wendt
contended that he had a right of publicity in his fictional television persona. The court
agreed, finding the robots a form of commercial speech.[38]

Still other plaintiffs have used the right of publicity tort to seek publication damages in cases where the First Amendment would almost surely bar damages if they
were to sue under either of the other two publication-based privacy torts, private facts
or false light. In 2000, the surviving family of Billy Tyne, the fishing boat captain
whose story is told in the book and movie *The Perfect Storm*, sued Warner Bros. under
a right of publicity claim when they were upset by the film's portrayal of Tyne as ex-
ceedingly reckless; in short, the family sought reputational damages.[39] The residents
of Dalbeattie, Scotland, wrested $5,000 from Twentieth-Century Fox, although they
did not actually file a suit, for the studio's depiction of William Murdoch, an officer
on board the *Titanic*. In the film of the same name, Murdoch is shown shooting pan-
icked passengers and then himself, when according to survivor reports Murdoch died
when he gave his lifejacket to a passenger. Similarly, boxer Joey Giardello settled out
of court with Universal Pictures when he sued the company for its depiction of him as
an undeserving champion in the film *The Hurricane*.[40]

There have also been cases involving more traditional news media in which plaintiffs seeking reputational damages have sued for misappropriation, and sometimes only that. Perhaps the best known of these is a 2000 New York case, *Messenger v. Gruner & Jahr*, involving a 14-year-old model who posed for several photographs only to have them appear in *YM* magazine under the headline, "I got trashed and had sex with three guys." The district court denied summary judgment on the grounds that the newsworthiness exception to New York's right of publicity statute did not extend to uses that were substantially false—allowing the plaintiff to proceed with what was effectively a false light action in a state where that tort is not recognized. The Second Circuit certified the case to New York's Court of Appeals, which ruled that so long as a photograph illustrates a newsworthy article and bears some "real relationship" to that article, there is no misappropriation.[41]

A year later, another New York court relied on *Messenger* to dispose of a case brought by the parents of a newborn whose photograph had been taken at the neonatal unit of a county hospital. The parents had authorized limited use of the photograph to accompany information about pulmonary problems in infants, but the photograph wound up in a *New York Times* article about mothers who pass AIDS along to their babies. The parents sued, but the court dismissed both their defamation claim and their misappropriation claim, in the latter noting that the article was not an advertisement in disguise and that there was a "real relationship" between the photograph and the *Times* article.[42]

These are not the only cases of this type, just some of the more well-known ones. Many misappropriation claims come packaged with false light claims, where that tort is recognized, and the two are frequently confused, as happened in *Messenger*. It is these kinds of cases, as some judges[43] and scholars[44] have argued, that give the right of publicity the potential to limit speech in ways that trademark and libel law cannot.

WHERE DOES JOURNALISM END AND COMMERCIAL USE BEGIN?

Of the recent cases that underscore the difficulty of distinguishing between journalism and commercial exploitation, the most colorful was the right of publicity claim brought by actor Dustin Hoffman against *Los Angeles Magazine* in 1999. The suit resulted from a 17-page fashion photo spread in the March 1997 issue of the magazine that employed digital photo manipulation to "redress" actors from famous film shots in modern designs and was published under the headline "Grand Illusions." The shoot, for example, included Marilyn Monroe's famous pose above a windy sidewalk grate from *The Seven Year Itch*, but with the actress dressed in a Valentino dress. Cary Grant, in a scene from *North by Northwest*, was digitally refitted in a Moschino suit, and the monster from *The Creature From the Black Lagoon* appeared in a pair of Nike athletic shoes. The still of Hoffman came from the 1982 film *Tootsie*, but the red sequined dress he had made famous in the film had been replaced by a "butter- colored silk gown by Richard Tyler and Ralph Lauren heels."[45]

To create the image, the magazine photographed a model posed as Hoffman had in the film, then digitally attached Hoffman's head to the new image and superimposed the original film background. Although the magazine noted in several places that all the images had been created with "digital magic," it had not sought permission to use the *Tootsie* image either from Hoffman or from Columbia Pictures, which owned the rights to the film.[46]

Hoffman's suit against the magazine claimed the use of his image from the film violated both his statutory and common law rights of publicity under California law, as well as the Lanham Act and another California statute against unfair competition.[47] He alleged that the photo layout made it appear as though he were promoting particular designers' fashions contrary to his "strict policy of not endorsing commercial products."[48] *Los Angeles Magazine* tried to raise both the First Amendment and the California laws in its defense, arguing that both provide exceptions for uses that concern "newsworthy events or matters of public interest."[49] U.S. District Court Judge Dickran Tevrizian did not buy it, and in 1999, after a 4-day bench trial, announced that Hoffman was "truly one of our country's living treasures"[50] and awarded that treasure $1.5 million in compensatory damages, the same amount in punitive damages, and another $270,000 in lawyer's fees. *Los Angeles Magazine*, Tevrizian wrote, "crossed over the line between editorial content and advertising. The photographs were manipulated and cannibalized to such an extent that the celebrities were commercially exploited and were robbed of their dignity, professionalism and talent. To be blunt, the celebrities were violated by technology."[51]

In rejecting the magazine's defenses, the district court relied on two separate cases brought by another actor, Clint Eastwood, against the *National Enquirer*. The first case, in 1983, had concerned a false story about Eastwood's love life,[52] and the second, in 1997, an "exclusive" interview with the actor that never happened.[53] But where the Eastwood cases had clearly involved the use of Eastwood's identity in a knowingly false manner—thus defeating any public interest privilege—the *Los Angeles Magazine* photo spread did not represent its digitally altered photographs as the real thing. Indeed, the presentation in the magazine made clear that the photos were, as the title of the layout suggested, "Grand Illusions," and the original film stills from which the digital creations were made appeared at the end of the layout.[54]

More significantly, although Los Angeles is a major center for the fashion industry, the district court simply did not see that the photo layout served any news interest, but instead characterized it as a commercial use. In the court's words, the article "provided no commentary on fashion trends and no coordinated or unified view of current fashions, ... no statement that any particular style of clothes is in vogue, that any particular color is becoming popular, or that any type of fabric is attracting the attention of designers.... The article is not really a presentation of fashion news or affairs."[55]

The court's reasoning on this point was certainly plausible. *Los Angeles Magazine* presented the layout not as a news story but a "fashion show" using mannequins with "classic looks."[56] Although other courts have ruled in similar cases that the kinds of information presented in the layout are important to consumers and thus newsworthy,[57] the key was that Hoffman never actually wore the dress in which he appeared in the layout. For that reason, the court concluded, the actor's name and likeness were "wholly unnecessary" to whatever message the magazine meant to convey to its readers.[58]

Two years later, the Ninth Circuit reversed the district court judgment, saying the magazine layout was not commercial speech and thus that the lower court decision could not be reconciled with the First Amendment.[59] Whatever commercial elements existed in the layout, the Ninth Circuit's opinion said, were inseparable from "humor and visual and verbal editorial comment.... [C]ommon sense tells us this is not a simple advertisement."[60] Applying its own precedent requiring a showing of actual malice to overcome the First Amendment defense, the court found none. The magazine, it concluded, had provided enough notification to its readers that Hoffman had not actually posed for the photograph, but that it was an altered version of the original movie still.

The *Hoffman* case is perhaps the most well known of several recent cases that raise interesting questions for journalists: What transforms a journalistic use of a person's name or likeness into a commercial one? Can the right of publicity tort be used to limit speech that would be protected under other forms of intellectual property law?

The first question has troubled even courts that, like the Ninth Circuit, have given substantial time and attention to it. In *Hoffman*, the Ninth Circuit relied on a narrow definition provided by the U.S. Supreme Court, that commercial speech is simply speech that "does no more than propose a commercial transaction," but of course the Court has in the last decade extended its protection of commercial speech to language that is merely informative.[61] In any case, the Ninth Circuit's words in *Hoffman* about "common sense" only underscore the fact that there is no clear and all-encompassing definition of commercial speech. Partly as a result, cases involving the right of publicity have long produced confusing results. In one 1961 case, for example, a New York court ruled the republication of a news photograph on a fabric used to manufacture clothing to be an incidental use and thus protected,[62] while the same court in the same year found a news photograph used by a private club to promote club membership a commercial use, and thus a violation.[63] In another New York case, a court found a comic book's rendering of a news story to be essentially amusement but nonetheless protected,[64] while an Illinois court found that the dramatized version of a news story in a detective magazine was unprotected because the magazine "makes a strong appeal to the idle and prurient."[65] The reasoning that distinguishes these cases can be hard to discern. Courts have disagreed not only on what kinds of uses are commercial, but also what constitutes a "likeness" sufficient to support a cause of action, and the bounds of a First Amendment defense.

Recently, for example, the Ninth Circuit revisited the issues from *Hoffman* in *Downing v. Abercrombie & Fitch*, a case involving several surfers who sued when their photographs appeared in the Spring 1999 edition of the clothier's quarterly publication, which is also the company's primary advertising vehicle.[66] The publication featured articles on the history of surfing that were illustrated with photos of the plaintiffs wearing the company's t-shirts; immediately next to the articles were pages showing similar shirts for sale. The company had argued that surfing was a matter of public interest, and the district court had granted summary judgment on the misappropriation claims. But the appeals court reinstated them, finding the photos to be mere "window dressing" in what was primarily a sales catalog. As such, the court ruled, it could appear that the surfers had endorsed the company's clothes. The court distinguished *Hoffman* by noting that the shopping guide in *Los Angeles Magazine* was placed far from the offending article, and that the magazine received no consideration from the designers. But the manufactured "endorsement" in Hoffman was in fact a contrivance; the surfers in *Abercrombie & Fitch Quarterly* were photographed in a public place wearing Abercrombie & Fitch clothes. In truth, they *did* endorse the company's products, and the photographs in the catalog were in no other way false. The difference between *Hoffman* and *Downing* is that *Los Angeles Magazine* is journalism and *Abercrombie & Fitch Quarterly* is a commercial. This distinction may make sense at one level, but it ignores the reality of the magazine business, where all but a small handful of general-readership magazines are conceived, created, and written to appeal to advertisers, who also supply the lion's share of industry revenues.

A case with similar conceptual confusion involved a Virginia orthopedic surgeon who was falsely accused by a local television news broadcast of sexually abusing his female patients. A producer had secured a grainy photograph of the physician by posing as a patient, and for a week before the story aired the station used the photo in broadcast and newspaper advertisements promoting its forthcoming story on "The X-Rated Doctor." The physician eventually won a $2 million defamation judgment, but the Virginia Supreme Court disallowed a $575,000 misappropriation award, saying that the report was not an "advertisement in disguise" for the station.[67] Such a ruling is consistent with the media's First Amendment protections under right of publicity claims, but it ignores the economics of broadcast television, where, so far as the financial transaction is concerned, advertisers are the customers and viewers are the product. The court's ruling also overlooked the fact that the promotional materials really *were* advertisements for a story later found to be false.

These cases raise several issues. One, outside the scope of this chapter, is what constitutes commercial speech and whether truthful speech, commercial or otherwise, should be judged by a lower First Amendment standard than political speech—assuming one can always tell the difference.[68] A second issue is who or what can legitimately claim to be engaged in journalism, especially when the institutional press is ever-more engaged in commercial activity unrelated to news and when the Internet makes it possible for individuals unaffiliated with the institutional press to investigate controversies and publish their findings.[69] And a third issue is how the right of publicity should apply in this new media environment. The increased use of the right of publicity tort in the last decade, combined with the kinds of "digital magic" at issue in *Hoffman*, have given new urgency to the need to find some test to resolve conflicts between property and free speech claims. The problem, in a nutshell, is that the intellectual property right in the right of publicity, like that in copyright and trademark, can conflict with free speech interests; unlike copyright law, however, the right of publicity does not include safeguards, such as copyright's fair use doctrine or trademark's "likelihood of confusion" test, sufficient to protect those interests.

In *Comedy III Productions, Inc. v. Gary Saderup, Inc.,*[70] the California Supreme Court attempted to overcome this problem by in effect borrowing from the fair use doctrine and examining whether an alleged infringement on the plaintiff's publicity right was "transformative." The case involved an artist who made and sold silkscreened t-shirts, one of which featured his own drawing of the Three Stooges. The artist, Gary Saderup, did not seek permission from Comedy III Productions, which owns the rights to the Stooges, and the company sued and won on a right of publicity claim. The state appeals court affirmed the essential part of the judgment, saying that the artist's work was commercial and thus not protected.[71]

The California Supreme Court also affirmed, but for a different reason. The court said that Saderup's work was not commercial speech—not an advertisement or an endorsement—but original expressive work, and worried about the damage to free speech rights that giving broad license to the right of publicity would encourage. Specifically, the court expressed concern about "the potential of allowing a celebrity to accomplish through the vigorous exercise of that right the censorship of unflattering commentary that cannot be constitutionally accomplished through defamation actions."[72] The court then borrowed from copyright's fair use doctrine to evaluate the "purpose and character"[73] of Saderup's use of the Stooges' images, to determine whether his work "merely 'supercedes the objects' of the original creation" or "adds 'something new.'"[74] The court announced a "balancing test between the First Amendment and the right of publicity based on whether the work in question adds significant creative elements so as to be transformed into something more than a mere celebrity likeness of imitation."[75] In applying this test, the court found no significant transformative quality to Saderup's work and denied him protection under what it characterized as a fair use claim.

Saderup's case is important because it establishes the idea that a commercial element by itself does not negate a First Amendment defense to a right of publicity claim. The Ninth Circuit also acknowledged the *Comedy III* analysis in its *Hoffman* decision, discussing the "significant transformative elements"[76] in the contested digital photograph. But other courts have not been as broad minded as the *Comedy III* court, upholding right of publicity claims in cases that, if evaluated under the mechanisms that protect First Amendment rights in other areas of intellectual property law, would likely be protected. In 2002, for example, the California Court of Appeals allowed rock-and-roll brothers Edgar and Johnny Winter to sue a comic book publisher for using the names Edgar and Johnny "Autumn" in what was an undisputed work of fiction (and even, as the court acknowledge, in tribute). The court dismissed the brothers' defamation claims, but with respect to their misappropriation claim decided it was a jury question whether the use of the brothers' names was "transformative."[77] In another troubling case, television personality Vanna White successfully sued the Samsung Corporation in 1992 when it aired a television advertisement featuring a robot in a blond wig standing on a game show set and turning letters—apparently as only Ms. White can.[78] Although the advertisement was clearly commercial in character, it was also clearly parody, which is protected under traditional intellectual property doctrines. White won not for the unauthorized use of her image, but from an image that was merely suggestive of an activity with which she is identified.

If the test employed by the California Supreme Court in *Comedy III* is a helpful step forward, it also suffers from the same kind of subjectivity that bedevils other tests courts have used in right of publicity cases, for example whether a use rises to the level of "social commentary,"[79] "provides a social benefit,"[80] or "promote[s] the dissemination of thoughts."[81] In *Saderup*, for example, the California Supreme Court took a turn in art criticism, distinguishing Saderup's use of celebrity images from Andy Warhol's by saying Warhol "was able to convey a message that went beyond the commercial exploitation of celebrity images and became a form of ironic social comment on the dehumanization of celebrity itself."[82] The court then congratulated itself on its ability to identify this "subtle" distinction.[83]

How any court is supposed to apply such a distinction in a principled way is another matter. In a recent and comparable New York case, an artist altered a photograph and inserted it into a silkscreen collage, leading the model pictured in the photograph to sue both the artist and the galleries that displayed her work (among them the Whitney Museum of American Art), promoted it through billboard advertising, and profited by it through the sale of souvenirs that contained the contested image. The court ruled the silkscreen *and* the ancillary products to be works of art fully protected by the First Amendment, in effect expanding the range of "newsworthy items" to include gift shop knickknacks.[84]

To be genuinely useful in future cases, the evaluation of fair use factors in right of publicity claims will have to get at the question of how much expression a work needs to be transformative, a question the court bulldozed through in *Comedy III*, where it described Saderup's art as "trivial" and not recognizably "his own."[85] Finally, effective use of a transformative test may benefit from analysis that more clearly separates the transformative elements of a work from its economic ones. In *Comedy III*, the court talked about economic considerations as a "subsidiary inquiry"[86] to transformation, but did not discuss just how and when such an inquiry would be required.

CONCLUSION

The right of publicity may prove to be just another tool that plaintiffs employ to seek damages unavailable to them under publication torts like private facts or libel, with their substantial First Amendment protections. If so, courts should have little trouble applying the First Amendment protections traditionally afforded to news and public affairs reporting under the tort.[87] But it is certainly conceivable that, as the district court did in *Hoffman*, courts will look with new skepticism on the claim that a certain use is in fact news, especially as news organizations are expected to leverage their work product for other nonnews uses, including some, such as films or television dramas, where the claim to serving the "public interest" will seem tenuous at best and the commercial elements will be harder to overlook. This is especially so as digital media give wider exposure to such use and make it easier for content creators to manipulate sounds, images, and text, and to link commercial content much more closely to the editorial choices of audiences.

The conflict between the right of publicity with commercial speech and intellectual property doctrines also raises questions about those areas of law. It does not make sense, for example, that a fashion magazine, without fear of liability, could run an untouched photograph of a famous actor wearing a designer jacket while standing in Times Square, but that the designer, if he were to use the same photograph in an advertisement, would be subject to a variety of statutory and common law claims, including a right of publicity violation. In neither case is the photograph imbued with any kind of falsehood; it is a true representation of what the actor was wearing in a public place. The fact that the photograph is used in the advertisement to promote a commercial transaction seems a curious distinction on which to hang liability, all the more so because the magazine is selling its own product, news. Where it is possible to clearly separate the commercial *purpose* of an appropriation from the issue of whether the *damage* is commercial it may be easier to limit or deny damages, although the proliferation of cheap and ubiquitous new media—from mass-produced videotapes like *Girls Gone Wild* to Web pages and other digital creations—may make this distinction harder to draw. On the other hand, the right of publicity seems at least to fit with the modern concern about privacy and the Internet, where the focus is on ownership of, access to, and control over personal information—in short, information as valuable property.[88] Whatever the shortcomings of that approach, it may be easier, for both First Amendment reasons and practical ones, to think about privacy rights in these kinds of terms than in terms of decency, falsity, or "newsworthiness."

NOTES

[1]Chris Rose, "Carnival Knowledge: The Case of the Coed Who Bared for Beads and Wound Up Starring in Voyeuristic Video," *New Orleans Times-Picayune* (January 10, 2002), available at <http://www.nola.com/printer/printer.ssf?/livingstory/rose10.html>, (last visited July 27, 2002).

[2]*Ibid.*

[3]*Ibid.*

[4]Mark J. Pescatore, *Here's Another Case That Argues for Privacy Where Privacy Shouldn't Be Expected*, available at <http://www.governmentvideo.com/2002/04/video_o402.shtml> (last visited July 27, 2002).

[5]See *Beverley v. Choices Women's Medical Center*, 16 Med.L.Rept. 1159 (2d Dep't), appeal dismissed, 536 N.Y.S.2d 743 (1988). The case involved a promotional calendar published by an abortion clinic and honoring important American women. The calendar

featured, without consent, the photograph of a woman physician opposed to abortion. The court awarded the plaintiff $50,000 for mental anguish but declined to fix an amount for "the appropriation value of plaintiff's name." The Court of Appeals agreed with the lower court that the calendar was a promotional item and sustained that judgment.

[6]See *Cardtoons v. Major League Baseball Players Association*, 95 F.3d 959 (10th Cir., 1996). The Court found that under Oklahoma law, the publicity right protects only economic interests, not personal anguish or humiliation.

[7]Pescatore, *supra*, note 4.

[8]For discussion on this point, see Steven Shiffrin, *The First Amendment and Economic Regulation: Away from a General Theory of the First Amendment*, 78 Northwestern U. Law Rev. 1212, at 1257, n. 275 (1983). Shiffrin asks whether any of the following situations are actionable:

> A magazine may have a profit motive in taking a particular position on a partic-
> ular subject, but the courts will ordinarily not count that motivation as signifi-
> cant. In thinking about profit motive and the dissemination of truth, consider
> these examples: 1) Without his consent, Mercedes Benz truthfully advertises
> that Frank Sinatra drives a Mercedes. Sinatra sues for misappropriation. Does
> it make a difference if Mercedes in its ad says, "We didn't ask Sinatra's permis-
> sion to tell you this" or "Sinatra doesn't want us to tell you this but … ?" 2) Sup-
> pose *Time* magazine writes a story on Mercedes Benz and puts Sinatra on the
> cover with a picture of his Mercedes. Suppose they put Sinatra on the cover
> purely for reasons of profit. 3) Suppose Time Inc. advertises: "Get the recent is-
> sue of *Time* with Frank Sinatra on the cover with his Mercedes." 4) Suppose
> *Time* truthfully advertises: "Sinatra doesn't want us to tell you this, but he is
> one of our regular readers."

[9]Restatement (2nd) of Torts, Sec. 652C.

[10]Ralph S. Brown, *Copyright and Its Upstart Cousins: Privacy, Publicity, Unfair Competition*, 33 J. Copyright Society 301 (1986).

[11]In New York, for example, the Court of Appeals has said unequivocally that there is no common law right of publicity. See *Stephano v. News Group Publications*, 64 N.Y.2d 174 (1984). Federal courts in New York, however, have found a separate common law right of publicity. See *Lerman v. Flynt Distributing Co.*, 745 F.2d 123 (2d Cir. 1984).

[12]See *Beverley v. Choices Women's Medical Center* (1988). See also *Pitt v. Playgirl*, BC 178 503 (Cal. Sup. Ct. 1997), in which actor Brad Pitt, in a misappropriation claim, sought and received a temporary restraining order stopping *Playgirl* from distributing an issue of the magazine that featured nude photographs of him and Gwyneth Paltrow that an unknown photographer had taken surreptitiously while the two were vacationing.

[13]See *Hicks v. Casablanca Records*, 464 F. Supp. 426 (S.D.N.Y. 1978), a case involving the heirs of Agatha Christie who sought to stop publication of a fictionalized account of the author's life.

[14]See *Carson v. Here's Johnny Portable Toilets, Inc.*, 698 F2d 831 (1983).

[15]See *Namath v. Sports Illustrated*, 48 A.D.2d 487 (1st Dep't 1975). New York Jets quarterback Namath sued for an advertisement the magazine ran seeking subscriptions, which featured a photograph of Namath taken from the magazine's own files. See also *Time Inc. v. Hill*, 385 U.S. 374 (1967); *Zacchini v. Scripps-Howard Broadcasting Co.*, 433 U.S. 562 (1977).

[16]See, for example, *Booth v. Curtis Publishing Co.*, 15 A.D.2d 343, 223 NYS2d 737, aff'd without opinion 11 NY2d 907, 182 N.E.2d 812, 228 N.Y.S.2d 468 (1962), involving a *Holi-*

day magazine photograph of actress Shirley Booth that the magazine later used in advertisements to promote the magazine's content); see also *Cher v. Forum*, 692 F2d 634 (1982), involving an interview with the actress that was later sold and published in *Forum* magazine, and which gave the false impression that Cher not only consented to the interview with the adult magazine but was a regular reader of the publication.

[17]The Lanham Act prohibits the misuse of a trademark—that is, a symbol or device such as a visual likeness, vocal imitation, or other uniquely distinguishing characteristic—that may confuse consumers as to a person's sponsorship or approval of a product or service. See 15 U.S.C. sec. 1125(a).

[18]See, for example, *Proctor & Gamble v Amway Corp.*, 242 F3d 539 (5th Cir., 2001).

[19]See David Bollier, "Can Serious Journalism Survive in the Marketplace of Ideas," *The Catto Report of Journalism and Society* 38–43 (1999).

[20]Louis D. Brandeis & Samuel D. Warren, *The Right to Privacy*, 4 Harvard Law Review 193 (1890).

[21]*Ibid.*, at 198–206.

[22]*Roberson v. Rochester Folding Box Co.*, 64 N.E. 442 (1902).

[23]This language is now part of New York's Civil Rights Law, sec. 50 and sec. 51. New York also recognizes the common law right of publicity tort.

[24]*Pavesich v. New England Life Insurance Co.*, 50 S.E. 68 (1905).

[25]*Haelan Laboratories v. Topps Chewing Gum, Inc.*, 202 F2 866 (2nd Cir., 1953).

[26]William Prosser, "Privacy," 48 *California Law Review* 383 (1960). See also *Restatement (Second) of Torts*, Sec. 652C, which provides: "One who appropriates to his own use or benefit the name or likeness of another is subject to liability to the other for invasion of privacy."

[27]*Carson v. Here's Johnny Portable Toilets, Inc.* (1983).

[28]See Cal. Civil Code, sec. 990. See also Jeff Barge, *Deceased Stars Haunting the Courtroom*, ABA Journal 33 (May 1995); and Henry Kaufman, *Right of Publicity Gets Support From Restatement: For the First Time, the Doctrine Is Recognized by the ALI as a Full-Fledged Property Right*, National Law Journal C6 (February 20, 1995).

[29]*Zacchini v. Scripps-Howard Broadcasting Co.* (1977).

[30]*Ibid.*, at 562.

[31]*Time Inc. v. Hill* (1967).

[32]*Ibid.*, at 388.

[33]*Zacchini v. Scripps-Howard Broadcasting Co.*, at 565.

[34]*Ibid.*, at 571.

[35]Ordinarily, promoters of sporting and entertainment events protect their rights by controlling access to the event and the terms of access. Performers like Zacchini, in turn, protect their rights through their contracts with the promoters.

[36]*Waits v. Frito-Lay, Inc.*, 978 F2d 1093 (9th Cir. 1992).

[37]*Midler v. Ford Motor Co.*, 849 F2d 460 (9th Cir. 1988).

[38]*Wendt v. Host International, Inc.*, 125 F3d 806 (9th Cir. 1987).

[39]*Tyne, et al. v. Time Warner Entertainment Co.*, 204 F. Supp.2d 1338 (M.D. Fla. 2002). See Richard Willing, "Can Hollywood Handle the Truth?" *USA Today*, available at <www.almenconi.com/news/jan02/012402.html.> (last visited January 24, 2002). See also Holly J. Wagner, *Judge Dismisses "Perfect Storm" Lawsuit*, available at <www.hive4media.com/news/html/theatrical_article.cfm?article_id=3098> (last visited July 27, 2002).

[40]Willing, *supra*, note 329.

[41]*Messenger v. Gruner & Jahr,* 994 F. Supp. 525 (S.D.N.Y. 1998), certification to the N.Y. Court of Appeals, 175 F.3d 262 (2nd Cir. 1999); certified question answered, 94 N.Y. 2d 436 (N.Y. 2000), answer to certified question conformed to and district court judgment vacated, 208 F3d 122 (2nd Cir. 2000), cert. Denied, 531 U.S. 818 (2000).

[42]*McCormack v. County of Westchester,* 731 N.Y.S.2d 58 (App. Div. 2001).

[43]See, for example, the dissents of Judge Alex Kozinski in the 9th Circuit's opinions in *White v. Samsung Electronics Am., Inc.*, 971 F.2d 1935 (1992) and in *Wendt v. Host International, Inc.*, 125 F3d 806 (1987).

[44]See Mark A. Lemley & Eugene Volokh, *Freedom of Speech and Injunctions in Intellectual Property Cases*, 48 Duke Law Journal 147 (1998). See also Diane Zimmerman, *Who Put the Right in the Right of Publicity*, 9 DePaul-LCA J. Art and Entertainment Law 35 (1998).

[45]"Grand Illusions," *Los Angeles Magazine* 118 (March 1997).

[46]*Ibid.,* 104.

[47]*Hoffman v. Capital Cities/ABC, Inc.*, 33 F. Supp. 2d 867 (C.D. Cal. 1999).

[48]*Ibid.,* at 870.

[49]See *Eastwood v. Superior Court*, 149 Cal. App. 3d 409 (1983), at 421–23.

[50]*Hoffman v. Capital Cities/ABC, Inc.*, 33 F. Supp., at 869.

[51]*Ibid.,* at 873.

[52]*Eastwood v. Superior Court* (1983).

[53]*Eastwood v. National Enquirer Inc.*, 123 F3d 1249 (9th Cir. 1997).

[54]"Grand Illiusions," 119.

[55]*Hoffman v. Capital Cities/ABC Inc.*, 33 F. Supp., at 874–875.

[56]"Grand Illiusions," 10.

[57]See *Stephano v. News Group Publications*, 64 N.Y.2d 174, 485 N.Y.S.2d 220 (1984).

[58]*Hoffman v. Capital Cities/ABC Inc.*, 33 F. Supp, at 874–875.

[59]*Hoffman v. Capital Cities/ABC, Inc.*, 255 F3d 1180 (9th Cir. 2001).

[60]*Ibid.,* at 1186.

[61]See *Rubin v. Coors Brewing Co.*, 514 U.S. 476 (1995), concerning the right to disclose alcohol content of beer on the label; *44 Liquormart v. Rhode Island,* 517 U.S. 484 (1996), concerning liquor price advertising.

[62]*Moglen v. Varsity Pajamas*, 213 NYS 2d 999 (1961).

[63]*Schneiderman v. New York Post*, 220 NYS 2d 1008 (1961).

[64]*Molony v. Boy Comics*, 98 NYS 2d 119 (1950).

[65]*Annerino v. Dell Publishing Co.*, 149 NE 2d 761 (1958).

[66]*Downing v. Abercrombie & Fitch*, 265 F.3d 994 (9th Cir. 2001).

[67]*WJLA-TV v. Levin*, 564 S.E.2d 383 (Va. 2002).

[68]See, for example, *Kasky v. Nike, Inc.*, 27 Cal. 4th 939, 45 P.3d 243 (Cal. 2002), in which the California Supreme Court adopted a definition of commercial speech that included press releases, letters to newspapers, letters to universities and their athletic directors, and other public relations materials.

[69]See, for example, the case of Vanessa Leggett. In re Grand Jury subpoenas, No. 01-20745 (5th Cir., August 17, 2001). A freelance and as yet unpublished book author, Leggett went to jail in Texas for 168 days after being found in contempt for refusing to provide the Justice Department with work materials concerning a murder case. The 5th Circuit found that even if a privilege existed to withhold the documents, Leggett—unpublished and unaffiliated with any institutional news organization—was not a journalist. See, by comparision, a 7th Circuit Case Builders Association of Greater Chicago v. Cook County, No. 96 C1121, 1998 U.S. Dist. LEXIS 2991 (E.D. Ill., March 10, 1998), where the court

found the Chicago Urban League—a non-profit, political advocacy organization—could qualify as a journalist for the purpose of claiming the reporter's privilege. The court suggested the privilege could also extend to "lecturers, political pollsters, novelists, academic researchers, and dramatists."

[70]*Comedy III Productions, Inc. v. Gary Saderup, Inc.*, 25 Cal. 4th 387 (2001).

[71]*Comedy III Productions, Inc. v. Gary Saderup, Inc.*, 80 Cal. Rpt. 2d 464 (Cal. Ct. App., 1999).

[72]Comedy III Productions, Inc. v. Gary Saderup, Inc., 25 Cal. 4th, at 398.

[73]See 17 U.S.C. Sec. 107(1).

[74]*Comedy III Productions, Inc. v. Gary Saderup, Inc.*, 25 Cal. 4th, at 404, quoting *Campbell v. Acuff-Rose Music, Inc.*, 510 U.S. 569, at 585 (1994).

[75]*Ibid.*, at 409.

[76]*Hoffman v. Capital Cities/ABC Inc.*, 255 F3d, at 1184, n. 2.

[77]*Winter v. DC Comics*, 99 Cal. App. 4th 458, 121 Cal. Rptr. 2d 431 (Cal. App. 2d 2002).

[78]*Vanna White v. Samsung Electronics Inc.*, 971 F 2d 1395 (9th Cir. 1992).

[79]See *Cardtoons, L.C. v. Major League Baseball Players Association*, 95 F3d 959 (10th Cir. 1996).

[80]*Estate of Presley v. Russen*, 513 F. Supp. 1339 (1981).

[81]*Groucho Marx Productions, Inc. v. Day & Night*, 523 F. Supp. 485 (1981).

[82]*Comedy III Productions, Inc. v. Gary Saderup*, 25 Cal. 4th, at 408.

[83]*Ibid.*

[84]*Hoepker v. Kruger*, 2001 WL 987937, 2001 Copr. L. Dec. P28, 336 (S.D.N.Y., 2001).

[85]*Comedy III Productions, Inc. v. Gary Saderup*, 25 Cal. 4th, at 408.

[86]*Ibid.*, at 407.

[87]See, for example, *Eastwood v. National Enquirer, Inc.*, 123 F.3d 1249 (9th Cir. 1997), at 1250. Eastwood alleged that the magazine invaded his privacy and misappropriated his name, likeness, and personality when it published a story about him and his newborn child. The magazine purchased the story from a freelance writer and published it under the byline of an *Enquirer* writer, touting it as an "exclusive interview" with the actor. Eastwood argued, in effect, that his reputation was damaged by the suggestion that he would grant an interview to a sensationalist tabloid, but the 9th Circuit denied the claim because Eastwood could not establish actual malice (at 1255). Eastwood succeeded, however, under a false light theory of liability, with the court observing that the jury could have found that "Eastwood's fans would think him a hypocrite … or essentially washed up … if he was courting publicity in a sensationalist tabloid" (at 1256).

[88]See, for example, *ETW Corp. v. Jireh Publishing, Inc.*, 99 F. Supp.2d 829 (N.D. Ohio 2000), in which Tiger Woods' merchandising company sued an artist who sold a limited edition signed print of Woods playing golf. Woods sued under the Lanham Act and Ohio's right of publicity tort. The Court found that Woods had not used his image as a trademark and that the work in question was an original art work deserving of full First Amendment protection.

See also National *Basketball Association v. New York Times* (N.Y. Sup. Ct., July 2000), one of several recent suits concerning the distribution of sports information and images over digital media. In this case, *The New York Times* sought to sell some of its news photographs of NBA games in violation of its contract with the league that use of such photos "shall be limited to news coverage of the game." The court denied the *Times*' motion to dismiss and the case was settled out of court.

The Contributors

Frederick Schauer is Academic Dean and Frank Stanton Professor of the First Amendment at the John F. Kennedy School of Government, Harvard University. He is the author of several books and more than 100 articles on legal theory, legal reasoning, constitutional law, and freedom of speech and press. He is a graduate of Dartmouth College, the Amos Tuck School of Business Administration at Dartmouth, and the Harvard Law School.

Randall Bezanson is the Charles E. Floete Distinguished Professor of Law at the University of Iowa College of Law. Prior to that he served as Professor and Dean of the Washington and Lee University School of Law. He is a well-known authority on speech and press issues, and has written widely on libel economics and reform. He has a B.A. from Northwestern University and his J.D. from the University of Iowa College of Law. From 1972 to 1973, he served as clerk at the U.S. Supreme Court for Justice Harry Blackmun.

Anthony Lewis joined *The New York Times* in 1955, and served the paper as a columnist from 1969 to 2001. He has twice won the Pulitzer Prize, once for coverage of the Supreme Court. In 1956–57 he was a Neiman Fellow at the Harvard Law School, where he has also served as a lecturer. Since 1983, he has held the James Madison Visiting Professorship at Columbia University. Lewis received his B.A. from Harvard College.

Anita Allen is Professor of Law and Philosophy at the University of Pennsylvania Law School, where she teaches in the areas of privacy, constitutional law, torts, jurisprudence, law and literature, and legal justice. She is the former Associate Dean for Research and Scholarship at the Georgetown University Law Center. Allen holds a Ph.D. in philosophy from the University of Michigan and a J.D. from the Harvard Law School.

Rodney Smolla is the George E. Allen Professor of Law at the University of Richmond's T.C. Williams School of Law. A former clerk to Judge Charles Clark on the U.S. Court of Appeals for the Fifth Circuit, Smolla writes and speaks extensively on constitutional law issues and is also active in litigation matters involving constitutional law. He is a graduate of Yale and the Duke Law School.

151

Jane Kirtley is the Silha Professor of Media Ethics and Law at the School of Journalism and Mass Communication at the University of Minnesota. Prior to that she was Executive Director of the Reporters Committee for Freedom of the Press for 14 years. Kirtley speaks and writes frequently on free press issues, both in the United States and abroad. She holds bachelor's and master's degrees from Northwestern University's Medill School of Journalism, and a J.D. from Vanderbilt Law School.

Craig LaMay is Associate Dean and Assistant Professor at Northwestern University's Medill School of Journalism, where he teaches journalism law and ethics, and topics in global journalism. He is a former fellow of the Annenberg Program in Communications Law and Policy, and the author of several books and monographs on journalism in postconflict and democratizing societies. He is a graduate of Brown University and the University of North Carolina at Chapel Hill.

Author Index

Numbers in parentheses are reference numbers and indicate that an author's work is referred to although the name is not cited in the text; numbers in italics indicate the page where the complete reference is given.

A

Alderman, E., 90(2), *101*
Allen, A. L., 7(29), *15*, 85(54), *87*
Altschull, J. H., 34(79, 80), *53*
American Society of Newspaper Editors, 69(2, 3), 76(15), 79(32), *85*
Anderson, D., 11(48), *16*, 17(10), *49*
Armstrong, D. M., 3(5), *14*
Auletta, K., 35(84), *54*

B

Baker, C. E., 17(6, 10), 27(37), *49, 51*
Baker, R., 33(68), 34(73, 74), *53*
Barge, J., 137(28), *147*
Bauer, S. M., 44(128, 130), *56*
Beatty, D., 116(127), *127*
Bentham, J., 5(14), *14*
Berger, P. L., 3(1), *13*
BeVier, L., 17(5), *49*
Bezanson, R., 7(23), *14*, 17(7, 10), 18(11), 18(13, 14), 21(20, 21), 22(23, 24), 24(34), 26(36), 28(42), 32(51, 52, 54, 57, 59, 61), 33(64), 34(79, 80), 35(83, 84), 39(101), 40(110, 112), 41(120), 42(123), 48(136), *49, 50, 51, 52, 53, 54, 55, 56, 57,* 92(20), *103*
Bible, J. D., 115(104), *126*
Bickel, A., 45(133), *57*
Blackstone, W., 4(6), *14*
Blasi, V., 39(101), *54*
Bloustein, E. J., 6(21), *14*
Bok, S., 63(10), *68*
Bollier, D., 136(19), *147*

Bork, R., 92(15), *102*
Brandeis, L., 7(32), *15*, 61(1), *68*, 100(56), *105*, 109(23), 136(20), *147*, 153, *122*
Brown, R. S., 134(10), *146*
Budnitz, M. E., 111(59), *124*
Byford, K. S., 10(44), *15*

C

Carey, J., 41(121), *56*
Cate, F., vii(3), *xiii*, 109(30), 112(72, 74), 118(150, 154, 155, 156), 119(167), *123, 125, 128, 129*
Cavallaro, J., Jr., 44(130), *56*
Cicero, 4(6), *14*
Clark, T. J., 11(50), *16*
Clausing, J., 120(184, 185), *130*
Coase, R. H., 109(22), *122*
Coleman, J., 4(7), *14*
Commission of the European Communities, 120(181), *130*
Connolly, W. G., 79(13), *86*
Cooley, T. M., 110(47), *123*
Crain, R., 34(76), *53*
Cranberg, G., 18(14), 24(34), 26(36), 32(61), 35(83, 84), 42(123), *50, 51, 53, 54*
Cunningham, B., 79(14), *86*

D

de Moraes, L., 77(19), *86*
Dendy, G., 91(9), 92(12), *102*
DePass, D., 120(190), *131*
Dilts, J. P., 17(10), *49*
Dworkin, R., 5(13, 18), *14*

153

Subject Index

A

ABC television network, 33–36, 44–46, *see also Food Lion v. Capital Cities/ABC, Inc.*
Access
  judicial constructions, 109–114
  trends, 113–117
Accountability, 78, 79–80
Advertisers, 26, 134, 136
AIDS, 70, 82, 139
American companies, databases, 118–120
American journalism, 11
American Society of Newspaper Editors (ASNE), 69, 76
Antitrust laws, 24
Appropriation, *see* Right of publicity
Arkansas Educational Television Commission v. Forbes, 28, 30
Arrest databases, 114
ASNE, *see* American Society of Newspaper Editors
Audience, 25
Australia, 11
Avrahami, Ram, 107–108

B

Bartnicki v. Vopper, 91, 95, 98–101
Baseball player, 136–137
Behavior, journalists, 80–81
Berger v. Hanlon, 36–40, 45, 80, 136
Blackmun, Justice Harry, 113
Brennan, Justice William, 7, 65, 107, 113

C

Cable News Network (CNN), 36–40, 45
Capitalist model, 23–25
Carter, President Jimmy, 118
Celebrity identity, 137
Cellular telephone transmission, 98–101
Cheers, 138
Cheney, Vice President Dick, 71
Children, 79
Civil disobedience, 36–40, 94
Civil lawsuits, 6, *see also* Lawsuits
Clinton, President William, 66, 84, 119
Code of Ethics, 69, 77–78
Cohen v. Cowles Media Company, 91
Cohen, Alexander, 84
Comedy III Productions, Inc., v. Gary Saderup, Inc., 143, 144
Comic books, 143
Commercial exploitation, 139–144
Commercial speech, 142–143
Common law, right of publicity, 134, 137
Common law tort rules, 21–22
Common sense, Court use, 141, *see also* Hoffman, Dustin
Communications media, privacy and access
  judicial constructions, 109–113
  news gathering and problems, 120–121
  push for, 117–120
  trend in right of, 113–117
Compensation, 47
Competitive model, 23, 29
Computer, 62
Condit, Congressman Gary, 73, 81
Condon v. Reno, 116–117
Confidentiality, 76, 91, 110

157